Environmental Protection at the State Level

Bureaucracies, Public Administration, and Public Policy

Kenneth J. Meier
Series Editor

Bureaucracies, Public Administration,
and Public Policy

Environmental Protection at the State Level

Politics and Progress in Controlling Pollution

EVAN J. RINGQUIST

M.E. Sharpe
Armonk, New York
London, England

Library of Congress Cataloging-in-Publication Data

Ringquist, Evan J., 1962–
Environmental protection at the state level: politics and progress in
controlling pollution / Evan J. Ringquist.
p.   cm. — (Bureaucracies, public administration, and public policy)
Includes bibliographical references and index.
ISBN 1-56324-203-6.—ISBN 1-56324-204-4 (pbk.)
1. Pollution—Government policy—United States—States.
2. Environmental policy—United States—States.
3. Environmental protection—United States—States.
4. Bureaucracy—United States—States.
I. Title.
II. Series.
HC110.P55R56   1993
363.7′056′0973—dc20
93-12298
CIP

Printed in the United States of America

The paper used in this publication meets the minimum requirements of
American National Standard for Information Sciences—
Permanence of Paper for Printed Library Materials,
ANSI Z 39.48-1984.

EB (c)   10   9   8   7   6   5   4   3   2   1

EB (p)   10   9   8   7   6   5   4   3   2

To Lois, Eric, Erling, and Laurie,
without them, none of what I have
accomplished would have been possible.

Contents

List of Tables and Figures

Tables

Figures

Foreword

The M.E. Sharpe series "Bureaucracies, Public Administration, and Public Policy" is designed as a forum for the best work on bureaucracy and its role in public policy and governance. Although the series is open with regard to approach, methods, and perspectives, especially sought are three types of research. First, the series hopes to attract theoretically informed, empirical studies of bureaucracy. Public administration has long been viewed as a theoretical and methodological backwater of political science. This view persists despite a recent accumulation of first-rate research. The series seeks to place public administration at the forefront of empirical analysis within political science. Second, the series is interested in conceptual work that attempts to clarify theoretical issues, set an agenda for research, or provide a focus for professional debates. Third, the series seeks manuscripts that challenge the conventional wisdom about how bureaucracies influence public policy or the role of public administration in governance.

Environmental Protection at the State Level: Politics and Progress in Controlling Pollution falls into the first category. It is a first-rate study of bureaucracy and environmental policy and can serve as a blueprint for how studies of public policy should be designed. Professor Ringquist provides a comprehensive view of the environmental policy process, covering adoption, implementation, and an assessment of the impact of current policies. Too many studies of public policy examine only a portion of the policy process. The current study demonstrates what should be the cutting edge of public policy analysis. It links the politics of adoption to implementation decisions and both of these to the quality of the nation's environment. The study illustrates that the public administration side of public policy (implementation) is crucial to understanding environmental policy in the United States. It also illustrates how the politics of policy adoption shapes and guides public administration.

Environmental Protection at the State Level also contributes to the wave of new studies that reestablish state governments and state politics as central concerns in political science. Environmental policy is only one of many policies that simply would not exist were it not for the active and aggressive role of state agencies. State governments have redefined federalism in the past twenty years. In many policy areas they are the coequal of the federal government; in environmental policy states are the source of much leadership and innovation.

All students of public policy face an inherent dilemma: do I want to contribute to the theoretical literature of political science or do I want to make a contribution to the substantive policy area? Professor Ringquist demonstrates that a scholar can do both. The enforcement of environmental regulations and their impact on the quality of our air and water are key substantive issues in environmental policy. The author addresses them using the theories and methods of a political scientist. As a result *Environmental Protection at the State Level: Politics and Progress in Controlling Pollution* says something important to both students of environmental policy and political scientists. Professor Ringquist has not resolved in this book all the tensions between substantive public policy and political science. No single book can. But he has provided a solid foundation for the effort.

Kenneth J. Meier
University of Wisconsin-Milwaukee

Preface and Acknowledgments

Why State Environmental Policy?

Many people who pick up this book are likely to hold one of three popular misconceptions concerning environmental regulation. The first misconception is that we fully understand the causes and consequences of environmental policy. Environmental protection has been a hot research topic on and off for over twenty years; what more could possibly be learned? The answer is that while we know a great deal about environmental politics at the federal level, we really know very little about the politics behind state environmental policy. We know even less about the consequences that environmental regulations have had for environmental quality (i.e., the extent to which these efforts have succeeded in protecting the environment). This book begins to fill these gaps in knowledge by analyzing state air and water quality regulations.

The second misconception deals with state efforts in environmental protection. The Clean Air Act, the Clean Water Act, the Resource Conservation and Recovery Act, and other flagship pieces of environmental legislation have been enacted at the federal level, and the federal Environmental Protection Agency plays the lead role in implementing these policies. Moreover, the EPA was created and these pieces of federal legislation passed largely because states had failed to protect environmental quality on their own prior to 1970. Of what relevance are state policies in an area dominated by the federal government? Besides, what effect could states possibly have on a problem as large and complex as protecting environmental quality? In fact, many states have tossed away their recalcitrant stance toward strong environmental programs, and in many instances state governments, not "the feds," are at the forefront in efforts to protect the environment. While state governments alone are not able to solve problems such as stratospheric ozone depletion, they are closer to many environmental problems; and after twenty years of federal policy leadership we have learned that flexibility in response to local conditions is a necessary (though not sufficient) feature of successful environmental programs.

The final misconception relates to state policy research in general. Research into state politics and policy has been criticized as holding little relevance for policymaking at other levels of government. The politics behind state environmental protection efforts and the impacts of these efforts are important, however, for evaluating the adequacy of government institutions in dealing with complex social problems, the potential for "capture" of state policymaking by economic interests, the representative nature of state governments, the responsiveness of democratic policymaking structures to ambient environmental conditions, and the ability of policy efforts at any level of government to attain their stated goals. Moreover, all indications are that the straitjacket of federal budgetary difficulties, increases in state government capacity, and a renewed emphasis on policy decentralization will make state efforts in policymaking increasingly important in the future (ACIR 1985; Gray and Eisinger 1991; Van Horn 1989).

The Plan of the Book

This book is intended to fulfill two purposes: first, to describe in some detail the role that states play in environmental policy; and second, to provide a rigorous empirical investigation into the causes and consequences of state air and water quality regulation. The introduction discusses the state of knowledge regarding environmental policy, or the questions that previous work in this policy area have left unanswered. Chapter 1 discusses the context of environmental policy. Any efforts at environmental protection, whether undertaken by the federal, state, or local governments, must take place within a complex interplay of scientific knowledge and uncertainty, political influence, and economic costs and benefits. We cannot understand environmental policy without understanding the context within which these policy decisions take place. Chapter 2 provides a brief history of pollution control policy and presents a fairly thorough discussion of the contents of these policies. Chapter 3 details the role states play in creating and implementing environmental policy, how this role has changed since World War II, and improvements in state governing capacity that have supported states' accepting an increased role in environmental protection.

An empirical analysis of the causes and consequences of state pollution control regulation begins with chapter 4, which presents an integrated theory of policy influence (accounting for policy outputs) and policy impact (accounting for policy outcomes). The empirical analysis is restricted to state air and water quality regulation because objective measures of the environmental impacts of hazardous waste regulations are simply not available (U.S. EPA 1988a). Chapters 5 and 7 focus on state air quality programs and water quality programs, respectively. The integrated model of policy outputs developed in chapter 4 is used to answer the question, why do some states have stronger pollution control regulations than others? The utility of the integrated model is also tested against three more traditional models often used to account for variations in state policy activity. Chapters 6 and 8 extend the empirical analysis to the outcomes of state air and water pollution control regulations. Here the research question becomes, do stronger state pollution control programs make a difference for environmental quality? Does pollution control regulation work? Finally, chapter 9 recaps the conclusions from the empirical analysis in chapters 4 through 8 and places these conclusions against the backdrop of future prospects for pollution control in the United States. Chapter 9 concludes with several recommendations for improving environmental policy in the states of the United States.

Acknowledgments

During a three-and-a-half-year project, one incurs many debts. The idea for this book germinated during discussions with Ken Meier at the University of Wisconsin-Madison. He, along with Cathy Johnson, John Witte, and others, helped the idea become a Ph.D. dissertation. I doubt many of them would recognize the final product, however. I am particularly indebted to Ken Meier, who not only provided the inspiration, but also freely shared his wisdom, countless Sprecher beers, and numerous carrots and sticks to push the project forward when I was in a rut. For all of these things, I am grateful.

The University of Wisconsin-Milwaukee and Texas Tech University gave me a supportive atmosphere in which to continue my research and writing. Most of the natural scientists with whom I discussed the project believed it was too ambitious, but to their credit they agreed to help me anyway. I am indebted to Tom Link and his staff at EPA's National Air Data Branch and Don Dolnack and his staff at the U.S. Geological Survey (USGS) for providing me with the air and water quality data presented in chapters 6 and 8. Furthermore, discussions with Dick Smith at the USGS were invaluable in helping me to refine the measures of water quality used in the analysis. Assistance in the tedious job of coding and formatting some of the data was provided by Bob Hummel at UWM and Nan Daugherty and Kim Ryan-Bosket at TTU. Penny Mclaughlin at TTU was especially helpful in preparing the manuscript to go to press, and she has my gratitude for this help. I also want to thank several anonymous referees who reviewed various portions of the manuscript. The book is much better than it would have been without their comments.

Special thanks go to Michael Weber of M.E. Sharpe for his unflagging belief in the book's scholarly contribution and to the copyeditor, Susanna Sharpe, for making me appear more lucid and better organized than I am in real life. Special thanks also go to my family for standing behind me during the long road that led to this book. My deepest debt is to my wife, Laurie, who listened to me ramble endlessly about state pollution control regulation, read several draft chapters with a critical eye, and endured the curses of a distracted husband and many evenings and weekends alone during the writing of this book. Finally, I want to acknowledge an unrepayable debt to Jimmy Buffett, whose companionship through long nights at the computer reminded me of the many important things in life that lay outside of academia. While I could not have completed the book without the inspiration and support of all of these folks, they remain blameless for any errors that remain.

Environmental Protection at the State Level

Introduction:
Unanswered Questions in
Environmental Policy

In thinking about environmental policy, professionals and laypersons alike seem fixated upon the role played by the federal government. We look to Washington for action and solutions to environmental problems, and blame the government there when environmental goals are not met. This federal focus obscures the fact that a significant amount of policy variation and activity takes place at the state level. Although the federal government sets general goals and guidelines, individual states have a significant amount of discretion as to the type and stringency of the environmental programs that they adopt. First of all, a majority of the oversight, implementation, and enforcement of environmental regulation takes place at the state level. Second, several states have used the discretion afforded by federal environmental legislation and the EPA to go beyond the requirements of federal environmental statutes in a number of areas. Finally, states often have significant environmental programs and responsibilities of their own, separate from those required by federal enabling legislation. A couple of examples might help to highlight the important role played by the states in environmental policy.

The upper reaches of the Delaware River contain one of the most pristine watersheds remaining in the eastern United States. Over the past several years, however, increasing pressure for riverfront development has begun to threaten water quality in the upper Delaware. After a five-year study, those states sharing the Delaware River watershed concluded that if the river was not protected soon, the substantial tourism and natural resource recreation industry benefits stemming from the unique water quality of the river would be lost. More importantly, these same states concluded that federal water quality regulations would not be sufficient to protect the river. In 1992, New York, Pennsylvania, New Jersey, and Delaware entered into a cooperative regulatory effort to protect water quality in the upper reaches of the Delaware. The regulatory program includes a series of development restrictions, but the most unique aspects of the program are that it requires water quality monitoring efforts that go far beyond what the EPA requires, and includes a set of water quality standards that are at minimum *twice* as stringent as those required under the Clean Water Act (Hanley 1992).

State innovations in environmental policy are not limited to protecting water quality. California's South Coast Air Quality Management District (SCAQMD, including San Bernadino, Los Angeles, Orange, and Riverside counties) has the worst air quality in the country. Pollutant levels here are three times as high as in any other region of the state. Responding to the state's unique air quality problems, California law requires the state's air quality regions to develop Air Quality Management Plans (AQMPs) that specify how air pollution will be controlled. These plans are revised every two years. By the late 1980s, however, it became clear that previous AQMPs were insufficient to deal with the exceptionally severe air pollution problems in the SCAQMD. Therefore, in 1989 the SCAQMD devised a radically different and more restrictive set of air pollution control regulations aimed at improving the region's air quality to federally determined minimum levels by the year 2010. The new three-stage regulatory framework imposes stronger pollution controls on industry, requires automobiles to run on cleaner fuels, promotes light rail mass transit, provides money for research into pollution-reducing technologies, and seeks to eliminate "drive-thrus," outdoor barbecue grills, and gasoline-powered lawn mowers (Kamieniecki and Ferrall 1991). The 1991 AQMP added an innovative industrial pollution emission trading scheme to these measures (Stevenson 1992a).

All of the regulations required under the 1989 and 1991 AQMPs go far beyond what is required by federal clean air legislation, but the SCAQMD and the state of California feel these restrictions are necessary. The twenty-year cost of these regulations is estimated to be over $7 billion, but they are predicted to produce $15 billion in benefits over this same period. Furthermore, not only do California's new air quality regulations exceed federal requirements, but several portions of the national 1990 Clean Air Act were borrowed directly from the California law (Kamieniecki and Ferrall 1991).

Protecting water quality on the upper Delaware River and state efforts to improve air quality in southern California are only two examples of the extensive variation present in state pollution control programs. In fact, over the past fifteen years, many states have been far more active in controlling pollution than has the federal government. By focusing most of our attention on federal efforts at environmental protection, we are missing some of the nation's most important and innovative efforts at pollution control.

The Origins of Environmental Concern

According to John Kingdon, research by interest groups and academics can be very important as a source of policy ideas and policy choices on the national political agenda (Kingdon 1984; see also Derthick and Quirk 1985). Kingdon's premise is borne out in examining the history of environmental concern. Early scientific and popular writings in the environmental area were crucial in elevating ecological concerns to national prominence (e.g., Carson 1962; Commoner 1972; Udall 1963).

Most of the initial environmental literature focused upon what have come to be known as "first generation" environmental problems. First generation environmental problems are most easily thought of as problems with clean air and clean water, and typically stem from pollutants that remain in one medium (in the air, in the water, or on the land). The earlier writings in environmental studies were buttressed by research focusing specifically on air and water pollution (Esposito 1970; Zwick and Benstock 1971). These writings, and their focus on first generation environmental problems, mobilized citizens behind environmental protection during the late 1960s and early 1970s. The national Clean Air Act, Clean Water Act, and Safe Drinking Water Act are all responses to first generation environmental problems.

"Second generation" environmental problems are caused by pollutants that readily move across different media (cross-media pollutants). Toxic and hazardous wastes are good examples of second generation environmental problems. Public attention was focused on second generation problems by episodes like the toxic contamination discovered at Love Canal in New York, and by warnings regarding the dangers of hazardous and toxic wastes in the popular and scholarly press (Michael Brown 1980; Epstein et al. 1982). Addressing the problems associated with cross-media second generation pollutants required a coordinated and integrated approach to environmental protection that the architects of traditional air and water quality regulations had not planned for. As a result, new environmental laws were enacted and applied to second generation environmental problems (e.g., the 1980 Comprehensive Environmental Response, Compensation, and Liability Act; the Resource Conservation and Recovery Act Amendments of 1984; and so forth).

During the late 1980s and early 1990s, environmental scholars focused most of their efforts on describing and discussing a new "third generation" of environmental problems (L. Brown 1989, 1991; Lyman 1990; Tuchman 1991; for earlier discussion of several third generation environmental problems, see Meadows et al. 1972; Mesarovic and Pestel 1974; and U.S. CEQ 1980). Third generation environmental problems also have cross-media impacts, but unlike second generation problems, third generation problems promise environmental effects on a regional or global scale. In fact, third generation environmental problems have the potential for altering or wiping out entire ecosystems. Acid rain, stratospheric ozone depletion, tropical deforestation, and global warming are all good examples of third generation environmental problems. Governments are only beginning to address the underlying causes of most third generation environmental problems. Recent events, however, such as the 1987 Montreal Protocol (in which most industrialized nations agreed to nearly eliminate the use of ozone-destroying chlorofluorocarbons) and the 1992 United Nations "Earth Summit" (where international global warming and biodiversity treaties were discussed), suggest that third generation environmental problems are beginning to occupy a more important position on governmental agendas.

Patterns of Research in Environmental Politics and Policy

Environmental Policy as Institutional Research

Political scientists arrived fairly late on the scene in studying environmental issues, and on those occasions when political scientists did take an interest, their work was criticized for being of low quality (C. Jones 1972; Kraft 1974). In a perceptive essay, Lynton Caldwell claims that political scientists were slow to recognize the political significance of environmental conditions because they habitually ignore the natural sciences as irrelevant to their discipline. An understanding of natural sciences and processes is crucial, however, if we are to comprehend the true scope and significance of environmental policy (Caldwell 1970).

Much early work by political scientists in the environmental area focused almost exclusively on political institutions and how they responded to the new demands placed upon them by environmental policy (e.g., Crenson 1971; Downs 1972; Edner 1976; C. Jones 1972, 1974, 1975; Thomas 1976). This research provided valuable information regarding institutional activity and coordination in a new policy area. Yet these authors offered few insights into the nature or scope of environmental problems, and failed to provide an adequate evaluation of public policy or convincing evidence that political science had something unique to offer in studying this area (e.g., C. Jones 1975).

Institutional research into environmental policy improved both analytically and substantively during subsequent years. We now know a good deal about the process behind the adoption of environmental policy (Ackerman and Hassler 1981; Calvert 1979; Mann 1982a). The administrative and judicial implementation of environmental regulations has also received extensive attention (Landy et al. 1990; Mann 1982b; Melnick 1983; Wenner 1982; B. Wood 1988). Because this research has continued to focus on political institutions, however, we are hard pressed to call it environmental policy analysis. (For a thorough consolidation of this research, see Lester 1989.)

Descriptive Policy Studies

During the late 1970s and early 1980s, research into environmental policy began to mature as researchers turned to focus upon environmental politics and the structure of environmental policy itself, rather than using environmental policy as an illustrative case study for institutional research. (For a general discussion of institutional, descriptive, and substantive policy research, see Gormley 1987).

Though generally descriptive in nature, these works did synthesize a large amount of valuable information regarding environmental policy, and many added substantially to our understanding of the politics that surround environmental policy (Mello 1987; Rosenbaum 1977, 1985; Smith 1992; Vig and Kraft 1984, 1990). Moreover, some of this research was quite analytic in nature, evaluating both environmental policy and the processes by which it was developed and implemented (Bosso 1987; Ingram and Goodwin 1985; Lester and Bowman 1983).

Substantive Policy Analysis: Economic Effects

Economists were the first to examine the social effects attributable to environmental regulations. Economists were also first to apply quantitative techniques to the study of environmental policy, and they have continued to be at the forefront of quantitative policy analysis in this area. Overall, the use of econometric tools to evaluate environmental policy has become quite common (see Johnston et al. 1988; Mills and Graves 1986). As might be expected, however, these scholars generally limit their analyses to the *economic* impacts of environmental policy. This research has concluded that the command and control regulations common in the environmental area are generally inefficient (Downing and Kimball 1982; Freeman and Haveman 1972; for a good review see Downing 1984), though in several cases the benefits of these regulations exceed their costs (Freeman 1982; Kneese 1984). Moreover, while environmental regulation has some significant negative impact on rates of inflation and industrial productivity, the absolute magnitude of these effects is small, and is in part offset by a net positive impact on employment levels. Overall, the macroeconomic effects of environmental regulations are not very large (CBO 1985; Portney 1981).

Social Critics and Environmental Policy

As more social scientists gravitated to the study of environmental programs, a small group of scholars questioned the entire pretense of environmental regulation. These writers discount as superficial the claims that pollutants are merely negative externalities that have been overlooked in the past. Instead, ecological problems are symptomatic of systemic deficiencies in social norms, values, modes of production, and institutions that value consumption and short-term profit at the expense of environmental integrity and long-term stability (Caldwell 1970; Heilbroner 1974; Ophuls 1977; see also Dryzek 1987; Sagoff 1988). Any attempt at addressing serious environmental problems using traditional regulatory schemes, or even economic incentive approaches, is doomed to fail. According to this view, environmental problems can only be addressed by changing the underlying structure of social values and institutions.

> Any change seeking to improve the environment will fail unless the goals of that change become integrated into the processes and value structure of society. . . . Thus, any change in environmental conditions requires a corresponding change in social structures and values. (Caldwell 1970, 144)

Caldwell is cautiously optimistic about the prospects for this type of change. Other scholars, however, envision a world characterized by resource scarcity, environmental devastation, and ecological totalitarianism (Ophuls 1977; for a similar potential scenario, see Lovins 1977). From this viewpoint, it is social norms and institutions, not government policies, that are in need of reform if the goal of environmental protection is to be realized. Thus, any environmental policy analysis that accepts present social norms and institutions as "givens" is dismissed as being shortsighted or irrelevant.

Substantive Policy Analysis: Social and Environmental Effects

Relatively little attention has been paid to the noneconomic effects of environmental regulation. These effects can be classified as general social effects and environmental effects. Seminal research in the first of these areas has discovered that in certain instances, there are definite negative social effects stemming from environmental policy decisions. For example, Bullard (1990) has identified severe inequities in siting hazardous waste facilities. Poor and minority communities receive a disproportionately large number of these facilities, and thus bear an unusually large share of the risks of these programs (see also Commission for Racial Justice 1987).

All of the institutional, descriptive, critical, and substantive research cited above has not told us what we most want to know with regard to environmental regulation: does it work? Have environmental regulations reduced air and water pollution? Have they protected and improved environmental quality? Ironically, these questions have received little attention from policy analysts. Government figures demonstrate that the emissions of several (but not all) criteria pollutants have declined substantially since the passage of the Clean Air Act in 1970, and ambient concentrations of these pollutants have declined as well (U.S. CEQ 1983, 1989). While less dramatic, the data suggest that overall water quality levels have remained stable over the past twenty years (no mean achievement), and discharges and concentrations of some pollutants have decreased significantly (ASIWPCA 1984; U.S. CEQ 1989; R. Smith et al. 1987).

While encouraging, these results do not demonstrate that environmental policies are having their desired effect. None of these studies attempts to evaluate changes in environmental indicators while controlling for nonregulatory variables such as changes in economic activity, changes in economic infrastructure, or changes in energy consumption. This makes inferring a causal connection between regulation and environmental improvements problematic. All of these factors (and potentially others) may have just as great an impact on environmental quality as does regulation.

We have a few rare examples of research evaluating the environmental effects of regulation controlling for other possible causal factors. First, when assessing U.S. emission regulations on new automobiles, White (1982) concluded that these regulations were responsible for significant decreases in nitrous oxide emissions. Second, in evaluating the effect of air quality regulations and other factors upon ambient pollutant measures in Western Europe, Knoepfel and Weidner (1982) found that these regulations did significantly reduce sulfur dioxide emissions. These researchers could not, however, demonstrate a correlation between reduced emissions and improvements in ambient air quality. Third, there is some evidence suggesting that wastewater treatment efforts in the states result in improved water quality in individual waterways (U.S. GAO 1986b; Magat and Viscusi 1990). Conversely, other research has concluded that government air pollution control efforts are less important in improving air quality than are changes in economic infrastructure and activity (Hanf 1982; MacAvoy 1979).

The institutional, descriptive, and substantive research recapped above has taught us volumes about environmental politics and policy. Some might even claim that we know more about the politics of environmental policy than we do about most other policy areas. While we are relatively well informed regarding the substance and efficiency of environmental regulations at the national level, we know relatively little about the politics surrounding state environmental regulation or the consequences this battery of legislation has had for environmental quality. Why do some states have stronger environmental regulations than others? Do varying levels of regulatory stringency and innovative state environmental programs have any effect on environmental quality? These important questions surrounding environmental policy have generally gone unanswered by policy analysts.

The Neglected World of State Politics

Over a decade ago, political scientists lamented the lack of research into "the neglected world of state politics" (Jewell 1980). Jewell and others claim that research into state politics, government, and policy receives too low a priority and too few resources in political science. This is unfortunate for a number of reasons. First of all, state politics and policy are areas of continuous change. The fifty state governments are often characterized as "laboratories of experimentation" where prospective federal policies may be tried out on a smaller scale and where existing federal programs can be adapted to the conditions and needs of individual states. States create and amend programs dealing with everything from education practices to revenue sources to social welfare reform at a pace that far exceeds the capability of the federal government. Moreover, the pace of these changes has been accelerated by the prodding of the last few presidential administrations. Second, because of the vast variety of programs and processes in the states, this level of analysis provides a perfect arena for testing hypotheses about politics and policy. Unfortunately, most of the research in comparative state studies has been handicapped by weak theoretical foundations and excessive reliance upon single-factor explanations for state variation in these areas (see chapter 4). Jewell (1980) concludes that political science would benefit greatly if more time, effort, and imagination were devoted to systematic, empirical explorations of politics and public policy at the state level.

Environmental policy analysis is hardly an exception to this general lack of state-level research. In every case, the research discussed in the previous section focuses upon institutions, process, and politics at the national level. State efforts are central to making progress in protecting and improving environmental quality, however. Thus, state-level research in environmental policy can be very fruitful, especially when we remember that most regulatory activities are undertaken by the states.

A small but growing body of literature takes the state as its unit of analysis. Similar to research at the federal level, early investigations into state environmental activities were descriptive and sought to improve our understanding of environmental institutions in the states (Hart and Enk 1980; Haskell and Price 1973; for updates to this material, see Jessup 1990; Rabe 1986; see also B. Jones 1991). More recent research by political scientists has undertaken quantitative empirical investigations of environmental programs at the state level. One likely reason for this quantitative emphasis is that the states exhibit variations in policies and programs not present at the national level. Whatever the explanation, quantitative approaches to studying state environmental policy are beginning to take hold (Game 1979; Lester et al. 1983; Lowry 1992; Williams and Matheny 1984).

Unanswered Questions in State Environmental Regulation

Policy Outputs in State Pollution Control

Policy outputs can be thought of as the strength and scope of state pollution control regulations and the resources devoted to carrying out these regulations. While we know a good deal about the politics behind environmental regulation at the national level, little is known about the politics behind the creation of state pollution control programs. Why should we be interested in why some states make greater efforts in environmental protection than others? What is so important about knowing why one particular policy is adopted rather than an alternative? These questions speak to more fundamental issues of political responsiveness and representation. First, in accounting for the determinants of state pollution control programs, we are able to discover whether state governments respond to organized interests in environmental policymaking and identify which interests are most influential. This allows us to say something about whose interests are served by the adoption of state environmental programs. Second, this analysis allows us to determine to what degree state policymaking is affected by political institutions. Finally, identifying the determinants of strong state pollution control programs allows us to evaluate the capacity of state governments in dealing with serious environmental problems.

In state hazardous waste regulation, both Lester et al. (1983) and Williams and Matheny (1984) attempt to discover why some states take a more aggressive regulatory stance than others. Unfortunately, these researchers come to conflicting conclusions regarding the capacity of state governments to regulate adequately the disposal of hazardous waste. The most comprehensive effort at explaining the vigor of state environmental regulations can be attributed to William Lowry (1992). Lowry examines the influences behind state efforts in controlling stationary source air pollution, mobile source air pollution, point source water pollution, and nonpoint source water pollution. In general, Lowry concludes that state efforts in environmental regulation are determined by the amount of discretion afforded states by the federal government, the level of state economic resources, and on occasion, the relative level of pollution in a state. While undoubtedly the best effort so far in explaining state environmental policy, Lowry's models explaining state regulatory strength do not account for the influence that organized state interests or the capacity of state political systems can have on state policy.

Policy Outcomes in State Pollution Control

Policy outcomes are the effects that state pollution control regulations have on environmental quality. We already have some evidence regarding why certain states enact stronger and more complete environmental programs than others. Even the most ambitious of these efforts, however, does not address the environmental outcomes of state environmental regulation. Are states with stronger pollution control programs rewarded for their efforts with greater improvements in environmental quality? No one knows. Our ignorance here is symptomatic of a general lack of knowledge regarding the environmental outcomes of pollution control regulation. What little research we have has either been conducted outside of the United States or comes to contradictory conclusions about the effect that regulations have on environmental quality. In effect, we remain in the dark as to whether this battery of regulation has made a difference in environmental quality. This is doubly true for environmental regulation at the state level.

Conclusion

The measures of environmental quality presented throughout this book focus strictly upon air and surface water quality. Only air and water quality regulations contain relatively unambiguous, measurable policy goals that can be quantitatively evaluated. We can measure progress in air pollution control by examining changes in pollutant emissions and airborne concentrations of pollutants. In water pollution control, we can also examine the concentration of certain benchmark pollutants. How can we measure progress in improving environmental quality in hazardous waste management? We might examine regulatory compliance rates or the number of abandoned hazardous waste dumps cleaned up, but these observations do not really measure changes in environmental quality. There are no benchmark or criteria pollutants, nor are there widespread monitoring networks associated with these regulations. A similar situation characterizes pesticide regulation. Finally, concerns over air and water quality directly touch more members of society than other areas of environmental regulation, and policymakers and citizens are most familiar with governmental involvement here. Moreover, the effects of regulation are not immediately observable, and changes in environmental quality come slowly. Air and water quality regulations have been in place longer than other environmental regulations, providing the extended time frame necessary for a research design aiming to examine the environmental outcomes of regulation.

This book is a start at filling gaps in our knowledge of the politics surrounding state air and water quality regulation and the substantive effects these regulatory efforts have had on environmental quality. This task requires the policy analyst to merge the skills of the political scientist with a sufficient understanding of the scientific information that underlies this policy area (Caldwell 1970). Combining the study of state policy and regulatory politics with substantive policy knowledge and natural science data will allow us to take a small step toward a more innovative and comprehensive method of analyzing environmental programs and public policy in general.

1

The Context of
Environmental Policy

State pollution control regulation is only one part of a larger body of environmental policy in the United States. Similarly, the politics surrounding state pollution control programs are embedded within a larger context of environmental policy at the national level. State efforts at protecting and improving environmental quality cannot be fully understood apart from this larger environmental policy context created by the interplay of scientific evidence, economic costs and benefits, and democratic political influence. Science warns us about the damage stemming from environmental pollutants (and thus the benefits of controlling pollution), while economics gives us estimates of the costs associated with realizing these benefits. In this context, political actors use scientific and economic data to craft policy solutions to environmental problems. This chapter highlights some of the more important features of the environmental policy context.

Because of environmental policy's close ties to economics and the natural sciences, the misconception exists that environmental policy should or can be developed simply by shaping legislation around objective scientific and economic information. If environmental policy varies from some "rational optimum," it is derided as "contaminated" by politics (see Greve and Smith 1992; Yandle 1989). This is simply not true. In the scientific context, for example, we rarely find indisputable "facts." Uncertainty is the rule. Concluding that a given level of a particular pollutant will cause significant harm to an ecosystem or a human being is sometimes as much a function of the assumptions (regarding the method of exposure and shape of the dose–response curve), values, and interpretation of the researcher as it is of physiology. Similarly, controversies over what one counts as a benefit or cost of environmental regulation, and how one counts and discounts these benefits and costs, mean that cost and benefit figures are equal parts political construct and empirical reality (for increasingly general discussions of the uncertainty surrounding scientific information, see Kuhn 1970; Lakatos and Musgrave 1970; Rosenbaum 1985, chapter 3; Stone 1988).

This is not to say that scientific and economic evidence are of no use in environmental policy, for this is obviously not the case. Good environmental policy decisions need to be informed by scientific and economic information. Moreover, we can make distinctions between generally good or useful and generally poor or irrelevant scientific and economic analyses. We simply need to remember that distinctions between "safe" and "harmful," and between economic costs and economic benefits, are based on somewhat subjective criteria agreed upon by groups of scientists, economists, and political representatives. Any piece of environmental regulation that successfully navigates the governmental gauntlet will necessarily represent a satisficing compromise among all the elements of the environmental policy context.

The Scientific Context: Threats to Environmental Quality

The premises of environmental policy rely heavily upon the state of scientific knowledge, and environmental regulations cannot be understood apart from this scientific context (see Caldwell 1990). Scientific evidence regarding the human health and ecosystem effects of different pollutants helps set the political agenda in environmental policy. Before undertaking a full-scale analysis of environmental policy then, we ought to describe in greater detail the effects of pollution and thus the need for regulation in the first place. The major concern regarding most pollutants is their effects upon human health. These effects can be acute, stemming from short-term exposure to large doses of pollutants, but chronic effects produced by long-term exposure to smaller concentrations of pollutants are much more common and much more difficult to identify or diagnose. In addition to these human health effects, nearly all pollutants exhibit some degree of "environmental toxicity," or toxic effects upon fish, birds, or other members of ecosystems.

Air Pollutants

The Clean Air Act requires the EPA to set air quality standards for six criteria pollutants: sulfur dioxide, nitrogen dioxide, photochemical oxidants (often referred to as volatile organic compounds), suspended particulates (particularly those less than ten micrometers in diameter), carbon monoxide, and lead. The bulk of EPA efforts in air quality regulation have focused upon controlling these six pollutants. The overwhelming majority of each of these pollutants comes from fuel combustion associated with electricity generation, transportation, and industrial processes.

Sulfur dioxide results primarily from burning high-sulfur fuels such as coal and some lower grades of fuel oil, though significant amounts are emitted from ore smelting as well. Sulfur dioxide can aggravate respiratory and cardiovascular conditions in sensitive individuals, and irritate the eyes and respiratory tracts of otherwise healthy persons. This pollutant can also increase human susceptibility to bronchitis, pneumonia, and viral infections such as influenza.

Nitrogen dioxide is one of two major nitrogen-based air pollutants, the other being nitric oxide. Nitrogen dioxide and nitric oxide are both produced during high-temperature combustion, and nitric oxides typically transform into nitrogen dioxide when emitted into the atmosphere. Unlike sulfur dioxide, which comes almost exclusively from stationary sources of pollution such as electric utilities and paper mills, half of the nitrogen dioxide entering the atmosphere comes from motor vehicles. Exposure to nitrogen dioxide can cause all of the same health effects as exposure to sulfur dioxide. In addition, nitrogen dioxide reacts with other air pollutants, compounding its danger to human health.

Volatile organic compounds (VOCs) are composed mainly of hydrocarbons, and are emitted from a number of diverse sources including automobiles, dry cleaners, bakeries, and chemical manufacturers. Many of these hydrocarbons have been linked to cancer and birth defects. More importantly, VOCs react with nitrous oxides and carbon monoxide in the presence of sunlight to produce peroxyacetyl nitrate (PAN) and other photochemical oxidants that can damage human health and vegetation. The most serious of these photochemical oxidants is ozone. Ozone is the major component of urban smog (nitrogen dioxide itself is a major smog constituent), and ozone directly affects more Americans than any other pollutant. Research has shown that exposure to ozone can aggravate asthma, bronchitis, and emphysema, and impair respiratory functions in otherwise healthy individuals. Ozone exposure also reduces immunity to a number of respiratory ailments, including pneumonia, and can aggravate chronic heart disease. Uncertainty regarding the level at which ozone produces these toxic effects, along with pressure from several industrial interest groups, led the EPA to relax national ozone standards in the early 1980s. Since that time, research has shown that ozone can lead to respiratory difficulties and permanent lung damage at exposure levels below currently required federal standards (Carney 1991; U.S. CEQ 1989). Recent research also suggests that these environmental and health effects of high concentrations of ozone in the lower atmosphere have been previously underestimated (U.S. EPA 1987).

Suspended particulates may vary in size from microscopic droplets to larger grit. The health effects of these particulates depends upon their size: larger particulates impair visibility but have few health effects, while the smallest particulates can cause severe health problems (Corson 1990). Particulates themselves include dust, smoke, ash, liquid droplets, and bacteria emitted into the air by factories, utilities, automobiles, and the like. Other sources of airborne particulates include forest fires and windblown dust that regulation can do little to prevent. Airborne particles cause eye irritation, and when inhaled they often become lodged in the lungs, creating respiratory problems. The U.S. Office of Technology Assessment estimates that present levels of atmospheric particulates and sulfates may cause up to 50,000 premature deaths each year (Corson 1990).

EPA regulations are especially concerned with controlling the smallest of these particulates, which can carry acidic, radioactive, and toxic compounds deep into the lungs.

Emissions of the final two criteria pollutants, carbon monoxide and lead, both come overwhelmingly from transportation sources. Most carbon monoxide is produced by the incomplete combustion of carbon-based fuels. Exposure to this pollutant interferes with the blood's ability to transport oxygen, and thus impairs perception, thinking, and coordination. Exposure to high concentrations of carbon monoxide can cause headaches, brain damage, cardiovascular ailments, and even death. Atmospheric lead is emitted chiefly as a by-product of burning leaded gasoline. It concentrates in certain body tissues (such as the liver and kidneys), and impairs the function of the cardiovascular, reproductive, and central nervous systems. Lead has also been tied to hyperactivity and mental retardation in children (French 1991).

In addition to their effects upon human health, air pollutants can inflict significant and far-reaching environmental damage. Nitrous oxides have been identified as greenhouse gases, and thus contribute to global warming. Sulfur dioxide and nitrogen dioxide are the primary sources of acid deposition or "acid rain." Acid rain decreases crop yields, causes forests to decline, attacks buildings and other exposed materials, and has acidified large numbers of unbuffered aquatic ecosystems, effectively destroying them (Mello 1987; Regens and Rycroft 1988). Man-made pollution is the number one cause of acidic degradation in most lakes and streams in the Unites States. Ozone is even more harmful to most plant species than are sulfur and nitrogen dioxides. Ozone interferes with photosynthesis in plants, damages plant cells, and recent evidence suggests that ozone pollution is a major cause of forest death in Europe (Corson 1990). The human health problems associated with each of these pollutants are replicated in all other animal inhabitants of the environment. Criteria pollutants are not the only pollutants that threaten human health and the environment. Each year, millions of tons of largely unregulated heavy metal and chemical "toxic air pollutants" are emitted into the atmosphere, and many of these pollutants exhibit toxigenic and carcinogenic properties. Finally, pollutants such as carbon dioxide and chlorofluorocarbons contribute to global warming and the destruction of the stratospheric ozone layer, and both of these environmental problems promise ecological alterations on a global scale.

Water Pollutants

Water pollutants are typically classified as either point source or nonpoint source. Point source pollutants are those emitted "end-of-pipe," coming from easily identifiable and relatively easy-to-control sources. Point sources of water pollution include industrial plants and factories and municipal wastewater treatment facilities. Nonpoint source pollution comes from diffuse sources including runoff from urban areas, construction sites, agricultural fields, and feedlots. Non-point source pollutants make up 65 percent of all pollutants reaching the nation's waterways (Rosenbaum 1991), and these pollutants pose the most serious water pollution problem in over half of the states (USDA 1987). Curbing water pollution from nonpoint sources is nearly impossible using traditional technologies and techniques. Alternative (and more invasive) measures such as land use planning and altered farming practices are the most promising control strategies here.

The effects of water pollutants on human health receive less attention than air pollutants, probably because they are less relevant. This is not to say that water pollution is either unimportant or not salient. Public attention is periodically focused upon water quality by serious episodes of surface water contamination. In the last few years, major metropolitan drinking water supplies have been contaminated by a large oil spill on the Monongahela River (in 1989) and by nonpoint source bacterial pollution (in Milwaukee in 1993). Threats to human health were also brought to public attention when the San Diego municipal sewage systems failed in 1992, spilling millions of gallons of partially treated sewerage off the southern California coast. Acute but localized contamination of municipal and private groundwater wells is also becoming fairly common. Unlike air, however, water is treated before it is consumed, removing nearly all of its harmful constituents.[1] While increased pollutant loads do increase the cost of water treatment and the likelihood of drinking water contamination, in general, surface water pollution affects people directly only through swimming and other forms of recreation, and by offending aesthetic sensibilities.

The most serious harmful effects of water pollutants are experienced by eco-systems. Sometimes these impacts are acute and dramatic: a 1991 pesticide spill in the Sacramento River in California effectively wiped out one of the most productive riparian ecosystems in the state (Bishop 1991). Typically, however, water pollutants contribute to more chronic effects. The traditional water pollutants of sediments and nutrients (e.g., nitrogen and phosphorus) can seriously upset aquatic systems. Sediments fill in river channels and cover spawning beds required for fish reproduction; nutrients choke these same systems with weeds and algae. Both pollutants vastly accelerate the eutrophication process in lakes, estuaries, and streams, destroying valuable fisheries or recreational resources in the process. A wide variety of other traditional pollutants increase the biological (or biochemical) oxygen demand (BOD) in lakes and waterways. As BOD increases, dissolved oxygen levels decrease and aquatic species, including fish and shellfish, die off. From 1977 to 1987, voluntary reports from the states identified over 6,600 fish kills, involving hundreds of millions of fish, and the primary causes of these kills were overabundant nutrient loads and low dissolved oxygen levels. Pollutants from agriculture and industry were the largest contributors to fish kills (U.S. EPA 1991a). The condition of low dissolved oxygen levels, or hypoxia, is compounded where the water is deep enough to stratify during the summer months. Sediments, nutrients, and oxygen-demanding wastes have been responsible for the impairment of large numbers of aquatic ecosystems, including Long Island Sound, Chesapeake Bay, and the Great Lakes of Erie, Ontario, and part of Lake Huron.

Similar to air pollutants, traditional water pollutants are not the only culprits that damage the ecological health of the nation's waters. Trace elements (e.g., arsenic), heavy metals (e.g., mercury and cadmium), and toxic substances including polychlorinated biphenyls (PCBs) and chlorinated solvents all interfere with several homeostatic systems in aquatic species. These compounds concentrate in bottom sediments, shellfish, and the fatty tissues and organs of several species of sportfish. Concentrations of these toxins have been high enough to cause states and localities to issue over 1,200 advisories or outright bans on the consumption of fish from contaminated waters, including most of the Mississippi and Ohio rivers and large sections of the Great Lakes (Schneider 1991a). Many of these traditional water pollutants have been tied to liver and kidney damage, and in some cases cancer, in humans. Moreover, most of these pollutants are unaffected by the treatment of either wastewater or drinking water.

Hazardous Wastes

The United States produces over 260 million metric tons of hazardous wastes every year (Corson 1990). In comparison to exposure to air and water pollutants, however, the EPA rates the risk of exposure to hazardous wastes as comparatively low (EPA 1987b). The term *hazardous waste* refers to a very large category of chemicals that exhibit corrosive, ignitive, reactive, or toxic characteristics. Approximately 98 percent of the chemical substances commonly used in industry are considered harmless to humans and ecosystems alike, though adequate information regarding toxicity is absent for about 78 percent of these chemicals (Rosenbaum 1991).

While most chemicals and chemical wastes do not pose serious human health or environmental problems, the inadequate disposal of millions of pounds of several dozen different hazardous compounds is cause for concern.

Waste oils, halogenated solvents, PCBs, benzene, trichloroethylene, cyanide, dioxins, toluene, and various pesticides are just a few examples of commonly produced hazardous wastes that are associated with everything from headaches and nausea to liver, skin, and gastrointestinal diseases to cancer. Recent research has demonstrated that one class of these wastes, the chlorinated organics (like DDT and PCBs) may also disrupt the hormonal systems governing reproduction in mammals by blocking receptor sites for normal sex hormones (Luoma 1992). Of particular concern is that up to 40 percent of hazardous wastes find their way into the air and waterways after disposal (Corson 1990). Hazardous waste disposal is a fine example of a second generation environmental problem, since these wastes often cross media boundaries to contaminate land, air, and water.

Scientific Context Summary

There is a large body of scientific evidence identifying significant human health and ecosystem effects from air pollutants, water pollutants, and hazardous wastes. For some pollutants (e.g., some dioxins) harmful effects are expressed at concentrations that make widespread human exposure unlikely. For most other pollutants, however, toxic effects occur well within likely human exposure levels. Moreover, we are only beginning to understand the health effects these pollutants have in combination with one another, and the effect these pollutants have on ecosystems. We rely upon environmental regulation to protect ourselves and our surroundings from the effects of these pollutants.

The Economic Context

Environmental protection is expensive, and several developments have contributed to the increasing importance of the cost of pollution control in environmental policy debates. A ballooning budget deficit requires policymakers to pay closer attention to all federal expenditures. Deregulatory pressures at the national level have elevated the practice of benefit–cost analysis so that now any government regulation must produce a positive benefit–cost ratio. (During this entire discussion of the costs and benefits of environmental regulation, we should keep in mind the serious limitations of benefit–cost analysis; see Meier 1983b, 1984 for a good review.) Finally, concern is routinely expressed that the costs of governmental regulation, and environmental regulation in particular, act as a drag on the economy and place American industries at a competitive disadvantage in the international market. While environmental regulations also produce economic benefits, it is the costs of regulation that typically receive the lion's share of attention from policymakers and the public. Economic costs and benefits, then, are an increasingly important part of the context within which environmental policy is made and implemented.

Government Spending for Pollution Control

The federal government spends several billion dollars each year for environmental protection, most of it through the EPA. Federal spending for pollution control has declined significantly over the past fifteen years, however (see table 1.1). This decline began in the late 1970s, and accelerated rapidly after the election of Ronald Reagan. From 1979 to 1983, pollution control and compliance spending at the EPA was cut by 60 percent in real dollars. From 1978 to 1983, the EPA's research and development budget was slashed 75 percent, and the total budget suffered a 56 percent reduction. Appropriations have been restored somewhat since the mid-1980s, but the buying power of the EPA's budget in 1992 was still only 55 percent of what it was in 1978, while the EPA's responsibilities increased signifi-

Table 1.1

EPA Budget Authority, 1978–95
(Constant 1982–84 $Million)

Year	Personnel and Expenses	Research and Development	Abatement, Control, and Compliance	Total Budget
1978	—	486.5	798.9	8,434.0
1979	—	458.4	937.9	7,448.1
1980	636.9	283.4	614.6	5,666.3
1981	617.9	275.6	588.3	3,328.9
1982	575.2	159.9	386.5	3,807.3
1983	557.8	121.5	370.6	3,702.8
1984	558.0	140.2	427.2	3,911.5
1985	618.7	175.6	446.6	4,039.0
1986	597.4	195.1	504.4	3,144.2
1987	640.0	173.9	536.7	4,704.2
1988	646.7	157.7	512.4	4,199.5
1989	657.3	163.3	580.3	4,097.6
1990	678.7	179.3	588.9	4,166.3
1991	705.5	187.8	708.2	4,344.4
1992	714.5	224.5	760.8	4,485.5
1993[a]	1,157.0	343.5	1,091.9	6,785.0
1994[a]	na	na	na	6,057.0
1995[a]	na	na	na	5,232.0

[a]Figures after 1992 are estimates, and are thus represented in current, not constant, dollars.
Source: U.S. Office of Management and Budget 1980–1993, *Budget of the United States Federal Government, Fiscal Years.*

cantly (see chapter 2). Finally, the EPA is no "budget buster." EPA expenditures peaked in 1977 at 1.2 percent of the total federal budget. By 1993, the EPA's appropriations accounted for only 0.4 percent of all federal expenditures (U.S. OMB 1992).

State governments spend less on pollution control than does the federal government, but they still spent nearly $4 billion in 1992 (EPA Administrator 1991). While federal spending for environmental protection was falling precipitously during the late 1970s and 1980s, state expenditures held the line, and in some areas actually increased slightly (see table 1.2). Local government spending for pollution control exceeds state government spending, but nearly all local government money goes for solid waste disposal (i.e., garbage collection and landfills) and other largely nonregulatory expenditures.

Capital Costs for Pollution Control

One of the most significant criticisms of environmental protection focuses on capital costs imposed on industry. Federal and state regulations require many industries to invest in air and water pollution control equipment (called "non-

Table 1.2

Federal and State Pollution Control Expenditures, 1972–89
(Constant 1982 $Million)

Year	Air Expenditures			Water Expenditures		
	Federal	Federal Capital[a]	State[b]	Federal	Federal Capital[a]	State[b]
1972	447	136	242	404	6,961	604
1975	442	169	250	845	8,916	599
1980	405	441	265	812	9,268	600
1985	405	359	227	953	7,120	533
1986	348	330	240	953	7,613	579
1987	338	328	255	893	8,527	576
1988	338	281	261	891	7,917	560
1989	344	261	277	900	8,179	606
1990	322	200	265	885	8,510	654

[a]Federal capital expenses reflect costs associated with fixed pollution control technologies, such as wastewater treatment plants.

[b]Local expenditures are included in these figures.

Sources: Compiled from U.S. Department of Commerce, Bureau of Economic Analysis 1981, 1992.

productive capital investment" by industry economists). These costs are not insignificant: industry spent just over $17 billion on pollution control capital investments in 1990 (industries in California and Texas accounted for 23 percent of this total; U.S. Department of Commerce, Bureau of Economic Analysis 1992). Critics of environmental protection fear that these capital costs will crowd out or displace more productive capital investments in new plant and equipment, and thus make American industry less competitive internationally. Leaving aside the question of whether or not investing in environmental protection is really "nonproductive," these crowding out concerns might be overstated. Capital outlays for pollution control peaked in 1975 at nearly 6 percent of total private capital investment (see table 1.3). By 1985, these capital costs of pollution control had dropped by one-third, and in 1990 industry spent just over three percent of total capital investment for pollution control. Capital investments for pollution control are substantial, but they have decreased significantly over time. Moreover, since both the federal and state governments provide significant tax advantages for the purchase of pollution control equipment, it is unlikely that these expenditures are driving out other forms of capital investment.

Total Costs of Environmental Protection

Government spending makes up only a small percentage of the costs of pollution control. Most environmental protection expenditures are made by private indus-

Table 1.3

Capital Outlays for Pollution Control as Percentage of Total Nonfarm Fixed Capital Investment, 1973–90

Year	Air Pollution	Water Pollution	Total Pollution Control
1973	2.51	2.43	5.20
1974	2.43	2.04	4.74
1975	3.04	2.30	5.60
1976	2.78	2.53	5.52
1977	2.50	2.33	5.10
1978	2.28	2.15	4.68
1979	2.23	1.96	4.55
1980	2.48	1.80	4.57
1981	2.46	1.37	4.13
1982	2.41	1.29	3.96
1983	2.19	1.40	3.82
1984	2.25	1.35	3.86
1985	2.08	1.25	3.62
1986	2.16	1.21	3.66
1987	2.15	1.13	3.60
1988	2.11	0.98	3.44
1989	1.88	0.99	3.21
1990	1.85	1.10	3.32

Sources: Calculated from U.S. Department of Commerce, Bureau of Economic Analysis 1981, 1992; U.S. Department of Commerce, Bureau of the Census 1976, 1981, 1991.

tries (e.g., capital investments) and consumers in the form of higher prices for goods and services. In constant-dollar terms, total spending for environmental protection increased from $26.5 billion in 1972 to $114 billion in 1992 (see table 1.4). The costs of environmental protection have also increased as a percentage of gross national product (GNP), from 0.9 percent of GNP in 1972 to 1.8 percent in 1985 to 2.3 percent in 1992. Initially, air and water pollution control were the two largest contributors to these costs, but recent solid and hazardous waste regulations are now absorbing a larger portion of environmental expenditures. Federal environmental regulations are not responsible for all of these costs, but they do account for a substantial portion.

Table 1.5 illustrates who pays the costs of pollution control. Private industry's share of these costs has remained relatively stable at about 60 percent, while the EPA's share more than doubled between 1972 and 1990. Both state and local governments pay a smaller share of pollution control costs in 1992 than they did in 1972, though in actual dollars these costs have increased substantially. The fastest growing element of pollution control costs is being paid by federal agencies other than the EPA, and most of this money is going to clean up Department of Energy and Department of Defense nuclear and chemical weapons facilities.

Table 1.4

Estimated Costs of Environmental Protection, Selected Years
(Constant 1986 $Billion)

	1972	1975	1980	1985	1987	1990	1992	1995	2000
Total Costs									
Air	7.9	10.9	17.6	23.3	26.7	27.6	29.7	31.9	37.5
Water [a]	9.1	14.0	22.8	30.4	34.4	38.5	41.5	45.4	51.6
Land [b]	8.4	9.8	13.6	15.9	19.1	26.5	33.0	37.2	46.1
HazWaste [c]	0.0	0.0	0.0	1.3	2.4	9.3	14.2	16.8	23.8
Total	26.5	36.8	58.0	74.0	85.3	99.9	114.2	129.4	147.9
Total as % GNP	0.9	1.2	1.6	1.8	1.9	2.1	2.3	2.4	2.6
Federally Mandated Costs	17.7	26.5	43.5	57.9	66.8	80.8	93.8	111.0	137.2
Total as % GNP	0.6	0.9	1.2	1.4	1.5	1.7	1.9	2.1	2.4
State Costs									
Air [d]	0.36	0.42	0.68	0.90	1.01	1.07	1.11	1.11	0.98
Water [e]	1.18	1.28	1.49	1.71	1.88	1.97	2.08	2.25	2.56
Total [f]	1.54	1.70	2.23	2.73	3.03	3.31	3.56	3.91	4.48

[a]Water quality efforts only; does not include drinking water costs.
[b]Includes both solid and hazardous waste management.
[c]Includes RCRA, Superfund, and LUST expenditures.
[d]Includes costs for both state and local governments.
[e]Water quality efforts only; does not include drinking water costs.
[f]Reflects all state pollution control costs, not only those for air and water.
Source: EPA Administrator 1991. Calculated from tables 3-3A, 4-3A, 8-3, 8-9A.

Table 1.5

Percentage of Environmental Costs by Funding Source, Selected Years

Funding Source	1972	1975	1980	1985	1987	1990	1992	1995	2000
EPA	3.69	4.72	7.89	7.96	7.96	7.88	7.45	7.33	7.04
Non-EPA Federal[a]	0.33	3.67	3.33	2.95	3.11	3.87	4.94	6.37	7.89
State	5.82	4.61	3.85	3.69	3.55	3.32	3.15	3.13	3.03
Local	28.98	26.60	22.18	23.09	22.47	21.81	21.81	22.32	22.03
Private	61.18	60.40	62.75	62.31	62.96	63.12	62.62	60.85	60.02

[a]Includes environmental costs incurred by other federal agencies, including the Department of Energy, Department of Defense, and Department of the Interior.
Source: EPA Administrator 1991, table 8-12A.

The Distribution of Pollution Control Costs

Benefit–cost analysis finds it very difficult to account for the distributional impact of public policies. Nevertheless, many econometric analyses have sought to estimate the allocation of the costs of environmental protection. Most researchers have concluded that because lower-income individuals spend a larger proportion of their income on goods affected by environmental regulation (i.e., on consumption), these costs are slightly regressive (Baumol and Oates 1975). This finding has led some economists to conclude that even if there is no difference between the level of environmental concern expressed by lower- and upper-income individuals, the regressive cost structure of pollution control means that elites in the upper classes still benefit disproportionately from these policies (Mills and Graves 1986).

The problem with this conclusion is that it assumes an even distribution of environmental threats, and this assumption is unfounded. The environmental and health effects of air and water pollution are most severe in low-income areas (Asch and Seneca 1978; McCaull 1976). Poorer and especially minority communities are also exposed to higher levels of toxic pollutants and hazardous waste than are more affluent communities. There is little chance that this disproportionate exposure to hazardous wastes is random, since there is a strong relationship among income, race, and hazardous waste facility sighting decisions (Bullard 1990; Commission for Racial Justice 1987). Thus, while the distribution of the costs of pollution control may not be uniform, neither are the costs of environmental contamination. Lower-income individuals may pay a higher percentage of their income for pollution control, but this difference disappears when we look at costs in absolute terms, and these same individuals probably benefit disproportionately from pollution control regulation.

Macroeconomic Impact of Environmental Protection

Since the late 1970s there has been some concern that the costs of regulation— and environmental regulation in particular—would drive up inflation and unemployment and undermine growth in productivity and economic output in the United States. These concerns are receiving renewed attention because some analysts fear that these costs of regulation could place American industries at a disadvantage in the international marketplace. Literally dozens of studies have attempted to estimate these macroeconomic impacts of environmental regulation, and they have produced some surprising conclusions (see CBO 1985 for a good review).

Environmental regulation has produced statistically significant macroeconomic impacts in the United States, but the substantive size of these impacts has been very small. In 1975, inflation was 0.25 percent higher than it would have been in the absence of all environmental regulation, and by 1982 this had declined to 0.13 percent. The productivity of the U.S. economy may have been affected by environmental regulation as well. Our best estimates are that productivity may have been 0.10 to 0.28 percent lower by 1982 than it would have been in the absence of all environmental regulation, though the size of this impact has decreased over time (CBO 1985). Some economists suggest that over time environmental regulations may actually increase economic productivity by directing capital to more efficient industries. Good evidence also suggests that environmental regulations may have actually created more jobs than they have displaced, thus contributing to lower unemployment rates (Portney 1981). Overall, most econometric analyses have concluded that the aggregate economic impact of pollution control regulation has been very small, and this impact has declined since the mid-1970s.

The Costs of Pollution Control in Comparative Perspective

We spend a good deal of money on environmental protection in the United States, and environmental regulations may have some small negative effect on certain parts of the economy. It remains to be seen, however, if environmental regulations place the United States at a competitive disadvantage compared with other developed nations. It is difficult to compare the costs of regulation across countries, but our best estimates are that in 1985, the non-household sector of the U.S. economy spent 1.44 percent of gross domestic product (GDP) on environmental protection. During the same year, (West) Germany spent 1.52 percent of GDP on environmental protection, Finland 1.32 percent, Great Britain 1.25 percent, and France 0.85 percent (EPA Administrator 1991). Thus, the United States spent slightly less than Germany, but slightly more than other countries for environmental protection in 1985. These figures, however, do not take into account major environmental initiatives in the European Community since 1985. In terms of the macroeconomic impact of environmental regulation, researchers have found no evidence that these regulations have placed our country at an economic disadvantage vis-à-vis Japan, (West) Germany, or Canada (CBO 1985).

The Economic Benefits of Environmental Protection

There are two sides to the benefit–cost equation in environmental policy. The costs of environmental regulation receive much more attention, and there is general agreement that these costs are much easier to identify and quantify than are the benefits. In fact, even the EPA has not attempted full calculation of these benefits. Significant benefits do accrue from environmental regulation, however. The purpose here is not to present a full benefit–cost analysis of environmental regulation, but simply to give some economic perspective on the issue.

The most obvious benefits of pollution control are improvements in human health through reductions in disease, morbidity, and mortality rates. In addition, reducing pollution can improve the productivity of cropland, forests, and fisheries, and reduce cleaning and maintenance costs. Lowering ambient levels of certain pollutants can also reduce damage to buildings and other exposed materials. Finally, there are significant amenity benefits from environmental protection, such as improved visibility from cleaner air and more enjoyable recreation from cleaner water.

Though the benefits of environmental protection are difficult to measure, we do have several partial estimates of these benefits (see Portney 1990a for a good review). With respect to specific pollutants, it is estimated that acid rain causes more than $4 billion in damages to crops, forests, and buildings each year (Webb and Tryens 1984). Other research has concluded that ozone damage to crops and forestland alone cost the U.S. economy $5.4 billion a year (Corson 1990), and nonpoint source air and water pollution from agriculture is estimated to cost upward of $12 billion annually (USDA 1987). These pollution damages are only indirect estimates of the benefits of pollution control, however. Economist Myrick Freeman (1982) has made the most direct and extensive estimates of the benefits of environmental regulation to date. Freeman estimates that between 1970 and 1978, clean air regulations produced between $8.8 and $91.6 billion of economic benefits, while water quality regulations produced between $5.7 and $27.7 billion in annual economic benefits in 1985 (in constant 1984 dollars). Other researchers have concluded that the Clean Air Act produced between $22.7 and $67.1 billion in benefits from 1970 to 1981 (Public Interest Economic Foundation 1984), and that a stronger standard for atmospheric particulates would produce between $1.6 and $66 billion in benefits (Mathtech 1983).

The wide range in estimates for the benefits of pollution control illustrate the difficulty in measuring these benefits. When our best estimates of costs and benefits are compared, however, it is likely that the benefits of clean air regulations exceed their costs, and that the costs of clean water regulations are roughly equal to or slightly higher than their benefits (Freeman 1982, 1990; Portney 1990b). Only in hazardous waste management do the costs of regulation likely exceed the benefits by a wide margin, although the data supporting these estimates are weaker than in air or water quality regulation (Dower 1990).

The Political Context

A leading scholar of environmental politics claims that environmental threats are politically determined in that environmental degradation is not a problem until the government decides it is a problem (Rosenbaum 1985). This position is extreme, but it does underscore the reality that solutions to environmental problems are politically determined. Regulatory politics in general depend upon the distribution of costs and benefits in a particular regulatory arena (see Meier 1985; also J. Wilson 1980), and environmental regulations concentrate these costs on a small (but growing) number of industrial producers while the benefits from these regulations are widely dispersed. This quality makes environmental policymaking particularly difficult and contentious (J. Wilson 1980). The political context of environmental policy reflects the constant battle between organized producers of environmental externalities (regulatory cost bearers) and the unorganized general public (regulatory beneficiaries: see Hays 1987; Rosenbaum 1991).[2] The protagonists in this battle use public opinion, interest groups, political parties, and the legislative, executive, and judicial branches of government to try to control the substance of environmental policy.

Public Opinion

Twenty years ago, changes in public opinion regarding specific domestic policy concerns were described by way of an "issue-attention" cycle (Downs 1972). Downs suggested that public concern regarding a "social crisis" would peak rapidly with media exposure, then decline just as rapidly as people either became bored with the issue or became disillusioned at the cost of making significant progress on the problem. Public concern regarding environmental protection, it was suggested, would decline more slowly than concern over other domestic problems, but it would decline nonetheless. Two decades of survey research data shows, however, that public support for environmental protection has been one of the most stable elements of the political context surrounding environmental policy.

When discussing public opinion, researchers typically make the distinction between the *strength* with which a particular position is held and the *political salience* of the position (see Mitchell 1990). Whether one feels that a particular topic is one of the most serious issues facing the nation (i.e., political salience) is heavily dependent upon media coverage, and is much more volatile than the strength of public concern over an issue. For this reason, most researchers feel that strength (i.e., the public's response to a direct question regarding an issue) is a better gauge of public concern. Using a variety of measures, table 1.6 shows that public support for environmental protection has remained remarkably high. Increasing numbers of Americans feel that environmental protection regulations have not gone far enough, and a shrinking minority feel that these regulations have gone too far. The picture is even more striking with regard to spending for environmental protection: by 1990, seventeen times as many Americans felt that we were spending too little on environmental protection as felt we were spending too much. Finally, if faced with the mostly false trade-off between environmental protection and economic growth, solid majorities have always chosen environmental quality.

Early on, opponents of environmental regulation criticized environmentalism as an elitist concern of middle-class white people. Since that time, it has become clear that levels of environmental concern are very similar across economic, education, and racial classifications (Dunlap 1989; Ladd 1982; Mitchell 1984), and some research suggests that minorities may even express higher levels of environmental concern than whites (Mohai 1990). Age appears to be the only real defining characteristic regarding concern for the environment: younger generations are more concerned about the environment than are older people.

Table 1.6

Public Opinion on Environmental Protection: Percentage Responding Affirmatively, Selected Years

	1974	1976	1978	1980	1982	1984	1988	1989	1990
Environmental Protection Laws Have Not Gone Far Enough[1]	25	32	29[a]	33	37	48[b]	—	55	54
Environmental Protection Laws Have Gone Too Far[1]	17	15	24[a]	25	16	14[b]	—	11	11
Government Is Spending Too Little on Protecting the Environment[2]	63	57	55	51	53	61	68	70	71
Government Is Spending Too Much on Protecting the Environment[2]	8	10	10	16	12	5	5	4	4
Willing to Sacrifice Economic Growth for Environmental Quality[3]	—	38	37	41[c]	41	42	52	52	64
Willing to Sacrifice Environmental Quality for Economic Growth[3]	—	21	23	26[c]	31	27	19	21	15
Too Little Government Regulation in Environmental Protection[3]	—	—	—	—	35	56	53	58	62
Too Much Government Regulation in Environmental Protection[3]	—	—	—	—	11	8	12	9	16

[a]Response for 1979.
[b]Response for 1983.
[c]Response for 1981.
[1]Roper Organization
[2]NORC General Social Survey
[3]Cambridge Reports, Inc.
Sources: Compiled from Dunlap 1989; F. Wood 1990; and Dunlap and Scarce 1991.

Concern for the environment is a strong and stable conviction among the American public, but it rarely plays a major role in national elections. Millions of citizens that disagreed with Ronald Reagan's environmental positions still voted for him for president, and even President Bush's relatively poor environmental record probably did not harm him in the 1992 campaign. While environmental protection is not an overriding political concern of Americans, environmentalism has modified our society's basic beliefs and values. The natural environment, traditionally viewed only as a source of raw materials, is increasingly seen as valuable in its own right (Dunlap 1989). Environmental values have become a central element of American life, and will likely continue to play a significant role in decisions regarding environmental policy (Hays 1987).

Organized Interest Groups

Organized interest groups are a defining characteristic of the American political scene, and they are as important in environmental policy as in other policy areas. These groups provide public access to the policymaking process by functionally representing the interests of their members. Mancur Olson (1965) suggested that groups that focus on the provision of public goods (for example, environmental groups) would be beset by debilitating free rider problems (why would anyone join these groups if they could receive the benefits of group action without incurring the costs of membership?) and thus be small, politically ineffective, and transitory. The size, persistence, and political strength of environmental groups suggests that Olson's positive theory of group behavior underestimates the power of individuals' commitments to publicly valued goods.

When discussing environmental interest groups, we typically think of the impact that large national organizations like the Sierra Club, Greenpeace, and the Conservation Foundation can have on public policy. National conservation and environmental groups have been around for nearly a century, but these groups did not become politically active until the 1970s. A second wave of political activation occurred in the 1980s when traditionally apolitical groups like the Audobon Society and the National Wildlife Federation mobilized in response to the environmental initiatives of the Reagan administration. Member pressure is one of the most potent political resources available to these groups, and by 1990 the seven largest environmental groups boasted over 3 million members (a 60 percent increase over 1980 levels), though group membership has fallen off a bit since 1990 (Mitchell 1990; Schneider 1992c).

Environmental groups undertake strategies that vary from the direct action campaigns of Earth First! to public education programs by Greenpeace to expert scientific and technical reports prepared by the Environmental Defense Fund and the Natural Resources Defense Council. All of these strategies, however, are aimed at influencing public policy. Environmental groups attempt to influence the formation of public policy by mounting grass-roots lobbying and letter-writing campaigns, and more of these groups are following the lead of Environmental Action and the League of Conservation Voters by endorsing and helping support candidates for political office (Hays 1987; Ingram and Mann 1989). Environmental groups also help shape the implementation of public policy by participating in agency rulemaking processes and by acting as "watchdogs" over the activities of agencies charged with protecting environmental quality. In rare instances, environmental groups are provided insider access to environmental policy implementation. For example, President Carter appointed several environmental leaders to positions within his EPA and Department of Interior, and President Bush appointed William Reilly, president of the Conservation Foundation, to head his EPA.

Environmental interest groups have also attempted to influence public policy through the liberal use of litigation against polluters and government agencies alike. More expansive criteria determining who had "standing" to sue in federal court increased environmental groups' access to the courts, and litigation provided the environmental movement with several of its first political victories. Finally, through the citizen suit provisions in statutes like the Clean Water Act, environmental groups may act as "private attorneys general" and bring enforcement actions directly against those who violate pollution control laws. Though the actions of environmental groups in enforcing pollution control laws have been criticized as "environmental bounty hunting" (see Greve 1992), the EPA, environmental groups, and their congressional supporters believe that these actions serve to broaden the enforcement of pollution control regulations and increase public participation in the regulatory process.

The success of environmental groups in the legislative and judicial arenas during the early 1970s caught the industrial targets of environmental regulation off guard. These producer interests regrouped and launched an effective political counteroffensive in the late 1970s and early 1980s. Initial challenges that environmental groups were elitist and anti-capitalist were largely unfounded, but business groups have effectively countered environmental group influence using other means. Focusing terrific resources on lobbying and litigation in opposition to environmental regulations increased the effectiveness of business groups. Many industrial concerns also vastly increased their support of pro-business "think tanks" like the American Enterprise Institute and the Heritage Foundation, which produce research questioning the scientific and economic basis of environmental regulation. Several members of these think tanks were appointed to environmental positions in the Reagan administration or otherwise afforded insider access to policymaking (see Vig and Kraft 1984, 1990). Finally, producer interests have helped to organize grass-roots counterpoints to environmental groups. One such organization is Wise Use, a coalition of loggers, miners, and four-wheel drive enthusiasts opposed to environmental regulation and wilderness protection of public lands. Traditional national environmental groups have attempted to temper business group criticisms that they are environmental extremists by forging more cooperative relationships with industry. Many national groups are also paying less attention to environmental activism and more attention to the difficulties of running complex organizations and maintaining their legitimacy as political insiders. In the process, however, national groups are increasingly criticized for being environmental wimps by state and regional environmental groups.

We typically think of the states as a level of conflict more conducive to business interests (see Nice 1987), and manufacturing groups do rank among the most influential interest groups in state politics (Thomas and Hrebenar 1991). Environmental groups continue to find it difficult to compete with industrial interests at the state level (environmental groups rank twenty-third out of forty groups in terms of their influence, according to Thomas and Hrebenar 1991), but these groups have made steady gains in the states over the past several years. Increasing group diversification has created state-based environmental groups (e.g., Clean Water Action, Public Interest Research Groups, Citizens Clearinghouse for Hazardous Waste, and so forth) and state chapters of national groups that are much more activist than the national groups themselves. These groups are also growing faster than their more traditional national counterparts (Schneider 1992c). In many respects, these state groups now serve as the vanguard of the environmental movement, and they are highly critical of the compromises major groups have made regarding environmental protection.

The cast of interest groups surrounding environmental policy vividly demonstrates the struggle between the general beneficiaries of environmental regulation and those who bear the costs of these regulations. We have witnessed near routs by both environmental and industrial groups, though presently the struggle seems to be more even. In many areas, environmental and industrial groups are cooperating as they begin to recognize their common interests in environmentally benign economic growth and the market potential for controlling pollution. We ought not expect a new era of harmony between environmental and industrial groups, however, as the criticism of traditional environmental groups demonstrates. Both sets of interests will remain powerful political protagonists for the foreseeable future.

Political Parties

Political parties, much like interest groups, aggregate and articulate interests in the American political system. Unlike interest groups, however, parties run candidates for political office and can control the direction of government. In fulfilling these roles, political parties offer voters a choice between different conceptions of the "public good." Generally, the Democratic Party believes in using the government as an agent of positive social change, while the Republican Party adheres to an ideology emphasizing limited government and few restrictions on free enterprise. Environmental regulation reinforces these partisan splits, and as a result we find significant differences between Republicans and Democrats in their support of environmental protection.

The League of Conservation Voters (LCV) evaluates the environmental voting record of each member of Congress during each congressional term, with higher LCV scores representing a stronger environmental voting record. A spirit of bipartisanship has surrounded certain pieces of environmental legislation: the Clean Air and Clean Water acts were passed with strong bipartisan majorities. These bipartisan efforts notwithstanding, Democrats consistently receive higher LCV scores than do Republicans, and this gap increased during the 1980s, mirroring an increase in partisanship in general (Bruce et al. 1991). From 1973 to 1978, congressional Democrats received an average LCV score of 58 while Republican scores averaged 34, a gap of 24 points. From 1981 to 1985, this gap widened to 33.5 points (Democrats 66, Republicans 32.5; see Dunlap 1989). By the end of the 1980s, Republican LCV scores had increased somewhat, to an average of 36, while Democratic averages stayed the same (Hall and Kerr 1991).

These scores do not mean that all Democrats are stronger environmentalists than are all Republicans. There are significant regional variations in LCV scores, with representatives from both parties in the East receiving the highest scores and representatives from the Midwest, West, and South following in order. In fact, eastern Republicans usually have higher LCV scores than do southern Democrats. Empirical evidence shows that ideology has a stronger relationship with environmental voting records than does party affiliation: liberals have higher LCV scores (Dunlap 1989). Since ideology is causally prior to party affiliation, ideological differences account for this regional trend in partisan support. Nevertheless, we vote using party labels, and there is a very strong relationship between ideology and party affiliation, so discussing partisan differences in environmental support still makes a good deal of sense. Environmental differences between Republicans and Democrats carry over into state legislatures as well. In examining voting patterns in ten states over six years, Dunlap (1989) found that Democrats had stronger environmental voting records than did Republicans in each state during each year. Moreover, the partisan differences in state legislatures were roughly equal to differences at the national level.

There are significant differences between political parties regarding the level of environmental concern demonstrated by their representatives; Democrats are more supportive of environmental protection. These partisan differences are politically relevant, because changes in legislative party strength at the national or state level result in changes in the relative power positions of political players in environmental policy, and this can lead to real policy change.

Congress and the President

The president and Congress are the two most visible participants in the environmental political context. These two actors are discussed together because the actions of each institution are largely defined in opposition to the other's in environmental policy. Environmental legislation needs the support of both the president and Congress to be enacted into law, so focusing on the relationship and interaction between these actors is more interesting and more profitable than focusing on each in isolation.

Throughout the 1970s, Congress played a vigorous role in outlining the environmental policy agenda (Kraft 1989). Congress and President Nixon generally cooperated in a bipartisan and inter-institutional display of support for environmental protection that led to the passage of the National Environmental Policy Act (1969), the Clean Air Act (1970), the Clean Water Act (1972), the Safe Drinking Water Act (1974), and other pieces of environmental legislation. There were congressional-presidential disagreements, but the most celebrated dispute was over which body could develop the strongest Clean Air Act—the Nixon–Muskie battle over the CAA. In instances such as funding mechanisms for the Clean Water Act where there was genuine conflict between Nixon and Congress, Congress usually prevailed. A generally cooperative relationship in environmental policy continued through the presidencies of Gerald Ford and Jimmy Carter.

The election of Ronald Reagan as president in 1980 inaugurated an entirely new relationship between Congress and the presidency. Reagan's hostility toward environmental regulation and his commitment to significant policy retrenchment in this area alienated numerous members of Congress, and the previous spirit of joint presidential-legislative support of environmental protection was cast aside (Kraft 1984; Hays 1987). Bolstered by the first Republican-controlled Senate in twenty-five years and significant Republican gains in the House, President Reagan first pursued a legislative strategy to weaken the major pieces of environmental law. Public outrage, interest group pressure, and a lack of support from moderate Republicans thwarted this legislative strategy. In response, the president's staff decided to bypass Congress altogether and pursue a three-pronged administrative strategy of budget and personnel cuts, shrewd political appointments, and agency reorganizations to reform environmental policy.

While Reagan's legislative strategy was not successful, Congress itself was nearly paralyzed with respect to promoting any new environmental initiatives (Kraft 1990). Several pieces of environmental legislation were up for reauthorization in the early 1980s, but many members of Congress feared that these laws could be weakened if opened for debate and amendment. As a result, Congress took a defensive stance vis-à-vis the president, and contented itself with trying to mitigate presidential budget cuts and keeping a watchful eye on the activities of Reagan appointees at EPA and elsewhere. While Reagan remained opposed to much environmental protection, during his second term most of the more hostile (and embarrassing) environmental appointees had either resigned or been removed from office, and the president's deregulatory energies were focused elsewhere. Consequently, congressional-executive gridlock over environmental policy was loosened somewhat, and Congress managed to amend and strengthen hazardous waste regulation in 1986 and water quality legislation in 1987 (Vig and Kraft 1990).

During the 1988 presidential election, George Bush vowed to be an "environmental president" and promised a return to the traditional pattern of executive-legislative cooperation in environmental policy. For the first two years of his term, President Bush was as good as his word. Working with Congress, Bush reversed his previous position and signed legislation to phase out ozone-destroying chlorofluorocarbons faster than required by the international Montreal Protocol agreement (Hilts 1992). In 1990, the president and Congress together crafted the most far-reaching revision of the Clean Air Act since 1970. The act promised significant improvements in air quality over the next fifteen years. Overall, a surprising and refreshing harmony characterized presidential-congressional relations in environmental policy.

This period of harmony was short-lived, however. Pressures from a stagnant economy and the conservative wing of his political party prompted President Bush to abandon his cooperative relationship with Congress. Beginning in late 1990, members of the Bush administration advanced an increasing number of anti-environmental initiatives. First, Bush proposed redefining wetlands in such a way that half of all remaining wetlands could lose federal protection; a clear violation of his "no net loss of wetlands" campaign promise (Huth 1992). Next, a presidential commission compromised the Endangered Species Act to permit clearcutting the habitat of the northern spotted owl. Following in close succession were actions that allowed polluters to exceed emission limits for toxic air pollutants without public notice or comment; the proposed elimination of public hearings and court challenges to oil, coal, gas, mineral, and timber leases and sales on public lands; and the weakening of several elements of the 1990 Clean Air Act under the direction of Vice President Quayle's Council on Competitiveness (see chapter 2). Outside observers claim that this was the strongest assault on environmental rules and regulations since the early days of the Reagan administration (Battaile 1992; Waxman 1992). Many members of Congress felt outraged and betrayed, but there was little they could do to block these administrative actions other than resort once again to more stringent agency oversight.

President Clinton has promised a new and improved working relationship with Congress, and there is no reason to expect that this relationship will not carry over into environmental policy. Moreover, Vice President Al Gore is the strongest advocate of environmental protection ever elected to nationwide office in the United States. The election of Clinton and Gore, coupled with Democratic majorities in both houses of Congress, will likely return the White House and Capitol Hill to a smoother relationship in environmental policy.

We are unlikely to see again executive-legislative conflict on the scale of President Reagan's first term in office. These confrontations were based on Reagan's mistaken belief that environmental values were not deeply held by most Americans, and this conflict cooled after the public expressed its displeasure regarding the president's environmental initiatives. On the other hand, if we continue to have a divided government at the national level, we are unlikely to experience the executive-legislative harmony displayed during the 1970s. The policy area is no longer novel, and both parties have established positions on environmental issues that will likely preclude such close cooperation. Closer cooperation between a president and the congressional majority of the same party is likely, but we lack the experience with this state of affairs to make solid generalizations. In any case, it is clear that the presidential-congressional relationship will continue to be one of the most important elements in the political context of environmental policy.

Environmental Administration

Several different government agencies share responsibility for administering environmental protection programs, including the Council on Environmental Quality, the Department of Energy, the Department of the Interior, and the Nuclear Regulatory Commission (see Rosenbaum 1985, chapter 2, for a good review). Of all administrative actors, the Environmental Protection Agency is undoubtedly the lead agency in environmental policy implementation, and arguably the most important actor in the political context of environmental policy.

The EPA crafts regulations and fleshes out environmental legislation through administrative rule making, and attempts to meet statutory environmental quality deadlines by enforcing these regulations. The EPA has been severely criticized for failing to meet many of these statutory deadlines, but there is some evidence that the agency has recently improved in this regard (Rosenbaum 1989). The EPA also acts as the government's chief environmental science organization, using information from its research and development efforts to inform regulatory decision making. The EPA's research efforts have been criticized as being uneven and at times second-rate, and the agency admits a serious shortage of top-notch scientists and state-of-the-art laboratory equipment. William Reilly, EPA administrator under President Bush, has vowed to improve the agency's scientific research through solicitation of outside scientific advice, peer review of agency research efforts, and the creation of six "endowed chairs" to attract first-rate scientists to the agency (Leary 1992). Finally, the EPA serves as a repository for environmental data and provides advice and guidance to industry and other administrative agencies. The EPA carries out these functions through a set of medium-specific offices (e.g., the Office of Air and Radiation, Office of Water, Office of Solid Waste and Emergency Response) and programmatic offices (such as the Office of Policy, Planning, and Evaluation). This medium-specific organizational structure means that the EPA experiences difficulty in dealing with second and third generation environmental problems that cross media boundaries, but the agency is attempting to deal with this shortcoming through a new emphasis on cross-media pollutants.

Agencies have personalities, and the EPA has a reputation of being very supportive of environmental protection. This "sense of mission" is more or less self-perpetuating as environmentally minded public servants gravitate to the agency, and because agencies themselves can affect the outlook and values of their employees (Goetze 1981; Hedge et al. 1988). Historically, presidents have appointed individuals to leadership positions in the EPA that were both environmental professionals and supported this sense of mission. Breaking with tradition, Ronald Reagan appointed individuals with few environmental credentials who were admittedly hostile to environmental protection to head environmental agencies.[3] One of the most notorious of these appointees, Anne Gorsuch-Burford of the EPA, was finally held in contempt of Congress for her actions aimed at undermining environmental protection. There is significant evidence that even appointments to governmental scientific advisory committees were based on political rather than scientific grounds (Vig and Kraft 1984).

The appointment of individuals hostile to environmental protection was simply one element of a more general administrative strategy launched by the Reagan administration aimed at rolling back environmental regulation. All environmental agencies suffered large budget and staff cuts during Reagan's first term. The Council on Environmental Quality, for example, saw its staff reduced from sixty to six. Through the cost–benefit requirements of Executive Order 12291, Reagan also succeeded in centralizing all rule-making authority in the Office of Management and Budget. Reagan and his appointees reorganized the enforcement and compliance divisions of environmental agencies often, making it nearly impossible to implement and enforce environmental regulations. Environmental enforcement activities dropped off significantly in the early 1980s in response to these political efforts to control the bureaucracy (B. Wood 1988; Wood and Waterman 1991). Finally, agency heads such as James Watt at the Interior and Anne Gorsuch-Burford at the EPA significantly revised agency regulations, effectively changing environmental law and bypassing Congress in the process (Hays 1987; Menzel 1983; Tobin 1984).

During the presidency of George Bush, environmental administration returned to previous patterns. While the strength of Bush's commitment to strong environmental protection was questionable, his appointments to many environmental agencies received high praise. William Reilly, former head of the Conservation Foundation, was tapped to head the EPA immediately following Bush's inauguration in 1989, and Michael Deland, selected to chair the Council on Environmental Quality, also had strong environmental credentials. Other appointments, however, such as the selection of Manuel Lujan as secretary of the Interior, demonstrate that Bush's commitment to selecting appointees with solid environmental credentials was not unbounded. President Clinton and Vice President Al Gore can be expected to work in concert to extend and expand the tradition of appointing sympathetic environmental professionals to lead federal environmental agencies.

The preceding discussion leaves the impression that the EPA is a unitary

Table 1.7

EPA Regions and Associated States

EPA Region	States within Region	EPA Region	States within Region
Region 1 (Boston)	Connecticut Maine Massachusetts New Hampshire Rhode Island Vermont	Region 6 (Dallas)	Arkansas Louisiana New Mexico Oklahoma Texas
Region 2 (New York)	New Jersey New York Puerto Rico Virgin Islands	Region 7 (Kansas City)	Iowa Kansas Missouri Nebraska
Region 3 (Philadelphia)	Delaware District of Columbia Maryland Pennsylvania Virginia West Virginia	Region 8 (Denver)	Colorado Montana North Dakota South Dakota Utah Wyoming
Region 4 (Atlanta)	Alabama Florida Georgia Kentucky Mississippi North Carolina South Carolina Tennessee	Region 9 (San Francisco)	Arizona California Hawaii Nevada American Samoa Guam
Region 5 (Chicago)	Illinois Indiana Michigan Minnesota Ohio Wisconsin	Region 10 (Seattle)	Alaska Idaho Oregon Washington

agency stationed in Washington, D.C., but this impression is misleading. In addition to a headquarters in the nation's capital, the EPA has ten regional offices scattered across the country (see table 1.7). Most of the real work of the EPA is accomplished at the regional level. For example, regional offices undertake almost all federal inspections and enforcement actions, and act to coordinate different environmental policies. Regional offices are also much more important than the central office to states and regulated industries, since these entities interact with regional offices on a daily basis.

A system of regional offices helps the EPA to manage its work load, but it also serves a more political function. Regional offices and regional personnel are more apt to reflect the different political cultures and varying demands for environmental regulation across the country, and this means that regional offices can be more representative of subnational interests and more responsive to subnational needs. This system of regional offices can also lead to significant variations in enforcement, however. For example, there is some evidence that the stringency with which clean water regulations are enforced varies a great deal between regions (EPA Region 4 has the strongest enforcement record, while EPA Region 1 has the weakest; see Hunter and Waterman 1992).[4]

The final administrative players in environmental policy are the state agencies charged with implementing environmental regulations. In almost every area, the EPA allows states to take over the implementation of federal environmental protection programs, and states often run their own additional programs (see chapter 3). While the EPA helps to fund these programs and still exerts some oversight responsibilities, state environmental agencies are relatively free from federal control (Hedge et al. 1991; B. Wood 1991). States can organize the administration and implementation of environmental policies using one of three schemes. Early on, states housed environmental protection programs within public health agencies, where they had to compete with other health concerns for attention and resources. Eleven states still administer environmental programs in this manner (see table 1.8). After 1970, many states followed the lead of the federal government by creating "mini-EPAs" that centralize the administration of pollution control in a separate agency (some states, such as Minnesota and Oregon, actually created these agencies in advance of the federal government). These autonomous pollution control agencies improved the visibility and professionalism of environmental administration in the states, but most are handicapped by the same medium-specific organizational scheme that hampers the EPA in dealing with cross-media environmental problems. Nineteen states administer environmental programs using mini-EPAs. A third group of sixteen states administers environmental protection programs in "superagencies" that combine pollution control, energy and natural resources management, and fish and wildlife management. While "superagencies" can enhance comprehensive environmental management, it is equally likely that environmental protection may be de-emphasized in favor of an agency's natural resource development responsibilities (Haskell and Price 1973). A few states adopt none of these organizational schemes, opting for decentralized aggregations of boards and commissions. Finally, a small number of states have attempted to create integrated environmental management schemes to address increasingly severe cross-media environmental problems. Most of these state reorganizations, however, have been more successful at streamlining environmental permitting processes (thus decreasing the burden of regulation) than at improving integrated environmental management, however (Rabe 1986).

The Political Role of the Courts

Over the past twenty-three years, almost every regulation developed by the EPA has been challenged in court, and the agency's enforcement decisions have been

Table 1.8

Organization of State Environmental Protection Agencies

Health Agency	Mini-EPA	Superagency	Other
Colorado	Alabama	Connecticut	California
Hawaii	Alaska	Delaware	Texas
Idaho	Arizona	Georgia	Virginia
Kansas	Arkansas	Iowa	West Virginia
Montana	Florida	Kentucky	
New Mexico	Illinois	Massachusetts	
North Dakota	Indiana	Michigan	
Oklahoma	Louisiana	Missouri	
South Carolina	Maine	Nevada	
Tennessee	Maryland	New Jersey	
Utah	Minnesota	North Carolina	
	Mississippi	Pennsylvania	
	Nebraska	Rhode Island	
	New Hampshire	South Dakota	
	New York	Vermont	
	Ohio	Wisconsin	
	Oregon		
	Washington		
	Wyoming		

Source: Compiled from Jessup 1990.

routinely challenged as well. In these instances, the courts are called in to determine what the law is and how it ought to be enforced. This makes the courts a significant player in the political context of environmental policy. The central questions surrounding court involvement in environmental policy are, to what extent should the courts substitute their judgments for the judgments of agency administrators? And, to what extent should the courts defer to agency expertise on matters of environmental regulation? These questions are relevant largely for the federal courts, since state courts have little influence in pollution control decisions. All challenges to EPA regulations, state regulations, and the structure of state environmental protection programs are heard in the federal courts.

Emboldened by the court successes of civil rights groups in the 1960s, environmental groups launched an extensive and fairly successful campaign to change federal policy through the courts. Two reforms in court practice during the 1960s and 1970s made this strategy possible. First, federal courts liberalized the criteria for "standing," so environmental groups that were previously excluded from challenging government and industry activities could now sue these actors in court. Second, judges became increasingly willing to overturn agency decisions on substantive as well as procedural grounds (Stewart 1975). Broader criteria for standing, combined with this "reformation" in administrative law, meant that environmental groups found it easier to argue their positions in court and were relatively successful in challenging government enforcement and regulatory decisions once they got there. Many scholars have been critical of this expanded policy role of the courts, however, charging that the decentralized structure of the court system leads to inconsistent and uneven policy decisions across the country, and that judges are not trained to make policy decisions in the complex area of environmental policy (see Melnick 1983).

Three main actors participate in environmental court cases—environmental groups, industry groups, and government agencies. Contrary to popular perception, environmental and industry groups rarely meet face-to-face in court. Government agencies are by far the most frequent court participants, with their decisions being challenged by either industry or environmental groups (industry groups challenge the EPA slightly more often than do environmental groups) (Wenner 1982). Increasingly, in fact, the EPA finds its regulations challenged by industry and environmental groups simultaneously (Wenner 1989). Who wins these confrontations? In addition to being the most frequent court participant, the government has the highest success rate in environmental court cases. Historically, environmental groups have been slightly more successful in court than industry, but this may be changing. For example, the Supreme Court is now more likely to overrule EPA regulations on the basis of cost (an industry concern) than on the basis of protecting public health (an environmental concern) (Wenner 1989, 1990).

The character of environmental court cases has changed a great deal over the past fifteen years. After being caught off guard by environmental group litigation in the late 1960s and early 1970s, industrial groups have significantly increased their participation in these cases. Perhaps more important, however, has been the changing complexion of the federal bench. Using explicitly ideological criteria, Presidents Reagan and Bush appointed judges that are relatively hostile to environmental protection and regulation in general. There is ample evidence that the ideological positions of judges affects how they make decisions (Emmert and Traut 1992; Sheehan et al. 1992), and Reagan–Bush appointees now make up 70 percent of all federal judges (Kovacic 1991).

We can observe the impact of these judicial appointments in several areas. The Washington, D.C., circuit court of appeals hears all challenges to federal agency rules, and is thus by far the most important appellate court for environmental policy. The D.C. circuit also has a long history of being a friendly venue for environmental groups (Melnick 1983). Recent appointees have changed the makeup of the D.C. circuit, however, and the court is now much less supportive of environmental challenges and more willing to reduce the impact of environmental regulation (Kovacic 1991). The effects of judicial appointment spread far beyond the D.C. circuit court, however. Environmental groups are increasingly being denied standing in environmental suits (R. Marcus 1992; Stanfield 1988), and EPA regulations are being overturned more frequently on the basis of cost, inadequate scientific evidence, and exceeding legislative authority (Schneider

1992a). The Supreme Court has also protected federal agencies from being fined for violating clean water and hazardous waste regulations (Greenhouse 1992).

The courts have played a key role in the context of environmental policy since the beginning of the environmental movement, though the character of this role has changed in recent years. In essence, we see the same erosion in environmental strength in the courts that we saw earlier in interest group influence and the presidency. Furthermore, we can expect the impact of these changes to increase over time. As older judges retire, Reagan–Bush appointees will move up to take more senior positions in the federal courts, and these judges will be in a position to counteract the decisions of even the most environmentally minded appointees at the EPA and elsewhere. All indications are that President Clinton will reverse the ideological trend in court appointments, though it is doubtful if the president will select judges specifically sympathetic to environmental concerns.

Conclusion

A few concluding observations regarding the context of environmental policy are in order. First, though uncertainty surrounds much research in the environmental sciences, the quality of this research is improving, and there is scientific consensus that the pollutants targeted by air and water quality regulations can do significant damage to ecosystems and human beings. Second, public opinion, interest group strength, and the ideological dispositions of institutional political actors are of great consequence for environmental protection policy.

Finally, there is no question that environmental protection costs a great deal of money. The data are more ambiguous, however, as to whether or not environmental protection is too expensive. The costs of pollution control have risen over the past two decades, but the pace of this increase has slowed, and the governmental and capital costs of pollution control have actually declined in relative terms. Overall, the macroeconomic effects of environmental protection regulations are relatively small. This does not mean that the efficiency of environmental regulations cannot be improved, perhaps by adopting some of the many market incentive schemes for reforming regulation promoted by economists (Dales 1968; Downing 1984; Portney 1990a). What it does mean is that environmental protection is not a major drag on economic performance (indeed, it may enhance economic performance), and that it is extremely unlikely that the costs of these regulations place the United States at a competitive disadvantage vis-à-vis our major international trading partners.

Environmental policy cannot be understood apart from the scientific, political, and economic factors that create its context. Political actors use scientific and economic data strategically to craft environmental policy. Furthermore, the characteristics of actors within the context means that any change in this political context (e.g., changes in public opinion, interest group strength, elections, appointments, and so forth) can lead to changes in public policy regardless of the status of the scientific and economic data supporting these changes.

Notes

1. The federal Safe Drinking Water Act (SDWA) (1974) and its amendments cover protecting and treating drinking water. While this is an important piece of legislation, the SDWA is not addressed in this book.

2. Some observers feel that casting the costs of environmental regulation as "concentrated" is misleading, since most industrial costs are transfered to consumers through higher prices. In this sense, all costs and benefits of regulation are widely dispersed, and political and empirical distinctions between costs and benefits become meaningless (after all, industrial concerns benefit from a clean environment as well). For this reason, we focus on the immediate costs and benefits of pollution control regulations.

3. For example, Reagan appointed Anne Gorsuch-Burford, an anti-regulation right-wing activist, to head the EPA. Other Reagan appointees included: Rita LaVelle, a former lobbyist for the chemical industry, as head of the EPA's hazardous waste division; James Watt, an activist with the Mountain States Legal Foundation who believed in privatizing most public lands and the rapid exploitation natural resources, as secretary of the Interior (interestingly, Watt was also a member of a Christian fundamentalist denomination that believed Armegeddon was just around the corner; this might explain Watt's aversion to preserving natural resources for future generations); Robert Harris, who led Indiana's challenge to the federal Surface Mining Control and Reclamation Act, as head of the Office of Surface Mining; John Crowell, general council for Louisiana Pacific (the largest purchaser of federal timber), as chief of the Forest Service; and Ray Arnell, a realtor who felt environmental groups were illegitimate participants in the policy process, as head of the Fish and Wildlife Service. This last appointment was illegal, since Arnell had no professional qualifications as a scientist or wildlife manager. The mission orientation of federal civil servants at the EPA and other agencies helped to blunt the impact these officials had on environmental policy.

4. A quick look at table 1.7 suggests a possible paradox: EPA Region 4 covers those states least supportive of environmental protection, while Region 1 covers states generally supportive of environmental protection. If regional offices respond to state demands, the observed stringency of regional enforcement would most likely be reversed. In resolving this paradox, we have to remember that states can run their own clean water programs if they choose to do so. In this case, the EPA is brought in only for the toughest enforcement cases. Seven of the eight states in Region 4 run their own water quality programs, while only three of the six states in Region 1 have taken on this responsibility. One explanation for the observed regional variation in enforcement is that the EPA Region 4 office is called upon only to deal with difficult polluters, and thus has to use stronger enforcement actions to obtain results. While the stringency of enforcement actions may not vary as much as Hunter and Waterman (1992) suggest, regional responsiveness to subnational conditions is still evident, and states do feel that the regional offices are much easier to deal with than EPA headquarters (Tobin 1992).

2

A Brief History of Pollution Control Policy

In his excellent history of environmental politics, Samuel Hays (1987) identifies the pendular movement of policy authority from the state level, to the federal level, and back to the state level as one of the most remarkable features of environmental politics over the last forty years. Charles Jones (1974) also uses environmental policy to illustrate his contention that the history of federal-state policy relations has been one of increasing federal dominance. Martha Derthick (1985) has identified the same trend toward federal dominance in intergovernmental policy relationships. In contrast to Jones, however, she remarks on how states have managed to retain a significant amount of discretion in policymaking even in areas where the urge to centralize is strongest, like environmental protection. It is fair to say then that the history of pollution control regulation is a history of shifting levels of policy responsibility between the federal and state governments.

Prior to 1970, environmental protection was almost exclusively the province of state and local governments. Most states paid little attention to environmental protection, however, and the federal government stepped in and seized primary responsibility for pollution control beginning with the Clean Air Act of 1970. Four justifications for relying upon federal leadership in environmental policy have been offered. The first assumes that the pervasive nature and broad scope of pollution require federal action. Environmental pollution is a nationwide problem, the argument goes, and thus deserves a nationwide solution. Second, many believe that only the federal government can deal with the negative externalities produced by the sources of environmental pollution. Most pollution does not stay within the borders of the state where it is produced (for example, 90 percent of the sulfur and nitrogen dioxide that precipitates out in Minnesota originates outside of that state; MPCA 1992). In a variation on the tragedy of the commons, states may be able to export their pollution and capture the economic benefits of pollution-generating activities without suffering the associated costs.

States have little incentive to regulate these externalities independently, since this could put them at a competitive disadvantage with respect to neighboring states in attracting industry (Rowland and Marz 1982). Third, it was believed that the federal administration of competitive grant programs in environmental policy would stimulate environmental policy innovation in the states. Lastly, some policymakers believed that a uniform federal policy would be easier to administer, enforce, and evaluate (Davis and Lester 1989).

The 1970s have been called the "environmental decade," but this decade also witnessed another important trend in government: the handing over of increased policy responsibility to the states. Richard Nixon's "new federalism" was aimed at providing states and municipalities with more influence and control over federal programs implemented within their jurisdictions. While less forceful than Nixon, Presidents Ford and Carter continued to support this general devolutionary trend. State control over public policy was only half of the story of 1970s new federalism, however. New federal block grants and general revenue sharing provided large inflows of revenue to state treasuries (with few strings attached), and these programs were complemented by increased federal spending for categorical grants to the states. Thus, states received additional financial resources to back up and carry out new policy responsibilities under new federalism.

The goal of increased federal control over environmental policy and the devolutionary goals of new federalism were inherently conflictual. While federal control over environmental protection was the rule through the first half of the environmental decade, by the mid-1970s the goals of new federalism began to be reflected in environmental policy. With the reauthorization and amendment of the Clean Air and Clean Water acts, the state role in federally directed environmental policy continued to grow. States began to take control of some aspects of environmental policy during the 1970s, but always under careful federal supervision. Many states even passed their own environmental statutes, and nearly all states created their own environmental agencies to administer these programs (Haskell and Price 1973; Jessup 1990).

The justifications for returning policy authority to the states have been grouped into three categories. First, devolution (and the accompanying variation in state policy) is desirable because it reflects the diversity of American society. State policymaking is seen as more flexible, more responsive to local needs and conditions, and facilitative of increased citizen participation (identical justifications are given for retaining state and local control over traditional state issues such as education). Second, there is, theoretically, no reason to believe that a centralized policy will be any more effective or efficient than state policies. In fact, state policies may be more effective than those that are federally directed, depending upon the ideology and disposition of those controlling the levers of power at the national level. Third, as mentioned above, the ability of states to act independently allows them to develop new policy tools and experiment with policy development (Lester 1985). Recent research suggests that not only are states developing these policy tools, but the diffusion of these new tools to other states is taking place much more rapidly than in the past (Savage 1985).[1]

In the 1980s, President Reagan consistently advocated replacing federal policy authority with increased state responsibility, particularly in the area of environmental protection. Reagan's two top appointees in the environmental field were of the opinion that environmental programs were too centralized and too stringent. EPA administrator Anne Gorsuch-Burford believed strongly that nearly all responsibility for environmental regulation should be devolved to the states, and she acted to put these beliefs into practice. Secretary of the Interior James Watt, a self-styled champion of the states' rights "sagebrush rebellion" in the West, did the same. While the tenure of these two appointees was relatively short, the underlying commitment to administrative decentralization remained. To the three justifications mentioned above for returning power to the states, Reagan's "new federalism" added a constitutional justification; the devolution of policy authority acted to redress a historic imbalance in decision-making power between the federal government and the states.

President Bush continued to support, at least in principle, Reagan's commitment to devolution in environmental policy. We witnessed a fundamentally different type of policy devolution during the Bush presidency, however: the devolution of responsibility for environmental protection to private industry through the increased use of market incentives for pollution control. We will see this shift from federal to state to private authority in pollution control more clearly when we take a closer look at the history of air and water quality regulation in the following sections. As a former governor, President Clinton will likely continue to support state discretion in environmental regulation. Vice President Gore has called for increased federal activity on the environmental front, but any significant new federal efforts in this regard will be hampered by large budget deficits and an anti-regulatory mood in Congress.

Regulating Air Quality

Air Pollution Control Before 1970

We usually think of air quality regulation as a federal responsibility, but the federal government's entrance into this area of pollution control is fairly recent. As a matter of fact, the earliest air pollution control laws in the United States were passed by cities. As far back as the 1880s, Chicago and Cincinnati had laws regulating smoke emissions, and New York City and Pittsburgh followed suit in the 1890s. The first state regulation related to air quality was passed by Ohio in the 1890s and was aimed at reducing emissions from coal-fired industrial boilers. In 1952, Oregon became the first state to pass comprehensive statewide air pollution legislation, establishing a state air pollution control agency (U.S. EPA 1988a).

Air pollution was not high on the public or political agenda immediately following World War II, but as air pollution continued to increase, a number of governmental and private studies were commissioned to determine the causes of air pollution and the effect of air pollutants on human health. The results of these studies made clear the need for a national approach to deal with air pollution. The federal government responded to this need during the 1960s by passing the Air Quality Act of 1960, followed by the first Clean Air Act in 1963 and amendments to the Air Quality Act in 1967. The Air Quality acts and the first Clean Air Act contained no regulatory role for the federal government. Instead, they sought to induce states to voluntarily set air pollution standards and to develop plans for attaining these standards. The acts also empowered the new National Air Pollution Control Administration (within the U.S. Public Health Service) to create a set of Air Quality Control Regions across the country, study the effects of air pollution, and provide grants and training assistance to the states for air pollution control.

The states were in dire need of this help from the government in Washington, D.C. In 1962, state spending for air pollution control was a minuscule 0.006 percent of total state expenditures. When the initial Clean Air Act (CAA) was passed in 1963, thirty-two states has some kind of air pollution regulation on the books, but only fifteen of these had any control authority over air pollutants, and only four to six states were actually enforcing their air pollution regulations (depending upon how one defines the term "enforce"). By 1970, over 50 percent of all state pollution control agencies still had fewer than ten staff persons (Lowry 1992). In short, states were doing very little to regulate air quality voluntarily (C. Jones 1976).

The federal enabling legislation of the 1960s was intended to induce states to step up their own efforts in air pollution control, but these inducements fell far short of their intended effects. For example, though the Clean Air Act empowered the federal government to intervene in interstate air pollution problems, this intervention could only come at the request of the states. From 1965 to 1970, only eleven of these air pollution abatement actions were taken under the Clean Air Act (Smith 1992). A few states (and some localities) began to grapple successfully with air pollution control problems near the end of the decade (see C. Jones 1975), but for the most part states tended to ignore the suggestions and incentives for controlling air pollution provided by early federal legislation.

The Clean Air Act of 1970

An environmentally invigorated electorate and impatience with state inactivity in air pollution control combined to place tremendous pressure on the federal government for stronger air quality legislation. Electoral considerations played a part in how the federal government responded to these pressures, as President Richard Nixon and Democratic presidential contender Senator Edmund Muskie each proposed increasingly strong clean air programs in Congress. Congress eventually embodied most of the Muskie proposals in the Clean Air Act Amendments of 1970, which were passed by huge bipartisan majorities. The Clean Air Act (as it has come to be known) is recognized as the flagship piece of federal environmental policy and has set the tone for both federal and state efforts in air quality regulation.

First, the Clean Air Act required the newly established Environmental Protection Agency to set uniform emission standards for new stationary sources of pollution (e.g., smelters, coal-fired power plants, and factories). New source performance standards (NSPS) are established on an industry-by-industry basis and require these sources to install the best available control technology. Second, the CAA itself set strict emission reduction standards for mobile sources of air pollution (such as cars and trucks), and automobile manufacturers were to meet these emission reduction standards by 1976. Third, the CAA required the EPA to set National Ambient Air Quality Standards (NAAQS) for the criteria pollutants of nitrogen dioxide, sulfur dioxide, total suspended particulates, carbon monoxide, ozone, and lead. There are actually two standards for each pollutant: a primary standard designed to protect human health "with an adequate margin of safety," and secondary standards designed to protect property, crops, and the environment (these standards are found in chapter 6). Finally, the CAA empowered the EPA to study the effects of toxic air pollutants (e.g., benzene, vinyl chloride, heavy metals) and set emission standards and NAAQS for these pollutants as necessary.

Initially, the federal EPA held most regulatory and enforcement authority under the CAA, but the act was designed so that states would play an increasingly important role in air pollution control through the exercise of partial preemption authority. Under partial preemption, the EPA sets new source performance standards and holds primary enforcement authority, but each state can take over these federal responsibilities so long as its state programs are at least as stringent as federal efforts. In addition, under the CAA individual states are responsible for developing emission standards for existing stationary sources of air pollution within their borders. Finally, states are ultimately responsible for meeting national ambient air quality standards, whether it be through existing source performance standards, the acceptance of partial preemptive authority over federal air quality regulations, or the use of other innovative state programs.

A crucial element in air pollution control regulation is the State Implementation Plan (SIP). The CAA required every state to develop and file an SIP, approved by the EPA, detailing how it would meet NAAQ standards within its borders. If states failed to submit SIPs that met with EPA approval, the EPA could impose federal implementation plans on states or air quality control regions within states.[2] State implementation plans include existing source performance standards for the individual state, along with any partial preemption authority the state is seeking, and compliance schedules and enforcement standards for these regulations. There is a common misconception that state implementation plans are either approved or disapproved once and for all, and that once a state has its SIP approved it becomes responsible for all air pollution control regulation. This misconception was fueled by the CAA itself, which required states to file SIPs by 1972 and have them approved by 1977, and by some environmental policy scholars who discuss the number of states having "approved" SIPs. In reality, state implementation plans are filed and approved in sections. A state may submit plans to meet the NAAQS for a particular pollutant, submit NAAQS attainment plans for a particular metropolitan area, or request authority to set new source performance standards for a particular industrial category. Moreover, as new federal regulations are created, states seek to amend their SIPs to take responsibility for implementing these regulations. Dozens of revisions to state implementation plans occur each year, making the concept of a complete or fully approved SIP misleading.

After having a particular section of its SIP approved, each state becomes responsible for the implementation, enforcement, and maintenance of federal air quality standards. It is important to remember, however, that states can exceed federal NAAQ standards, enforcement schedules, and new source performance standards in their SIPs if they choose to do so. The federal government provides financial and technical assistance to states carrying out these responsibilities. The CAA was designed to be flexible to local conditions in the enforcement of the NAAQ standards. While severe sanctions awaited those states failing to attain required air quality levels (including the loss of federal pollution control and highway funds), these sanctions are mandatory only for those states that fail to try to meet the standards, not for those that have tried and failed.[3]

The CAA Amendments of 1977

The Clean Air Act was reauthorized in 1977. Amendments in the 1977 legislation relaxed many of the 1970 standards, altered federal new source performance standards, and extended clean air regulations to areas that were already meeting or exceeding NAAQ standards. As the reauthorization deadline approached, it was clear that many of the goals of the CAA of 1970 would not be reached, and several of the 1977 amendments either relaxed the stringency of air quality regulations or rolled back the dates for attaining clean air goals. For example, the 1977 CAA delayed SIP approval deadlines from 1977 to 1982, and delayed the deadline for meeting NAAQ standards from 1979 to 1987. Schedules for attaining automobile emission reductions for hydrocarbons and carbon monoxide were extended, and mobile nitrous oxide emission standards were relaxed.[4]

A number of coal-fired utilities met the emission reduction requirements of the 1970 CAA without installing pollution control equipment. This was possible because many stationary sources of pollution could meet the emission standards simply by switching from more polluting high-sulfur coal to less polluting low-sulfur coal. This strategy did not sit well with either high-sulfur coal interests or environmental groups, and the 1977 amendments closed this "loophole" by requiring all new stationary sources of pollution to adopt the best *technological* system of continuous emission reductions (that is, smokestack scrubbers), and by requiring each new source to reduce pollutant emissions by a certain percentage regardless of how high or low emissions would be in the absence of pollution control technology.

The 1970 CAA required strong pollution controls only in areas that were not currently meeting NAAQ standards. Environmental groups feared that this would induce polluting industries to locate in areas with clean air (to avoid pollution control costs) and lead to the pollution of areas with exceptionally clean air across the country. To prevent this, the Sierra Club sued the EPA in federal court, and in 1972 the Supreme Court ruled that SIPs must include provisions to prevent the degradation of air quality in those areas that currently exceeded federal air quality standards (*Sierra Club* v. *Ruckleshaus* 1972). The EPA responded by developing prevention of significant deterioration (PSD) regulations in 1974, and the 1977 CAA amendments formalized these regulations as a set of legislative PSD requirements. Under PSD, all air quality control regions (AQCRs) attaining NAAQ standards were designated Class I, Class II, or Class III. Almost all AQCRs were originally designated Class II, which allows some degradation of air quality. States can reclassify Class II areas (with EPA approval) to either Class I (for pristine areas around national parks or wilderness preserves) or Class III (where air quality is allowed to degrade to NAAQS levels).

The CAA of 1977 had varying implications for the states. Relaxed mobile source regulations were of little relevance to the states, because regulating mobile sources of air pollution was almost completely a federal responsibility. Both the altered new source performance standards and prevention of significant deterioration requirements affected the states, however. Many western states saw these regulations as attempts by the high-sulfur coal–producing and industrialized states of the East to hamstring industrial development in the wide open (and relatively clean) spaces of the West (Ackerman and Hassler 1981). Finally, the 1977 CAA formally recognized the interstate nature of air pollution problems and required states to provide "adequate assurance" that stationary sources of pollution within one state's borders would not prevent the attainment of NAAQS in neighboring states (Freedman 1987). This prohibition has not been supported in practice, however. During the 1980s, Wisconsin sued Illinois, and states in the Northeast sued states in the Midwest over cross-boundary air pollution, but in each case the courts refused to take substantive action (Lowry 1992).

Criticisms of the 1970 and 1977 Clean Air Acts

The Clean Air acts of 1970 and 1977 were criticized from a number of perspectives. Environmentalists felt that several of the pollution control provisions in the acts were not strong enough. As evidence of these weaknesses, environmental groups pointed to automobile emission standards that had either remained the same or been relaxed since 1970, a lack of progress in reducing urban air pollution (chiefly nitrogen dioxide and ozone), and the absence of pollution controls aimed at acid rain and toxic air pollutants. Environmental groups also pointed to the periodic rolling back of SIP approval and NAAQS attainment deadlines as evidence that enforcement efforts under the acts were too weak.

Many economists argued that uniform emission reduction standards and the "command and control" provisions characteristic of environmental regulation in general were inefficient—because they required the same level of pollution control regardless of differences across firms in the costs of this control—and often ineffective. Most economic policy analysts suggested an increased use of economic incentives and market-based pollution control mechanisms to overcome the problems of inefficiency and ineffectiveness. Some of these same economists, along with representatives of heavily industrialized states, claimed that CAA regulations were too restrictive, and decried the negative impact these regulations had on local economies and unemployment levels.

Finally, there were numerous criticisms that the 1977 CAA was not a piece of environmental legislation at all, but was simply intended to satisfy the distributional goals of a variety of special interests harmed by the 1970 legislation. For example, requiring scrubbers on all new coal-fired utilities did little to improve air quality, but it did much to save the jobs of thousands of high-sulfur coal miners in the eastern and midwestern states (Ackerman and Hassler 1981). Similarly, PSD standards have been criticized for slowing the relocation of polluting industries from non-attainment to attainment areas, thus exposing persons in the industrialized cities of the East and Midwest to more dangerous levels of pollution. Overall, the 1977 CAA has been criticized for increasing electricity prices, increasing dependence upon imported oil, increasing sulfur dioxide emissions, and placing southern and western states at a disadvantage in industrial development and coal production (Navarro 1981).

Disagreements over how a new CAA should address these criticisms led to intense political debates throughout the 1980s. President Reagan briefly attempted to weaken the act when it came up for reauthorization in 1982, but this effort was quickly abandoned when it became clear that congressional support for the act was strong enough to thwart this executive initiative. While congressional support for the Clean Air Act was strong, powerful figures such as Senator Robert Byrd from West Virginia and Representative John Dingell from Michigan prevented Congress from strengthening either the acid rain or automobile emission provisions of the act. Furthermore, even if Congress could have developed a new Clean Air Act acceptable to a majority of members, there was not enough support to override a certain presidential veto. Thus, the provisions of the 1977 act were kept in place during the 1980s through a series of congressional continuing resolutions.

The Clean Air Act Amendments of 1990

The deadlock over clean air policy was broken in 1990 when Congress and the Bush administration were able to agree on reauthorization of the CAA. The 1990

CAA amendments significantly strengthened the act, and it is clear that the architects of the law listened carefully to critics of the earlier legislation. First of all, the 1990 amendments seek to address urban air problems by requiring that all automobiles sold after the 1993 model year reduce their emissions of nitrogen dioxide by 60 percent from 1990 levels and hydrocarbons by 35 percent from 1990 levels, by doubling the mandated life span of automobile pollution control equipment (from 50,000 to 100,000 miles), and by requiring the use of reformulated automotive fuels in those cities with the worst smog problems. These requirements will be tightened again in 2003 unless the EPA deems that they are unfeasible or unnecessary. The 1970 and 1977 Clean Air acts prohibited all states other than California from adopting mobile source emission standards stronger than those of the federal government, but the 1990 CAA gave the states the option of exceeding federal requirements in this area as well. As of November 1992, eleven northeastern states and Washington, D.C., had decided to exceed federal mobile source emission standards. Finally, all ozone non-attainment areas have been placed on strict attainment schedules. Cities with relatively small ozone problems must reduce ozone concentrations to safe levels by 1993, while cities with severe ozone problems have until the year 2010 to meet these standards.

Second, the 1990 CAA makes a concerted effort to control toxic air pollutants. Beginning in 1993, all sources that emit significant amounts of toxic pollutants into the air must obtain a permit from the EPA. If toxic polluters exceed the emissions allowed by their permits, they are subject to civil fines and criminal prosecution by the EPA or empowered state agencies. Environmental agencies are not the only toxic pollutant watchdogs under the 1990 CAA, however. The act contains a provision modeled on the Clean Water Act that allows any citizen (or environmental group) to sue an industry for excessive toxic air pollutant emissions. The goal of this air pollution permit program is a 75 percent reduction in the emission of over 180 toxic chemicals.

Third, the 1990 amendments take aim at the acid rain problem by targeting a 50 percent reduction in sulfur dioxide emissions (baseline = 1980) and significant reductions in nitrogen dioxide emissions by the year 2000.[5] Importantly, these reductions are to be realized in large part through the use of marketable emission permits, which will allow electric utilities to buy and sell the right to emit sulfur and nitrogen dioxide. For example, if utility A can reduce pollution emissions more cheaply than can utility B, utility A reduces its emissions more than required by clean air regulations and sells utility B the right to emit more pollution than allowed by regulations. In this way, total pollution is still reduced, and reduced more cheaply than if both utilities A and B had to reduce their pollution by equal amounts. Initially, 110 of the nation's dirtiest utilities will be able to trade these permits, and by the year 2000 nearly all coal-fired utilities will be allowed to trade in the emission permit market. Over time, the number of permits (and thus the level of allowable pollution) will be reduced, though the EPA does have the authority to issue more permits if necessary (Cushman 1991).

Finally, the 1990 CAA provides a $250 million grant fund to retrain workers displaced by these regulations, and accelerates emission reductions of ozone-depleting chlorofluorocarbons.

Implementation of the 1990 CAA has been uneven, and it is in this implementation that we see the increased influence of state activities in air pollution control. The first sale of emission permits under the 1990 CAA took place in May 1992. The Tennessee Valley Authority (ironically, a federally owned utility) purchased the rights to 10,000 tons of sulfur dioxide emissions from Wisconsin Power and Light for between $2.5 and $3 million (Wald 1992a). The second sale of emission permits took place barely a week later, this time between Wisconsin Power and Light and the Duquesne Power Company in Pittsburgh. For both the TVA and Duquesne, the emission permits they purchased cover only a fraction of their required emission reductions under the 1990 CAA, but the purchases do buy them more time to comply fully with the regulations. Interestingly, it was the stricter air pollution control regulations in Wisconsin that turned Wisconsin Power and Light's extra emission reductions into a valuable asset that the utility could sell. Finally, in March 1993, a futures market for sulfur dioxide permits opened on the Chicago Merchantile Exchange, institutionalizing a trading scheme for implementing the 1990 CAA amendments.

The remainder of the implementation experiences under the 1990 CAA are not nearly so positive. Carrying out the provisions of the law was blocked by President Bush's election year moratorium on all new federal regulations and by the objections of Vice President Dan Quayle's Council on Competitiveness. These objections caused the EPA to miss CAA deadlines for issuing toxic pollution permit guidelines, new car pollution equipment requirements, automobile inspection and maintenance requirements, and standards for reformulated automotive fuels (Wald 1992c). The regulations that have been promulgated have made it easier for industries to exceed toxic air pollution emission limits and have exempted a number of utilities from having to participate in the marketable emission permit program (Cushman 1991). Several states have become impatient with what they perceive as federal efforts to delay or weaken new clean air regulations, and nine states brought suit against the federal government in 1992 for failing to carry out the provisions of the 1990 CAA (Wald 1992b). New CAA regulations did begin to be issued in late 1992, and all expectations are that President Clinton will release the remainder of these regulations in a more expeditious manner.

Regulating Water Quality

Water Pollution Control before 1972

Beginning with the Rivers and Harbors Act of 1889 and the Refuse Act of 1899, policymakers have sought ways to prevent the pollution of the nation's waterways.[6] The first piece of legislation reflecting an interest in water quality as an environmental and health issue, however, was the Water Pollution Control Act of 1948. Much like the early pieces of air quality legislation, this statute did little but recognize water pollution as a potential problem and provide limited federal funds for studying the situation. The Water Pollution Control Act of 1956 strengthened efforts at water pollution control by creating a grant program whereby the federal government would pay 55 percent of the construction costs of municipal wastewater treatment facilities. The 1956 act also authorized states to develop water quality standards for interstate waters within their borders and to develop implementation plans to meet these water quality standards. Once again, however, early federal legislation relied upon the states to carry out water pollution control efforts. The U.S. Public Health Service was only able to enforce water quality requirements through voluntary agreements between polluters and the states, so protecting water quality remained a serious problem (Freeman 1990).

The 1965 Water Quality Act was the first federal law to mandate state action to protect and improve water quality. The act now *required* states to set quantitative water quality criteria for interstate waters within their borders and to develop implementation plans to meet these water quality standards. These implementation plans were to estimate how much of a particular pollutant a particular body of water could safely absorb, and then place limits on individual polluters to make certain that this pollutant load limit was not exceeded. Detecting permit violations, prosecuting these violations, and issuing fines were all responsibilities left to the states, with minimal federal oversight. Detecting specific water quality permit violations and setting the water quality–based permit standards themselves were beyond the technical capacity of most states, however. In addition, most states ignored federal admonitions to devise and enforce a system of water pollution permits, and once again the federal government stepped in to take over primary responsibility in pollution control.

The Federal Water Pollution Control Act of 1972

The present set of surface water quality regulations are firmly rooted in the watershed Federal Water Pollution Control Act (typically referred to as the FWPCA or the Clean Water Act, CWA) of 1972. Like many pieces of environmental legislation, the FWPCA was passed largely in response to a series of highly publicized events such as the "death" of Lake Erie, and the Cuyahoga River in Ohio becoming so polluted that it periodically burst into flames. The Clean Water Act received strong bipartisan support in Congress (though President Nixon threatened a veto over its cost) and the act is perhaps the most ambitious piece of environmental legislation ever passed at the federal level. When developing the CWA, however, Congress also took pains to recognize and preserve the primary responsibilities and rights of the states in reducing, preventing, and controlling water pollution (Freedman 1987). The objective of the act is to restore and maintain the chemical, physical, and biological integrity of the nation's waters (U.S. EPA 1987). The Clean Water Act was intended to attain the very ambitious goal of zero pollutant discharge into the nation's waters by 1985. As an interim standard, the act set a goal of all waters being fishable and swimmable by 1983. These goals have not been met, however, and the goal of zero discharge likely never will be.

The first step in protecting water quality is deciding what use a particular body of water is intended to serve. Water quality designations range from industrial use (low water quality) to human consumption (high water quality), with the vast majority of waters being classified as fishable-swimmable (i.e., suitable for recreational activities). Each state is responsible for assessing its waters and assigning each body to a water quality use category. These assignments are done under the supervision of the EPA, and there has been significant pressure in recent years to phase out all water quality use categories below fishable-swimmable (95 percent of all waters are now categorized as fishable-swimmable or better). States still have wide latitude in placing use assessments on waters within their borders, however, and states utilize over one hundred different use categories across the country. In addition, states are responsible for determining what level of water quality counts as fishable-swimmable, or any other use designation. The water quality levels deemed to support a particular use can vary tremendously from state to state. For example, a level of water quality determined to be fishable-swimmable in Georgia might not meet the requirements for that same designation in Oregon.[7] Finally, all states make use of a set of anti-degradation criteria to protect particularly high quality watersheds (U.S. EPA 1988c).

The Clean Water Act provides two major tools that state and federal water quality officials use to protect and improve water quality: the Municipal Wastewater Treatment grant program, and the National Pollutant Discharge Elimination System (NPDES). Prior to 1972, most municipalities dumped untreated sewage directly into lakes, rivers, and oceans, creating serious quality problems in these bodies of water. Many municipalities that did treat their wastes before disposing of them provided only primary treatment (e.g., settling ponds) that left many pollutants unaffected. Under the 1972 municipal wastewater grant program, the federal government contributed 75 percent of the cost of constructing municipal wastewater treatment plants that would meet the Clean Water Act's goal of providing all municipalities with secondary wastewater treatment levels (i.e., removal of 85 percent of most pollutants and nutrients).[8]

The municipal wastewater treatment grant program was probably equal parts environmental policy and development policy. Serious water quality problems were limiting the potential for growth in some municipalities, and wastewater treatment plants removed this obstacle to growth. In addition, every state was entitled to at least one-half of 1 percent of the total wastewater treatment grant budget, regardless of need, which reinforced the distributive (some would say pork barrel) character of the program. While amendments to the Clean Water Act in 1981 reduced the federal government's share of treatment plant construction costs to 55 percent, the municipal wastewater treatment grant program remained by far the single largest budgetary expense of the federal EPA. (From 1972 to 1988, the EPA provided over $45 billion in grants to municipalities; U.S. EPA 1989a.)

Under the NPDES, state and federal regulators provide permits to all industrial and municipal facilities that discharge wastes into public waterways. The permits stipulate the amount and type of pollutants each facility is allowed to discharge, and the condition of this discharge.[9] The permits, which must be renewed on the average of every five years, also impose a strict set of reporting requirements on each facility. Periodically (though infrequently), state and/or federal regulators inspect both the facility and its reporting records for compliance and accuracy. The CWA, like the CAA, has a partial preemption provision that allows the states to accept responsibility for implementing their own NPDES programs. The EPA was initially reluctant to grant primacy to the states in water pollution control, but by 1992 thirty-eight states were setting permit requirements and undertaking facility investigations under the CWA (see chapter 3).

Municipal wastewater treatment grants and the NPDES permitting program are intended to control the amount and type of pollution entering any particular waterway in order to assure that the waterway meets its designated use. The CWA provided two sets of standards, or two methods, by which these permits could be given. The first method, the one originally envisioned as standard operating procedure by many federal regulators, relies upon water quality standards like those called for in the 1965 Water Quality Act. When using water quality standards, the safe carrying capacity of waterways receiving discharges is established for a number of pollutants. Permits are then issued to industrial and municipal dischargers so that the total amount of pollutants entering the waterway does not exceed its safe carrying capacity.

The water quality–based permitting system is ecologically sound, but it is extremely difficult to implement. Determining pollutant-carrying capacities for waterways requires complicated water quality models and an expensive and extensive system of water quality monitors. Furthermore, pollutant-carrying capacities vary with changes in ambient water conditions such as temperature and flow levels. These conditions make it very difficult to divide up the pollutant-carrying capacity of a body of water among a large group of municipal and industrial polluters. Water quality standards were quickly abandoned in favor of technology-based standards for issuing permits to dischargers. Under the technology-based approach, determining the safe carrying capacity of waters is bypassed, and instead the EPA places uniform technical treatment requirements on all polluters in a particular industry or all polluters using a particular manufacturing process. In order to receive an NPDES permit under technology-based permitting, each source has to install a specific set of pollution control equipment. The technology-based approach to permitting has produced a mind-boggling number of complex requirements for industrial and municipal dischargers, but implementing and enforcing uniform pollution control equipment standards is much easier than implementing and enforcing water quality–based permits. Moreover, because a technology-based permitting system is easier to set up, this scheme also produced results more quickly than the competing water quality–based approach.[10]

Under technology-based standards, all municipalities discharging effluent into public waters were to obtain a secondary level of sewage treatment by 1977. This deadline was extended to 1988 by the 1981 Clean Water Act Amendments, and extended again in 1987 by the Water Quality Act. Industrial dischargers were required to adopt the best practical control technology (BPT) by 1977 and the best available control technology economically achievable (BAT) by 1981. Although these deadlines were extended by amendments to the CWA in 1977, 1981, and 1987, many industries have not yet installed BAT controls. One reason for the failure of industry to meet BAT deadlines is the snail's pace at which EPA has promulgated BAT regulations. From 1979 to 1987, only twenty-nine BAT regulations were developed. The EPA cannot be held completely responsible for the lack of BAT standards, however, because nearly every standard proposed by the agency has been delayed in court by industry litigation (U.S. EPA 1987).

The Water Quality Act of 1987

Experience with federally directed water quality regulation identified and clarified a number of shortcomings of the Clean Water Act and its amendments. First of all, nearly all federal regulation under the CWA focused on point sources of water pollution, but by the late 1980s nonpoint source pollution accounted for nearly two-thirds of the pollutants reaching American waterways (Rosenbaum 1991), and was the leading pollution problem in a majority of states (U.S. EPA 1990). Second, though the CWA required EPA and the states to regulate toxic water pollutants, controlling these pollutants was generally ignored during the 1970s and 1980s. Third, several policy observers and legislators had become concerned about the excessive cost of the federal municipal wastewater treatment grant program. And fourth, most indicators suggested that progress toward improving water quality was very slow. The Water Quality Act (WQA) of 1987, passed nearly unanimously over the veto of President Reagan, sought to address these concerns regarding previous water quality legislation. The WQA also expanded the role of the states in water quality regulation, and returned authority to the states that had been removed to the federal level twenty years earlier.

The CWA of 1972 identified both point source and nonpoint source water pollution as problems, but nearly all efforts at controlling water pollution have focused upon point sources (i.e., the municipal wastewater treatment grant and NPDES programs both apply only to point sources of water pollution). The

Water Quality Act of 1987 addresses nonpoint source water pollution by directing the states to assess the seriousness of nonpoint source pollution and to minimize the impact of these pollutants on the environment. The states have always had primacy over nonpoint pollutant efforts. The WQA simply refocused state attention in this direction. Under the WQA, states are required to prepare a nonpoint source pollution assessment that identifies waters severely affected by nonpoint source pollutants and the major sources of nonpoint source pollution in these waters, including stormwater runoff. States (and localities) are then directed to devise implementation plans incorporating the "best management practices" that will control these nonpoint source pollution sources (U.S. EPA 1990; Hansen et al. 1988).[11] The states are assisted in their nonpoint pollution control efforts by an EPA nonpoint source pollution task force (which published its final guidelines in late 1989), the Departments of Agriculture and Commerce, and the U.S. Geological Survey (U.S. EPA 1990).

Prior to the mid-1980s, surface water regulation emphasized traditional pollutants such as bacteria, nutrients, sediments, and oxygen-demanding wastes. The 1987 WQA, however, focuses more attention on trace toxic elements in water such as pesticides and heavy metals. Toxic pollutants are the most significant remaining problem in industrial and municipal effluent (U.S. EPA 1990). Under pressure from environmental groups, the EPA has significantly stepped up its efforts at regulating toxic pollutants from industry.[12] States have increased their toxic pollution control efforts as well. The WQA requires states to develop lists of waters impaired by toxic pollution, and then develop individual impact control strategies (i.e., new NPDES permits) for each of the point sources contributing to this toxic pollution (U.S. EPA 1990). States were supposed to have these toxic discharge control programs in place by 1990, and while only thirty-five had done so by 1991, all states are expected to have completed toxic discharge control programs by 1993 (Schneider 1991a).

The 1987 WQA also seeks to control toxic water pollution through an aggressive industrial pretreatment program. In pretreatment, industries that produce toxic pollutants are required to treat their effluent to remove these toxins before releasing the remainder of their waste stream into municipal sewage systems. The rationale for pretreatment stems from the fact that an increasing number of industries are discharging their wastes into municipal sewer systems and most municipal treatment facilities are not equipped to handle toxic substances. At best, the substances pass through the municipal facility unaffected, and at worst they can damage the facility itself, rendering the treatment of other wastes difficult or impossible. It has been estimated that 35 percent of all toxic chemicals reaching the nation's waters do so by passing through municipal treatment systems (U.S. EPA 1988b). Pretreatment programs are developed and implemented by municipalities, with some state aid, and the EPA has begun enforcing federal pretreatment program standards on recalcitrant municipalities (U.S. EPA 1990).

The 1987 Water Quality Act also made significant changes in how the construction of municipal wastewater treatment plants is funded. The municipal wastewater treatment grant program was replaced by a series of one-time grants to the states for municipal wastewater treatment. States use these one-time grants to set up revolving loan funds, and municipalities that want to build or upgrade wastewater treatment facilities receive loans out of these funds. The loan fund greatly reduces federal support for municipal wastewater treatment (all federal wastewater treatment grants are scheduled to end by 1995), but most municipalities presently have secondary-level treatment plants or better, and the loan fund allows the states to follow their own funding priorities when constructing wastewater treatment plants. Thirteen states had fully operational revolving loan funds by 1990 (U.S. EPA 1990). In a final municipal treatment note, the EPA expects to issue a set of rules in 1993 to regulate the toxic pollutant content and disposal of the 7 million metric tons of sludge produced annually at municipal wastewater treatment plants.

Finally, EPA and U.S. Geological Survey data, along with steadily improving state water quality reports, suggest that progress toward improving water quality is moving along rather slowly. The Water Quality Act provides additional tools for those states having a particularly difficult time meeting water quality standards. Monitoring technology and water quality modeling have both improved tremendously over the past two decades, and these technical improvements are reflected in an increased use of water quality–based permits (as opposed to technology-based permits) at the state level. If states identify bodies of water that will not be able to meet their use designations with BAT permit compliance, they may, if they wish, develop a special water quality–based permitting scheme for these waters. Furthermore, if municipal facilities are responsible for a body of water not meeting its designated use, states are authorized to impose tertiary treatment requirements on these facilities (tertiary treatment removes between 95 and 98 percent of most pollutants and nutrients from wastewater).

Summary

Understanding the substance of environmental policies is at least as important as understanding the context within which those policies are made. Moreover, knowledge of both policy context and policy substance is essential for a thorough understanding of environmental policy analysis. This chapter has provided a brief overview of the substantive content of air and water pollution control legislation. Air and water quality regulations have a long history. In both cases, initial efforts at controlling pollution were made by states and municipalities. As evidence mounted regarding the scope of environmental damage, and as public opinion responded to this evidence, state efforts at environmental protection were judged to be insufficient. The Clean Air Act of 1970 signaled the start of an era of federal dominance in pollution control, but this era was short-lived. Each revision of the Clean Air Act and Clean Water Act sought to address shortcomings and criticisms of previous legislation, and one common method of redressing these shortcomings was to return more policy responsibility to the states. The discussions that follow regarding the roles states play in environmental policy and the environmental consequences of state policy activities assume an understanding of the context and substance of pollution control policy.

Notes

1. These justifications for devolving policy authority to the states are not easily reconcilable with the justifications given earlier for centralizing environmental policy responsibility at the national level. Decisions regarding the level of government best suited for environmental protection depend in large part upon the importance one attaches to environmental protection and assumptions regarding the capacity of state governments. This question is returned to in chapter 3.

2. The EPA is reluctant to develop and impose its own federal implementation plans on the states, for obvious political reasons. Under pressure from environmental groups, however, the EPA has devised CAA implementation plans for Phoenix, Arizona; Los Angeles, California; Chicago, Illinois; and several smaller cities (Z. Smith 1992).

3. As of 1987, only Cleveland had lost federal highway funds for failing to meet Clean Air Act requirements (Lowry 1992).

4. The CAA of 1977 was not the first extension of most of these deadlines. The EPA extended many of the deadlines administratively in 1973, 1974, and 1975 (Z. Smith 1992).

5. The acid rain provisions require that sulfur dioxide emissions be reduced 10 million tons and nitrogen dioxide emissions reduced 2 million tons by 1995. Limits on sulfur dioxide emissions will be reduced to 8.9 million tons by 2000 through the use of the marketable emission permit system.

6. The original purpose of the Refuse Act was to prohibit sawmills, slaughterhouses, and even steamboats and garbage barges from tossing so much physical garbage into rivers that they posed a hazard to navigation. Any actor wanting to dispose of refuse that had the potential for obstructing navigation had to obtain a disposal permit from the Army Corps of Engineers. In the late 1960s and early 1970s, environmental groups attempted (with little success) to invoke the Refuse Act when seeking to prohibit the dumping of raw wastes into the nation's waters.

7. These variations in state water quality use designations are not always due to less stringent regulations. There are many bodies of water, mostly in the South and Southwest, that could never meet water quality standards in other areas of the country, even in their natural state. The character of surface water quality within a state is largely determined by the characteristics of the physical environment and the ecosystem or ecoregion that predominates in that state. These differences across states in "natural" levels of water quality are one reason for the large amount of discretion afforded to state regulators in determining water quality use designations. These natural variations also make evaluating water quality on a national scale a very difficult task.

8. The municipal wastewater treatment grant program only provides money for construction costs, not for operation and maintenance costs. This has led many municipalities to build "cadillac" treatment facilities that they cannot afford to operate or maintain. Problems with maintenance and a lack of skilled operating personnel lead many of these plants to operate inefficiently and below their full capacity (Ingram and Mann 1984).

9. Because industries and municipalities do not have to pay for these permits, many critics of federal surface water regulation, from environmentalists to free market econo-

mists, have denounced the permits as little more than free licenses to pollute.

10. Quick results notwithstanding, the voluminous set of technological regulations and requirements has been criticized by students of public policy as a humongous bureaucratic morass. In addition, most economists maintain that such a uniform system is inherently inefficient because it places pollution control burdens on polluters that are either too heavy or too light, and because it discourages the use of innovative pollution control technologies that may be cheaper, more efficient, or more effective than those technologies required by the permits.

11. "Best management practices" in nonpoint source water pollution control include public education efforts (e.g., admonitions not to overfertilize lawns or dump waste oil in street gutters), as well as more technological requirements such as altered agricultural practices, new construction runoff regulations, stabilization of abandoned surface mining operations, and treatment of stormwater runoff.

12. The 1972 Clean Water Act required the EPA to set toxic pollutant effluent standards for fifty industrial categories, but by 1990 the EPA had only developed toxic water pollutant regulations for twenty-four industries. After being sued by the Sierra Club and the Natural Resources Defense Council, the EPA agreed to set toxic pollutant standards for sixteen additional industrial categories by 1996 (Schneider 1992b).

3

State Roles in Environmental Policy

State responsibilities in pollution control have increased significantly in the last twenty years. This expansion of state policy responsibility did not occur in a vacuum, however. Important changes in state political systems predisposed the states to successfully handle increased authority in pollution control, whether these policies were developed spontaneously by the states or thrust upon them by national political figures. This chapter briefly recaps national and state-level political changes that led to the greater role of states in environmental policy. The chapter then closely examines the specific roles played by the states in pollution control policy and notable state policy initiatives in these areas.

"New Federalism" in Environmental Policy

President Reagan's "new federalism" program, launched after the 1980 election, was the most far-reaching domestic policy initiative in twenty-five years. Federal activities under new federalism can be grouped into two general categories. First, the government in Washington, D.C., devolved increased policy responsibility to the states (where, it was argued, responsibility for most domestic programs belonged). A good deal of pressure was placed on state governments to accept greater responsibility in several policy areas (e.g., the "great swap," whereby the federal government proposed that the states take full responsibility for medicaid programs in return for the federal government taking over the much smaller Aid to Families with Dependent Children program). Exceptional devolutionary pressure was brought to bear in environmental policy, however. In a three-year period (1981 to 1984), the delegation of environmental programs to the states doubled from 33 percent to 66 percent of all eligible programs. With new federal programs, the delegation of new policy responsibilities, and a decrease in voluntary compliance resulting from the changed political climate, work loads in state environmental agencies doubled between 1980 and 1984 (Stanfield 1984).

Second, the federal government slashed federal fiscal contributions to devolved programs in an effort to shrink governmental domestic expenditures. During President Nixon's new federalism push of the 1970s, the federal government provided increased financial assistance to carry out increased state policy responsibilities. Reagan's new federalism, on the other hand, *cut* federal funding for both federal and state domestic policy activities. For example, federal grants as a percentage of total state expenditures fell from 28 percent in 1978 to just under 18 percent in 1990. The overall value of federal aid to the states dropped 39 percent from 1980 to 1987 (ACIR 1991). Cuts in federal support for state activities went even deeper in environmental policy. In 1979, federal grants to the states made up 43 percent of the EPA's budget. By 1988, federal grants made up only 31 percent of a much smaller EPA budget (see chapter 1). Over this same period, federal support for state air pollution control programs fell by 54 percent, while support for state water pollution control activities declined by 68 percent (CBO 1988).[1]

Members of the Reagan administration promoted what they saw as the two main virtues of new federalism. First, returning responsibility to the states was supposed to render policymaking and implementation more efficient, effective, and responsive to citizen demands. Second, these initiatives would redress a constitutional imbalance in policy authority between the federal government and the states.

Debates about federalism and the "proper" level of government authority are commonly cast in constitutional terms. Conflicts regarding the intentions of the founding fathers find their roots in the contradictions between Article 1, Section 8 and the Tenth Amendment, and between the Fourteenth and Tenth amendments. Casting federalist debates in constitutional terms suggests that one and only one correct distribution of policy authority is possible, and that all other distributions are illegitimate. More often than not, however, posturing over the constitutional fidelity of increasing or decreasing the degree of "federalism" in a policy area is mostly a ruse for camouflaging the true policy agenda of the participants. Questions of federalism are really questions over the proper scope of conflict, and as the scope of conflict changes (i.e., at the local, state, or national level), so does the balance of power among policy participants. Debates about federalism and the "proper" level of government authority are usually policy debates in disguise, because by controlling the scope of conflict, one can heavily influence the substance of public policy (Nice 1987).

Many researchers have questioned the proposed benefits of Reagan's new federalism. Most of this research concludes that new federalism was in fact a guise for an underlying goal of significant policy retrenchment in the areas of social welfare, occupational safety and health, and environmental protection (Nathan and Doolittle 1987). The Reagan administration tried to achieve this goal by devolving policy authority for these programs to the states (a scope of conflict traditionally less friendly to social and environmental policy advocates and less active in these areas), and by simultaneously cutting federal funding for these programs (Nathan and Doolittle 1983). Devolutionary new federalism initiatives were not always applied consistently, however. Where state policy activity and innovation ran afoul of Reagan administration policy objectives (e.g., AFDC quality control, nuclear emergency evacuation plans, and state liquor laws), the heavy hand of federal preemption was brought down to coerce state compliance (see Eisinger and Gormley 1988). While the effects of the new federalism strategies were significant in some areas, they were also uneven (Peterson et al. 1986).

The states became increasingly important in environmental policy during the 1980s. Increases in state policy responsibility are not simply a function of Reagan's new federalism, however. As we saw in chapter 2, state responsibilities in pollution control have been expanding since the mid-1970s, and the importance of the states in environmental policy did not wane during the presidency of George Bush. Moreover, as Bill Clinton, a former governor, takes over the presidency, state responsibilities in pollution control will likely remain of critical importance through the 1990s.

State Capacity

The performance of a state's political system depends to a great extent on the capacity of that system's governmental institutions. With states taking over a significant amount of responsibility for environmental programs, as well as numerous other policy areas, an important question arises over the ability and competence of the states to administer these programs. Research in the 1950s and 1960s generally concluded that the states were ill suited to accept or carry out an expanded role within the federal system. State governments labored under outmoded constitutions and revenue systems, unrepresentative and unprofessional legislatures, weak governors, and weak and disjointed administrative agencies. State governments were criticized as being racist, incompetent, and unwilling to change, and for routinely ignoring their policy responsibilities (Davis and Lester 1989; Sanford 1967). State activities in pollution control fit this description rather well (see chapter 2). A few researchers, however, claimed that states were unfairly charged with fiscal irresponsibility and administrative incompetence (see Elazar 1974).

The capacity of states to accept and administer expanding policy authority has increased in the past few decades. Over the past twenty-five years, almost every facet of state government structures and operations has been transformed (ACIR 1985). Beginning in the late 1960s and continuing through the 1970s, state governments underwent a metamorphosis from which they emerged stronger, smarter, and more willing and able to undertake significant policy responsibilities. A 1981 report by the Advisory Commission on Intergovernmental Relations summed up this process nicely:

> State governments have been transformed. Continuing a reform period unparalleled in their history, they are emerging, for the most part, as competent, vigorous, and assertive governments. They are more open, more responsible, and more accountable than they were in the past. While all are not equally so, and much work remains to be done, the change has been phenomenal. (Reeves 1981, 5)

Reagan's new federalism initiatives prodded the states to continue reforming and improving their governmental institutions through the 1980s (Bowman and Kearney 1986, 1988).

State capacity has been described as "the ability to anticipate and influence change; make informed and intelligent decisions about policy; attract and absorb resources . . . and evaluate current activities to guide future actions" (Honadale 1981, 578). When discussing the capacity of state governments to accept significant policy responsibilities, however, one has to be specific about what type of "capacity" one is talking about, since capacity is a multi-dimensional concept (see Bowman and Kearney 1988). Charles Warren (1982) has categorized state abilities in this area as fiscal capacity, managerial capacity, and political capacity. All three forms of capacity are necessary if states are to adequately carry out policy responsibilities. Fortunately, these three types of capacity have all improved over the past twenty-five years. In terms of policymaking and implementation, states are more representative, responsive, activist, and professional today than they ever have been (ACIR 1985).

Fiscal Capacity

Fiscal capacity refers to revenue levels, revenue sources, and the use states make of these revenue sources. Excluding social security, states spend far more on civilian domestic programs than does the federal government, and this gap has been increasing (Gray and Eisinger 1991). Developing and administering these policies takes money, and states lacking adequate fiscal capacity will find both of these tasks difficult. State governments have also been forced to increase their fiscal capacity in the face of reduced aid from the federal government, and they have responded. State governments are using many more revenue sources in the 1990s than they did in the 1960s. Of particular note is the tremendous increase in the use of state personal and corporate income taxes, which by 1990 were responsible for 40 percent of state revenues—nearly double the level of the 1960s (ACIR 1991). The corresponding decrease in reliance upon sales taxes, personal property taxes, and user fees resulted in state tax systems that were not only more stable, but more progressive as well.

Increased spending for policy programs accompanied this increased utilization of revenue sources. States spent nearly $600 billion in 1990, compared with only $73 billion in 1964 (constant 1987 dollars). Per capita state spending has risen faster than spending at any other level of government, increasing a whopping 269 percent in constant-dollar terms between 1959 and 1979 (Davis and Lester 1989). This increase in expenditures continued during the 1980s; from 1980 to 1990, total per capita state government expenditures increased 27 percent in real terms (ACIR 1991). States face limits in increasing their fiscal capacity, however. Recent economic downturns had many states running large general fund deficits between 1988 and 1992. States have been covering these deficits using surpluses in state social insurance funds, but this cannot go on much longer. In the near term, states must either hold the line on spending, or increase taxes and revenues again—an unlikely prospect given the present political climate (U.S. Department of Commerce 1992).

Managerial Capacity

Clearly, state fiscal capacity has improved over the past few decades, but what of state managerial capacity? Managerial capacity refers to the ability of states to successfully carry out their charges in program design, policy execution and implementation, and the delivery of public services (Warren 1982). Managerial capacity then is closely tied to the capacity of state governmental institutions. Without a doubt, the office of governor has been strengthened throughout the nation. Fewer term limitations and an increased reliance upon professional staffs have created more professional state chief executives. Moreover, state governors hold increased powers to control state agency appointments, increased budgetary responsibilities, and stronger veto authority. State governors are not only exercising more power within their home states, but they are increasingly active in national policy matters as well (Beyle 1988; Sabato 1983).

Governors have not been the only actors affected by reforms in state governments; state legislatures are also more active and much more professional than in decades past (Rosenthal 1989). These legislatures were rebuilt nearly from scratch during the 1960s and 1970s. Some of this restructuring was the result of federal judicial mandates (e.g., *Baker* v. *Carr*, 369 U.S. 186, 1962). Other modernizations have originated at the state level, however. State legislatures experience less member turnover, have longer legislative sessions, and provide better compensation for legislators. State legislative staffs have been vastly expanded as well. In 1988, there were approximately 20,000 individuals working for state legislatures—a more than 200 percent increase from the 1960s (Rosenthal 1989). These reforms have turned state legislatures into the most powerful and important force in the policy environment of state administrative agencies, and the most influential actors in state policymaking in general (Brudney and Hebert 1987). (Some have questioned whether this increased professionalism and policy activity has actually been translated into improved policymaking, however; see Rosenthal 1988).

Perhaps no institution of state government has been transformed to the degree of state bureaucracies. Administrative reorganizations and constitutional revisions have rationalized bureaucratic structure in many states. State administrators are better educated, more professional, better compensated, and more representative of the general public than their counterparts of just a decade or two ago. This increase in professionalism has led to a higher degree of policy competence among state administrators (Haas and Wright 1988; Hebert and Wright 1982). In an interesting argument, Gormley (1989) suggests that much of the improvement in state bureaucratic capability has resulted from federally required levels of bureaucratic staffing and competence that have accompanied the increased devolution of policy authority to the states. In environmental policy, for example, many states feel that their environmental administrators now have more knowledge and experience than officials at the EPA (Lowry 1992).

Political Capacity

State political capacity is more difficult to define, but it relates to the ability of state governments to "articulate needs, weigh competing demands, establish priorities, and allocate resources" (Warren 1982, 37). From this definition, political capacity appears to overlap the institutional improvements associated with managerial capacity. At heart though, political capacity refers to a state's ability to make difficult, necessary, and innovative policy decisions. Skeptics of devolving increased policy responsibility to the states are most concerned about questions of political capacity. Many critics of state capacity openly wonder whether state governments have improved *enough* to adequately handle their new policy responsibilities (ACIR 1985). State governments have been increasingly prominent in policy innovations, however, suggesting that some of the worries of these critics may be unfounded. In the words of Carl Van Horn (1989, 7):

> By the late 1980s, state governments were the driving force in policy innovation. . . . State policy leadership is perhaps best illustrated by recent developments in four policy domains—economic development, education, welfare, and environmental protection. In each instance, the states, not the federal government, have initiated successful policy experiments that have eventually been copied or endorsed by the national government. And in each case, state governments are providing the lion's share of funds to carry out new public strategies.

State governments have moved to the forefront in tackling the tough issues of toxic substances regulation, low-level radioactive waste disposal, gun control, comparable worth, AIDS, homelessness, surrogate motherhood, education for persons with disabilities, drug abuse, living wills, sexual harassment, rights for homosexuals, economic development, welfare reform—the list appears endless. States are also stepping in to fill the federal withdrawal in antitrust litigation and First Amendment protections, and scholars of state government and politics expect states to continue their policy leadership in consumer protection, urban enterprise zones, sunset laws, and many other policy areas (ACIR 1985; Gray and Eisinger 1991).

State Responsibilities in Pollution Control

Government activities in environmental policy can be grouped into five areas of program responsibility: setting goals and standards, designing and implementing programs, monitoring and enforcement, research and development, and funding (see CBO 1988). States have the opportunity to take the lead in each of these progam areas, and while they must meet certain federal minimum requirements in their environmental programs, few obstacles prevent states from developing programs that exceed these federal minimums.

The EPA was initially very reluctant to devolve authority over environmental programs to the states, mainly because federal officials did not trust the states to handle the job. Changes in environmental statutes and improvements in state government capacity during the 1970s, coupled with Reagan's new federalism initiatives of the 1980s, prompted the EPA to increase the devolution of policy authority to the states, however. States take over the implementation of federal environmental programs through the process of partial preemption, or *primacy* (see chapter 2). A large majority of states have accepted primacy responsibilities in environmental protection, and states are extremely reluctant to relinquish primacy authority to the federal government.[2] A few state policy scholars claim that partial preemption is little more than regulation by federal fiat, and that states deeply resent this federal intrusion into state policymaking. These same scholars believe that primacy minimizes the role of state legislatures, governors, and courts, weakening state policymaking systems and turning the states into little more than administrative arms of the federal government (see Crotty 1987 for a good example).

The debilitating effects of primacy on state environmental policy capacity are grossly overstated. To one degree or another, states are almost always uncomfortable with federal agencies meddling in state policy affairs. Environmental policy is not exceptional in this regard. Furthermore, many state administrators feel that federal-state relationships in environmental policy improved only marginally even after significant increases in state authority under Reagan's new federalism (Tobin 1992). Still, state officials are very satisfied in their contacts with EPA regional offices and three-quarters of all state contact with the EPA is through regional offices. Moreover, research into the attitudes of state environmental administrators shows that states recognize and appreciate federal assistance in enforcement and research and development, and a majority of state environmental officials feel that they could not get along without the EPA (Tobin 1992).

States have responded to increased state capacity and increased policy devolution from Nixon to Reagan by sharply expanding their policy activity in pollution control (see below). Even when the federal government has tried to circumscribe state activities in environmental protection, states have been able to maintain significant autonomy in enforcing environmental regulations (Hedge et al.

1991; B. Wood 1991). Recent increases in independent state policy activity and state administrative autonomy hardly serve as evidence that federal oversight of primacy marginalizes state legislatures, governors, and courts, or hampers state policy efforts in environmental protection.

Setting Goals and Standards

The Clean Air Act and Clean Water Act contain fairly specific goals for environmental quality, and emission and effluent standards are developed in an attempt to meet these goals. Governments have two options when setting standards; they may set uniform standards or flexible standards. Uniform standards set levels for emissions, effluent, and environmental quality that are enforced universally across the country. They are the same in Jackson, Mississippi, as they are in Missoula, Montana. The justification for uniform standards is that each citizen has an inherent right to the same level of environmental quality (or the same level of environmental risk). In short, uniform standards reflect the ideal of equal protection under the law. Flexible standards, on the other hand, are designed to be adapted to local environmental and economic conditions. The first justification for flexible standards is found in the great variation in ecosystem types found across the United States. Some ecosystems are better able to handle pollutant loads than are others, and it makes little sense to hold these ecosystems to identical protective standards. Second, the difficulty and cost of pollution control varies from situation to situation because of differences in industrial processes, products, ambient environmental conditions, and so forth. Pollution control standards that ignore these differences (i.e., uniform standards) produce requirements that are too stringent in some situations, too lenient in others, and economically inefficient across the board.[3] The final justification for flexible standards lies in the ideal of a responsive government. If a majority of citizens desire a level of environmental quality that is higher or lower than the federally mandated level, then these preferences should be reflected in local or state environmental protection standards (so long as these standards do not affect citizens in other localities or states).

We find examples of both kinds of standards in air and water quality regulation. The Clean Air Act requires the EPA to set uniform mobile and stationary emission standards, uniform national emission standards for hazardous pollutants, and uniform NAAQS for the six criteria pollutants. Atmospheric conditions vary comparatively little across the country, and air pollutants travel easily across state boundaries. As a result, Congress felt compelled to adopt the "equal protection" justification for uniform standards in air pollution control. States can enact air quality standards that exceed federal minimum standards, however. In surface water protection, states have the authority to determine water quality designations and set flexible water quality standards that reflect differences in the natural conditions of these aquatic ecosystems.

Many states have taken advantage of their opportunity to exceed federal air pollution standards. In 1991, eleven northeastern states and the District of Columbia agreed to adopt California's strict guidelines for new car emissions (recall that the CAA of 1990 allows state variation in mobile source emission standards). Policymakers in the Northeast believe that these mobile source emission controls are a relatively inexpensive way to reduce pollutants contributing to urban smog problems. The enactment of these standards means that one-third of the population of the United States is now covered by mobile source emission standards more stringent than those required by the federal government (Wald 1991a, 1991b). Even Texas has gotten into the act by requiring that 90 percent of all state-owned vehicles run on compressed natural gas by 1996. Stronger mobile source pollutant standards present a clear example of how environmental groups have successfully lobbied state governments after being stymied at the federal level.

In the mid-1980s, eight northeastern states, acting together through the Northeastern States for Coordinated Air Use Management, voted to adopt California's tough clean fuel requirements. The EPA initially threatened to preempt these requirements, but eventually the federal agency acquiesced to the state rules (Kritz 1989). These state requirements later became the basis for the reformulated fuel requirements in the 1990 CAA. States have continued to push the boundaries of clean fuel requirements in the 1990s. The California Air Resources Board announced in 1991 that it was adopting new standards on gasoline even tougher than those required under the 1990 CAA. While these cleaner fuels will be more expensive (costing about fifteen cents more per gallon), they will reduce automobile pollution 30 to 40 percent and are expected to be more cost-effective than other methods of controlling air pollution. The group of northeastern states is now debating whether or not to adopt these new California regulations (Wald 1991c). Finally, this same group of northeastern states has agreed to impose new nitrogen dioxide emission standards on power plants that are stronger than the standards required by the 1990 CAA. While these requirements are relatively inexpensive ($1,000 to $5,000 per ton of nitrous oxides removed), they will require extensive pollution control retrofits on most coal-fired utilities (Wald 1991a). One is struck by the fact that states required these new controls, in response to new scientific evidence regarding nitrogen dioxide's contribution to urban smog, at the same time the Bush administration was blocking the implementation of the new federal regulations these state standards were designed to exceed.

While some states have laws prohibiting state regulations from exceeding federal standards (Colorado and North Carolina, for example), Arkansas, Hawaii, Maine, North Dakota, Florida, and several other states have passed NAAQ standards more stringent than those required by the EPA (Jessup 1990). States can also bring significant pressure to bear on the EPA for changing national air quality standards. In 1991, New York, Connecticut, and three other states joined the American Lung Association (ALA) and the Natural Resources Defense

Council in suing the EPA over the NAAQS for ozone. The CAA requires the EPA to set air quality standards that protect human health with an adequate margin of safety, and to review these standards every five years. The EPA relaxed the NAAQS for ozone from 0.08 parts per million to 0.12 parts per million in the early 1980s, but had never reviewed that standard. The states and the ALA felt that the ozone standard was dangerous and outdated, citing evidence that ozone has significant adverse health effects below the current EPA standard of 0.12 parts per million (Schneider 1991b).[4]

Finally, state innovations in pollution standards are not limited to criteria air pollutants. States have literally hundreds of water quality classifications, and many of these are more stringent than minimum EPA requirements (U.S. EPA 1988c). In addition, a handful of states currently regulate carbon dioxide emissions, and a few more have taken steps to reduce their emissions of chlorofluorocarbons. Finally, prior to the CAA of 1990, every state in the union regulated air toxins as stringently or more so than the federal government (Kritz 1989).

Designing and Implementing Programs

In designing and implementing programs, states determine what techniques will be employed to meet policy goals and standards. Both the Clean Air Act and the Clean Water Act embody a federal oversight role in program design and implementation, chiefly through partial preemption of these programs. Each act, however, envisions that the states will take over primary responsibility in pollution control. In addition to their own responsibilities under the Clean Air Act, states may accept primacy for regulating new stationary sources of pollution (48 had done so by 1992), hazardous air pollutants (47 had done so by 1992), and the prevention of significant deterioration (35 had done so by 1992; see table 3.1). Under the Clean Water and Water Quality acts, states may take over responsibility for the NPDES and industrial pretreatment programs, issue general water quality permits for entire water basins, and regulate federal facilities in water pollution control. As of November 1992, twenty-four states had accepted primacy in all four of these areas (see table 3.2).

Variations and innovations in designing and implementing state pollution control programs go far beyond accepting regulatory responsibilities under partial preemption. While some states are prevented from exceeding federal environmental standards (see above), almost every state "fills in the holes" in federal environmental protection regulations with innovative pollution control programs. In air pollution control, "bubbles," offsets, and emissions trading were all innovations pioneered by state governments. The state of New York passed the nation's first law aimed at controlling acid rain (several years before the federal government), and the states of New Hampshire, Minnesota, Massachusetts, and Wisconsin soon followed suit.

The Wisconsin Air Toxics Task Force (WATTF), created in 1983, presents a good example of state innovation in developing air pollution control programs.

Table 3.1

States with Primary Administrative Responsibility under the Clean Air Act, October 1992

State	NSPS[1]	HAZ[2]	PSD[3]	State	NSPS[1]	HAZ[2]	PSD[3]
Alabama	X	X	X	Montana	X	X	X
Alaska	X	X	X	Nebraska	X	X	X
Arizona	X	X	X	Nevada	X	X	
Arkansas	X	X		New Hampshire	X	X	
California	X	X		New Jersey	X	X	X
Colorado	X	X		New Mexico	X	X	X
Connecticut	X	X		New York	X	X	
Delaware	X	X	X	North Carolina	X	X	X
Florida	X	X		North Dakota	X	X	X
Georgia	X	X		Ohio	X	X	
Hawaii	X	X	X	Oklahoma	X	X	X
Idaho	X		X	Oregon	X	X	X
Illinois			X	Pennsylvania	X	X	X
Indiana	X	X		Rhode Island	X	X	
Iowa	X	X	X	South Carolina	X	X	X
Kansas	X	X	X	South Dakota	X	X	
Kentucky	X	X	X	Tennessee	X	X	X
Louisiana	X	X	X	Texas		X	X
Maine	X	X	X	Utah	X	X	X
Maryland	X	X	X	Vermont	X	X	
Massachusetts	X	X		Virginia	X	X	X
Michigan	X	X	X	Washington	X	X	X
Minnesota	X	X	X	West Virginia	X	X	X
Mississippi	X	X	X	Wisconsin	X	X	X
Missouri	X	X	X	Wyoming	X		X

[1]New source performance standards.

[2]Hazardous air pollutants.

[3]Prevention of significant deterioration. Some states are authorized to undertake PSD reviews and issue PSD permits, with the EPA regional office giving final permit approval. These states are included with those that have full PSD authorization.

Sources: U.S. Code of Federal Regulations, 40 CFR 60.3b and 40 CFR 61.3b; and U.S. EPA Office of Air and Radiation, FOIA Request RIN-5949-92.

The WATTF was made up of environmentalists, industrialists, and public officials, and was charged with developing a state policy to control toxic air pollutants not covered by federal legislation. Under the supervision of the Wisconsin Department of Natural Resources, the WATTF created one of the first and most comprehensive toxic pollution control programs in the country. The Wisconsin program has been emulated by other states, though there is still remarkable variation in state toxic pollutant control programs. For example, in 1991 the toxic air pollution control program in Connecticut listed 853 toxic pollutants, while a similar program in Texas listed none (Lowry 1992).

Table 3.2

States with Primary Administrative Responsibility under the Clean Water Act, October 1992

State	NPDES[1]	GEN[2]	PRE[3]	FED[4]	State	NPDES[1]	GEN[2]	PRE[3]	FED[4]
Alabama	X	X	X	X	Montana	X	X		X
Alaska					Nebraska	X	X	X	X
Arizona					Nevada	X	X		X
Arkansas	X	X	X	X	New Hampshire				
California	X	X	X	X	New Jersey	X	X	X	X
Colorado	X	X			New Mexico				
Connecticut	X	X	X	X	New York	X			X
Delaware	X				North Carolina	X	X	X	X
Florida					North Dakota	X	X		X
Georgia	X	X	X	X	Ohio	X	X	X	X
Hawaii	X	X	X	X	Oklahoma				
Idaho					Oregon	X	X	X	X
Illinois	X	X		X	Pennsylvania	X	X		X
Indiana	X	X		X	Rhode Island	X	X	X	X
Iowa	X	X	X	X	South Carolina	X	X	X	X
Kansas	X			X	South Dakota				
Kentucky	X	X	X	X	Tennessee	X	X	X	X
Louisiana					Texas				
Maine					Utah	X	X	X	X
Maryland	X	X	X	X	Vermont	X		X	
Massachusetts					Virginia	X	X	X	X
Michigan	X		X	X	Washington	X	X	X	
Minnesota	X	X	X	X	West Virginia	X	X	X	X
Mississippi	X	X	X	X	Wisconsin	X	X	X	X
Missouri	X	X	X	X	Wyoming	X	X		X

[1]National pollutant discharge elimination system.
[2]General permitting authority.
[3]Industrial pretreatment permitting authority.
[4]Authority to regulate federal facilities.
Source: U.S. EPA Office of Water, FOIA Request RIN-05949-92.

States have also taken the lead in developing and implementing innovative water pollution control programs. In controlling point sources of pollution, the North Carolina Division of Environmental Management relies extensively upon water quality criteria to issue NPDES permits. North Carolina is able to do this by relying upon information from over 340 ambient water quality monitors scattered around the state (this is nearly as many monitors as the U.S. Geological Survey uses to measure water quality across the entire country). North Carolina also has the nation's premier water pollution prevention program (Lowry 1992). In nonpoint source pollution control, Massachusetts, Pennsylvania, North Carolina, Illinois, Indiana, Wisconsin, Wyoming, and the states surrounding Chesapeake Bay all have extensive and innovative nonpoint source programs (U.S. EPA 1988c).

Washington's Centennial Clean Water Program (CCWP), launched in 1986, presents a nice mix of innovations in controlling both point source and nonpoint source water pollutants. The CCWP is funded by a state tax on tobacco, and this money can be used to upgrade municipal wastewater treatment systems, control nonpoint source pollution, protect and restore lakes and streams, separate storm sewers from waste sewers, and fund several other approved projects. Under the CCWP, localities submit water pollution control plans to the Washington Department of Ecology, and the state provides the localities with grant money to carry out the projects. Localities must match this state grant with local funds, labor, or the contribution of materials. State funding decisions are based upon the seriousness of the problem to be corrected and the level of local support (i.e., funding focuses on the most important and popular programs) (U.S. EPA 1988c).[5]

Monitoring and Enforcement

Enforcement activities include monitoring emissions, effluent, and environmental quality; inspecting facilities; levying and collecting fines; issuing notices of violation and administrative orders; invoking civil and criminal penalties; and revoking permits. Both the Clean Air and Clean Water acts expect states to adopt primary responsibility for enforcing pollution regulations, and this level of state responsibility increased during the 1980s. States undertake far more monitoring and enforcement actions than does the EPA. In 1988, the states regulated twice as many "major" NPDES permittees as did the EPA (5,000 versus 2,500) and over three times as many "minor" NPDES sources (40,000 versus 12,000). In addition, state backlogs in issuing NPDES permits were only one-half as long as federal permit backlogs (U.S. EPA 1988b). In air pollution control, the states completed 28,000 inspections and monitoring actions in 1988, while the federal EPA conducted only 2,800 (Lowry 1992). Moreover, state enforcement activity remained relatively constant during the mid-1980s as federal enforcement actions declined precipitously (B. Wood 1988, 1991). Still, the federal EPA retains both the authority to oversee state enforcement actions and concurrent enforcement authority, and typically takes the lead role in the most difficult enforcement activities at the state level.

States conduct the majority of monitoring and enforcement activity in pollution control, and both Minnesota and New Jersey have an "environmental bill of rights" that allows all citizens, industries, and political subdivisions to file enforcement suits against polluting firms (Jessup 1990). In addition, twenty-two states have programs in which citizens help state environmental agencies to monitor water quality (U.S. EPA 1990). States have also been aggressive in enforcing pollution control regulations on federal facilities. Federal governmental facilities, such as Department of Defense and Department of Energy installations, include some of the largest polluters in the nation, and states have sought to enforce federal environmental regulations on these facilities. The Supreme Court ruled, however, that these federal facilities have sovereign immunity from state prosecution and civil penalties under the Clean Water Act and related hazardous waste statutes. In 1992, the states and the National Governors' Association successfully lobbied Congress, and both the House and Senate passed bills allowing the states to prosecute and fine federal agencies under the terms of the Clean Water Act (Greenhouse 1992).

Finally, states have also been innovative in pushing back the frontiers of pollution monitoring technology. In a major advance, California's South Coast Air Quality Management District is planning to switch to *continuous* pollutant monitoring of industrial emissions sometime in late 1993 or early 1994. Traditionally, states and the EPA have relied upon industry self-monitoring and infrequent governmental inspections and audits to keep tabs on industrial pollutant emissions. New laser scanning technology, however, allows pollution detectors to be placed directly in smokestacks. These detectors are connected to the pollution control agency's central computer, and allow the agency to quickly and accurately measure how much of a particular pollutant is being produced by large industrial sources. The inability to accurately and continuously monitor pollutant emissions has been the single largest hurdle to widespread reliance upon emission fees and emission trading programs in pollution control, and the continuous monitors now being field tested in California were developed specifically to support that state's innovative emission trading scheme (Stevenson 1992b).

Research and Development

Research and development are integral to progress in environmental protection. Government activities here include supporting the development of innovative pollution control strategies and technologies, developing and providing guidance for standard setting, and assisting the states in program design and enforcement. While some states have significant research programs of their own, the resources of the federal government are necessary to answer most questions in this area. State research and development efforts are hampered by a lack of resources, and deterred by the possibility that other states might act as "free riders" on their technological advances. Occasionally, states have undertaken significant research and development programs in acid rain, toxic air pollutants, and biomonitoring technology in water quality (i.e., using aquatic species to measure water quality). Overall, however, the federal government retains more program responsibility here than in any other element of environmental policy. (As an example, in 1989, the EPA spent $770 million on research and development in pollution control, while the states spent only $33 million; U.S. Department of Commerce 1991.)

Table 3.3

Federal Grants to States for Environmental Protection Programs, 1978–95
(Constant 1982–84 $Million)

Year	Total Grants	Abatement, Control, and Compliance Grants	Construction Grants	Superfund Grants
1978	5,199.4	311.3	4,888.0	0
1979	5,458.7	283.7	5,173.6	0
1980	5,586.2	315.5	5,270.6	0
1981	4,599.6	330.0	4,269.5	0
1982	4,226.9	331.6	3,892.2	3.1
1983	3,279.1	271.1	2,995.0	13.1
1984	2,811.4	236.8	2,520.7	54.9
1985	2,971.2	243.5	2,684.9	43.7
1986	3,119.5	237.2	2,836.7	44.7
1987	2,861.8	255.3	2,569.5	37.0
1988	2,447.2	249.4	2,125.1	65.9
1989	2,255.6	241.1	1,898.4	96.8
1990	2,198.9	260.9	1,752.1	151.5
1991	2,222.1	258.3	1,728.7	189.6
1992	2,080.0	326.9	1,516.6	193.1
1993[a]	2,976.0	459.0	2,159.0	288.0
1994[a]	3,068.0	503.0	2,197.0	300.0
1995[a]	2,995.0	500.0	2,120.0	310.0

[a]Figures after 1992 are estimated in current dollars.
Source: U.S. OMB, *Budget of the United States Government,* fiscal years 1980 to 1993.

Funding

We clearly see the changes in the federal-state partnership in environmental policy when we look at who funds these programs. States vary widely with respect to their dependence upon the federal government in financing environmental programs. Federal support for environmental protection ranges from 81 percent of state spending in Rhode Island to 24 percent of state spending in California (Davis and Lester 1989). During the early years of federal policy leadership, the EPA provided a majority of the funds for all pollution control activities at the state level (except for solid waste management). Over the past twenty years, however, the states have come to rely increasingly upon their own treasuries for funding of these programs (see table 3.3). Overall, federal grants to the states for environmental protection declined 60 percent in real terms between 1980 and 1992. Most of this decrease was felt in the municipal wastewater treatment grant program, but real declines were observed in other areas as well.

State environmental officials resent reductions in federal assistance for environmental protection (Tobin 1992). As federal dollars have disappeared and environmental protection responsibilities increased, however, states have become increasingly innovative in funding pollution control initiatives. For example, the Arizona Department of Environmental Quality has set up revolving loan funds for air and water quality improvements in the state. The air pollution program is funded by a $1.50 surcharge on annual motor vehicle registrations, while the water pollution program is funded by a surtax on hazardous waste generators (Jessup 1990). Overall, the National Governors' Association identified 431 alternative financing schemes for environmental programs being used in forty-four states, and these financing schemes generated over $3.2 billion in revenues (National Governors' Association 1989).

The Need for a Federal Role in Pollution Control

With little guidance from Washington, states increasingly set the environmental agenda during the 1980s. As we have seen, a significant number of states enacted regulations more stringent than required by the EPA in several environmental areas, in effect wresting policy leadership away from the federal government (Kritz 1989). Moreover, these innovations were developed much more frequently and were of higher quality during the 1980s (Council of State Governments 1986). Many states did an admirable job in mitigating the effects of new federalism on environmental protection programs by protecting personnel, increasing state spending, and increasing policy activity.

While most states have done a remarkable job in environmental protection, a strong federal role in environmental policy is still necessary. First, states rely upon the federal EPA for research, development, and technical assistance on a scale too large for individual states to handle alone. A strong federal role is critical here. Second, many states must rely upon the threat of an EPA lawsuit to get polluters to comply with regulations. The threat of an EPA lawsuit has been likened to a "gorilla in the closet" that state officials can bring into play during particularly difficult enforcement cases (Stanfield 1984). An EPA emaciated through budget cuts and staff reductions will be a less credible enforcement threat, compounding state problems in this area (Mosher 1982). Third, though many grumble considerably, most state administrators appreciate EPA sanctions and deadlines. The prospect of federal intervention provides state agencies with a gun to the head of state legislatures when attempting to get them to enact state programs to meet these deadlines.

Despite remarkable increases in state capacity and state commitment to environmental protection, state efforts alone are not always sufficient to address cross-boundary pollution issues. In the example cited earlier, Connecticut is the only northeastern state that has refused to adopt stricter emission controls on new automobiles. The other states in the Northeastern States for Coordinated Air Use

Management coalition feel that Connecticut is acting as a "free rider" in this instance, receiving the benefits of neighboring states' efforts at pollution control without paying any of the costs. Massachusetts, which is downwind of Connecticut, is particularly upset by this state's refusal to join the coalition (Wald 1991b). Nor are these cross-boundary problems restricted to air pollution. Arkansas's water quality regulations are weaker than Oklahoma's, and water flowing out of Arkansas sometimes causes rivers in Oklahoma not to meet Oklahoma's water quality standards. In 1992, Oklahoma sued the state of Arkansas for polluting its waterways, but the Supreme Court has refused to provide judicial relief, upholding Arkansas's right to have weaker water quality regulations because these regulations equaled national minimum requirements set by the EPA (Schneider 1992a). Finally, the federal government occasionally needs to prod the states into action, as when the EPA threatened to impose federal water quality rules on those states not regulating toxic chemical discharges under the Water Quality Act (see chapter 2). The characteristics of environmental problems that required a leading role for the federal government in the first place—their pervasive nature, broad scope, and cross-boundary impacts—still exist, and at minimum require strong federal research, coordination, and oversight activities.

Explaining States' Responses to "New Federalism"

Assuming that one goal of new federalism was the reduction of governmental activity in environmental protection, we have to ask why the states responded in a fashion so unpredicted by Reagan administration officials? First, remember that President Reagan did not initiate the devolution of policy responsibility to the states; he simply accelerated this devolution. States had been accepting increased authority in pollution control for several years, and thus were experienced in dealing with the responsibilities tossed their way after 1980. Second, significant improvements in the capacity of state governments allowed the states to handle greater policy responsibility. Third, environmental policy retrenchment was strongly opposed by a coalition of state citizens, state environmental groups, state environmental professionals, and state political officials. Finally, and most importantly, many of the retrenchment goals of new federalism were turned aside by state political cultures more supportive of environmental protection than they had been in the past. New federalism's strategy of retreating from environmental policy goals by devolving policy responsibility to the states might have worked fifteen years earlier, but not in the 1980s and 1990s.

The improvements in state capacity and policy activity during the 1980s were not unique to environmental policy. The twin goals of devolution and defunding that were so prominent in Reagan's new federalism campaign actually helped to energize state governments in a way that undermined the president's superordinate goal of policy retrenchment. While some political observers reacted to this state response with mild shock, political scientist Richard Nathan (1989) claims that this response was predictable, and not without precedent. Nathan explains the aggressive response of state governments by arguing that historically there has been a cyclical relationship between states and the federal government in policymaking. During liberal periods (e.g., the 1930s through the late 1970s), proponents of governmental activism focus their efforts on the federal government. The success of these efforts through the middle half of this century led many students of federalism to describe the state-federal relationship as a one-way flow of policy authority from the states to the federal government. During periods of national conservatism, however, this picture of federal-state policy relationships looks much different. During conservative eras, pro-government forces do not disappear but instead refocus their lobbying efforts at the state level.

A number of states have developed reputations for innovation in domestic policy (Gray 1974; Savage 1985; Walker 1969). These innovative states have historically taken the lead in policy activism during periods of conservatism at the federal level. For example, in the late nineteenth century state governments pioneered programs aimed at education reform, civil service reform, child labor standards, and the regulation of private industry. Several of these state programs provided the basis for similar pieces of federal legislation during the more liberal Progressive era. This same pattern of state policy activity appears in the conservative late 1910s and 1920s, when states took the lead in instituting workers' compensation, unemployment insurance, and public assistance programs. These state-level initiatives were transformed into federal programs that became hallmarks of the New Deal. The leading role played by the states was less noticeable after the New Deal, but a resurgence of conservatism at the national level and an increased emphasis on state policy authority caused this pattern to repeat itself in the 1980s.

Conclusion

States are much more than administrative arms of the federal government. They are finally fulfilling their role as "laboratories of democracy," expanding their political vitality and increasing the number and the quality of their policy experiments. Furthermore, citizens see state governments as more concerned, attentive, responsive, trustworthy, and efficient than the national government in Washington, D.C. This chapter has highlighted the role state governments play in environmental protection, and the tremendous variation exhibited by these state programs. The potential for variation was present in the initial pieces of federal pollution control legislation, but state policy responses to Reagan's new federalism initiatives (made possible because of notable increases in state government capacity) have created greater variation among state programs than ever before. These variations in state air and water pollution control programs make this policy area an excellent laboratory for comparative state policy analysis. Program variation allows us to evaluate the politics behind state policy decisions in pollution control (i.e., what conditions and influences make for stronger pollution control programs). Cross-state variation also provides us the unique opportunity to evaluate the effects (if any) that different levels of regulatory effort have on environmental quality.

Notes

1. Deep cuts in federal support for state environmental programs were especially hard for the states to deal with because these funding decreases came while the states were facing increased responsibility for regulating hazardous wastes under the Resource Conservation and Recovery Act (RCRA) and the "Superfund" legislation.

2. As of 1987, there were only three instances where states gave back primacy over EPA-directed programs. The EPA took over Idaho's clean air program in 1982, but returned program responsibility to the state a year later when a private firm agreed to oversee state implementation of clean air regulations. The EPA took over Iowa's drinking water program in 1982, but federal enforcement of safe drinking water regulations in Iowa fell far below the level of state efforts that the EPA had deemed insufficient in the first place. Program responsibility was returned to Iowa in 1983. Finally, California gave authority over the municipal construction grant program back to the EPA regional office in San Francisco after concluding that the EPA required more of primacy states than of its own regional offices. In a related area, the Department of the Interior relieved Oklahoma and Kentucky of their environmental protection responsibilities in surface mining reclamation.

3. Environmental protection standards are economically efficient if the marginal cost of controlling a unit of pollution equals the marginal benefits of control. Most economists argue that uniform pollution control standards prevent this balancing of costs and benefits.

4. States have an additional reason to pressure the EPA to promptly adopt strong clean air regulations. The states are subject to penalties if they do not meet CAA guidelines, and it is very difficult for the states to induce industries to reduce pollution without threatening EPA regulations as a sanction. States are subject to these penalties regardless of whether or not the EPA promulgates regulations at the federal level. Thus, miscommunication and delay in promulgating EPA regulations tend to annoy state environmental officials (Wald 1992c).

5. Policy variation in pollution control does not end at the state level. Detroit has its own rules regarding air quality, as does Los Angeles. In Tennessee, state pollution control offices in Memphis, Nashville, Chattanooga, and Knoxville all issue their own permits. Finally, communities in Washington can adopt more stringent environmental standards and enforcement provisions than are required by the state Department of Ecology (Jessup 1990).

4

An Integrated Theory of State Policy

In developing an integrated theory of public policy, we really have two goals. First, we must compose a model that allows us to account for cross-state variations in policy outputs. A model of policy outputs gives us much more than a tool to answer the relatively uninteresting question of "why do some states have stronger pollution control programs than do other states?" however. By identifying the determinants of stronger state environmental programs, we are addressing fundamental questions of state government responsiveness (do state governments respond to organized interests in policymaking?), accountability (which groups do state governments respond to?), and capacity (can state governments develop strong environmental regulations when they need to?).

Our second goal is to create a model of outcomes in state pollution control policy. In modeling policy outcomes, we are not satisfied with explaining the strength of governmental programs, or even the aggressiveness of governmental enforcement efforts. An analysis of state policy outcomes asks the important question, what *impact* or *effect* have state programs had on the problems they were intended to address? In investigating this question of state policy effectiveness, we are essentially evaluating the promise of governmental activity in solving social problems.

The politics, processes, and influences that surround policy outputs and policy outcomes are very different, and should be modeled separately (see Appleton 1985). This chapter develops separate models explaining policy outputs and policy outcomes. In combination, these models provide a comprehensive system for evaluating environmental policy, and by extension, public policy in general, in the states.

Modeling Policy Outputs: Traditional Theories

In comparative state policy studies, a particularly contentious debate rages between political scientists who see wealth and economic development as the key determinants of state policy outputs, and another group of scholars who posit a paramount role for political institutions in policymaking. Economists have devoted a good deal of effort to analyzing the origins of public policy as well. More often than not, however, they focus their attention on the influence of dominant industrial interests in the policy process. Finally, pluralist political scientists also see organized interests as key actors in the creation of policy outputs, albeit with a more inclusive view than economists of what constitutes a policy-relevant group. Before presenting an integrated model of policy outputs, we must discuss the attributes and theoretical shortcomings of these other attempts at accounting for policy variation in the states.

The Economic Model

The first systematic, empirical investigation into the influences behind variations in state policy outputs is generally attributed to Dawson and Robinson (1963). Their research concluded that interparty competition had little effect on welfare programs across states, and that the observed variation in policy could be explained by levels of economic development alone. The implications of Dawson and Robinson's findings were stunning. Conventional wisdom in political science held that in a representative democracy, governmental activities and public policies remained responsive to the wishes of the citizenry through political parties. Voters could express their policy preferences through elected representatives, and the choice between candidates was usually based upon the cue of a candidate's party affiliation. In addition, as early as 1949, V.O. Key claimed that high levels of interparty competition would (and should) lead to more expansive government programs as parties competed for the swing vote of the economic have-nots in the population (Key 1949; see also Downs 1957). If political parties and interparty competition had no influence on the sort of public policy produced, many of the normative benefits claimed for political parties could be questioned.

Dawson and Robinson instigated a rush of research activity by political scientists in the area of comparative state policy studies. Most of this work has used quantitative analysis to examine differences in state policy outputs and institutional structures. For instance, Richard Hofferbert (1966) discovered that expenditure variations in education policy, welfare programs, and unemployment compensation at the state level were better explained by differences in socioeconomic conditions among states than by a state's political institutions. The only significant political variable in the analysis, interparty competition, dropped out when controlling for socioeconomic conditions. Thomas Dye, arguably the godfather of the economics-determines-politics camp, comes to similar conclusions in his opus *Politics, Economics, and the Public* (1966). Here again, socioeconomic variables are the best and often the only significant predictors of state policy outputs.

If political structures and institutions had no impact upon state policy in the aggregate, perhaps politics was important at the margins of policymaking. Levels of economic development could provide states with the resources to enact more expensive public policies, but politics could be important in influencing changes in state programs over time, or in instigating a state to adopt new programs. Alas, both Walker (1969) and Gray (1974) found that socioeconomic conditions overwhelmed the influence of political institutions when it came to explaining policy innovation in the states. Wealthier, more industrialized states were more innovative, and that was that. Economic conditions seemed to cause changes in redistributive policy over time as well. In a pooled time series analysis, Richard Winters (1976) concluded that political variables, particularly political parties, were unrelated to changes in budgetary redistribution levels.

In a possible attempt to demonstrate that while public *policy* may be determined by socioeconomic factors, political *institutions* were not, political scientists delivered what might have been a crippling blow to their own relevance as researchers. In three separate analyses, Dye found economic development variables to be the most significant factors in explaining variation among states with respect to the powers of the governor, levels of party identification, and interparty competition (although these analyses are clearly classic examples of backward causal reasoning, see Dye 1966, 1969, and 1984). Here, economic development explained not only government policy but political institutions as well.

With the above research as precedent, the claim was made that "the burden of proof now rests on those who hypothesize a politics-policy relationship" (Sharkansky and Hofferbert 1969, 868). In response to this challenge, Sharkansky and Hofferbert obtain results that display a strong and (they hypothesize) causal relationship among affluence, industrialization, and public policy in the states. They also find party competition and voter turnout to be significant factors in accounting for variations in state welfare and education programs. This apparent victory for politics is misleading, however, since the political factor representing party competition and voter turnout is itself largely determined by economic development. While their results are more ambiguous than Dye's, the bulk of the evidence still suggested that socioeconomic conditions strongly influence the characteristics of both political structures and public policy.

The most common theoretical explanation given for the influence of economic variables on policy outputs is that economic development (i.e., wealth, industrialization, and so forth) provides a state with the resources to devise more expensive public programs. A related argument is that economic development creates an expanded set of demands upon policymakers, demands to which state policymakers respond. The single greatest shortcoming of this branch of research is its lack of a plausible theory of influence. How is it that income, industrialization, and the like affect public policy? Certainly these conditions cannot influence public policy and political structures on their own. There must be an intervening mechanism. The process whereby economic development is turned into political influence is rarely if ever discussed by the economics-determines-policy cohort. While the connections between economic development and policy outputs seem reasonable, proponents of this system of influence still provide no mechanism whereby increased demands are translated into policy or increased resources are channeled into governmentally sanctioned areas.[1] For this reason, the consistent results presented by these researchers begin to look less like revelations of underlying patterns of political behavior and more like fortuitous correlations or examples of misspecified models of policy influence.

A final theoretical concern stems from the correlation between economic development and the structure of political institutions within a state. This relationship is never adequately examined. Does economic development determine the structure of political institutions? Much of the work cited here indicates that it does. An affirmative answer to the question "Do economic factors determine the characteristics of the political system?" has important implications. First, such results could lend empirical support to the Marxist doctrine of social substructures (i.e., economic relationships) determining superstructures (i.e., sociopolitical systems). Less radically, it could provide support for Lindblom's argument regarding the pervasive influence of the business sector over the political system in capitalist democracies (Lindblom 1977). Finally, these results suggest one possible method by which economic influences are incorporated into the political system. Each of these implications poses interesting and important questions for students of democratic government.

Researchers supporting the economics-determines-policy-and-political-structure relationship generally do not respond to these important questions. The failure of these researchers to advance and support a plausible explanation for the influence of economic variables over public policy and institutions leaves the economics-determines-politics position theoretically moribund. A more sophisticated and satisfying explanation for policy variation among the states is clearly needed.

The Political Model

Political scientists have made efforts toward resurrecting political structures and institutions as important factors accounting for policy outputs, rescuing the relevance of institutionally oriented policy research at the same time. Armed with solid hypotheses and more sophisticated theoretical and methodological models than their more economically inclined brethren, they have had a significant degree of success in this endeavor. The first signs of the resuscitation of political institutions as relevant policy variables came from Sharkansky and Hofferbert (1969) as mentioned above. Fry and Winters (1970) also provided evidence that political variables may have policy relevance when controlling for economic conditions. How they arrived at these conclusions has been criticized, however (Sullivan 1972).

In a thoughtful and well-conceived essay, Jennings (1979) exposes an important role for party control of government in determining levels of welfare expenditures. He argues that party labels are less useful for understanding policy variation than are the characteristics upon which party cleavages are based. Categorizing party systems according to whether or not they divide the electorate along class lines revealed that parties with different constituency bases produce different welfare policies once in office. Plotnick and Winters (1985) also find that political variables play an important policy role in state policymaking: even when controlling for economic factors, interparty competition and levels of need influence state AFDC benefit levels. Plotnick and Winters argue persuasively for a more integrated view of policy influence that contains multiple measures of both economic and political concepts. Finally, other researchers have demonstrated that the structure of political institutions has a direct effect on public policy and representation in municipal governments (Engstrom and MacDonald 1981; Lineberry and Fowler 1967; Meier, Stewart, and England 1989), and even that patterns of class participation in elections are reflected in the scope of the social safety net states choose to adopt (Hill and Leighley 1992).

The most convincing evidence for claiming a unique role for the influence of political variables in state policymaking comes from a body of work by Erikson, Wright, and McIver, who make the persuasive argument that the socioeconomic measures so prominent in economic models are actually surrogates for public policy demands, or public opinion. Consequently, these researchers set out to measure public opinion directly. In doing so, they find that state opinion liberalism has a strong and significant impact upon public policy in the states. Moreover, in the presence of state public opinion, the traditionally dominant economic development variables lapse into insignificance (Wright, Erikson, and McIver 1987; see also Nice 1983). In a further treatment of the same theoretical structure, Erikson, Wright, and McIver (1989) model and explicitly test one channel of influence for public opinion—political parties. They find that public opinion influences public policy directly and indirectly through the intervening factors of party identification, party elites, and the composition of the state legislature. One senses satisfaction in their conclusion that state political systems respond through institutional intermediaries to the demands of the public. Politics, it seems, does matter, even when controlling for levels of wealth and economic development.

The recent research in comparative state policy analysis has satisfactorily illustrated that political institutions and conditions do matter in the policy process. As well as being methodologically sound and professionally reassuring, these studies are satisfying from a theoretical standpoint. Still, these works alone do not provide an adequately rich and integrated representation of the policy process. Most of the research, even that by Erikson, Wright, and McIver, effuses a kind of "*either* economics *or* politics" conception of policy influence in the states. This is understandable, since much state policy research over the last decade has sought to reestablish a role for political variables in the policy process. There are, however, alternatives to this either-or position (see Plotnick and Winters 1985).

Any comprehensive and realistic model of policy influence should include selected political and economic explanatory variables. They are obviously important. · On the other hand, assuming that all relevant policy influences are economically derived or are channeled exclusively through governmental or quasi-governmental institutions such as legislatures and political parties is politically naive. In short, there has to be a greater recognition of the role organized interests play in shaping public policy in the states. For this, we turn to a discussion of group theory and the politics of regulatory policy.

Group Theory and Regulatory Policy

The idea that public policy is the product of a competitive compromise among organized (and some unorganized) groups is hardly new to political science. Just after the turn of the century, Arthur Bentley (1908) claimed that not only public policy, but all political activity was the result of group interaction and competition. Decades later, Truman (1951) and Dahl (1956) argued that group exchange (i.e., pluralism) was the dominant method of political decision making, and implied that it should be. According to pluralist group theory, democratic participation and responsiveness in a mass society are preserved through the functional representation of citizen interests in organized groups.

Early on, political scientists and sociologists began questioning both the empirical and the normative claims of pluralism. Certainly all groups were not equal in terms of their resources and influence, and if the process of decision making under these unequal conditions could somehow be justified as pluralist, the results could not. Moreover, dominant groups and interests had the ability to control the political agenda, preventing pluralist debate over a full range of policy options in the first place (Bachrach and Baratz 1962; Crenson 1971; Lindblom 1977; Mills 1956). Mancur Olson (1982) goes so far as to argue that the increasing influence of organized interest groups may actually be dysfunctional, ossifying a nation's political system and undermining its economic base. Many political scientists, however, have questioned the contention that government institutions are incapable of contributing anything more than a neutral arena for group conflict when it comes to making public policy (Evans et al. 1985; Schattschneider 1960).

The tenets of group theory have been evaluated most explicitly in analyses of regulatory policies. Nearly all attempts at explaining the politics of regulation hinge in large part upon some conception of group politics (Lowi 1979; Meier 1985; Stigler 1971; J. Wilson 1980). At its extreme, group theory suggests that regulatory policies emerge from a political equilibrium produced by coalitions of the regulated industries and their customer groups. The most explicit example of this position is attributable to Richard Posner, who states that "regulation serves the interests of politically effective groups" (Posner 1974, 343).

With respect to economic price and entry regulation, the most common position taken is that regulations almost inevitably serve the interests of the regulated industries, opposite to the popular conception of their intent. Several researchers have argued that the industrial benefits stemming from regulation are intentional. Stigler (1971) claims that industries demand or seek out regulation from political "suppliers" in order to restrict the entry of competitors into the marketplace. This allows producers to reap economic rents from the constricted supply of goods and services in the regulated areas. Similarly, Posner (1974) claims that these groups craft policy compromises with legislative/bureaucratic regulators, extracting benefits from the regulations at the expense of the unorganized and hence ineffective public.

Slightly more sophisticated, but no less cynical, are the works of political scientists Murray Edelman and Theodore Lowi. Edelman argues that the regulation of industry is largely symbolic. A gullible public is mollified by the enactment of regulatory legislation while the regulated industry, through sly legislative craftsmanship or administrative neglect, is generally left unaffected (Edelman 1964). For Lowi, regulatory politics is categorized by weak, vague statutes allowing for the exercise of tremendous amounts of bureaucratic discretion. Because of the close ties between regulated industries and the implementing agencies, agencies use this discretion to develop rules and regulations that are weak, or even serve the interests of the regulated (Lowi 1979).

An alternative view of regulatory politics suggests that while regulations may be intended to protect and serve the "public interest," the realities of implementing these regulations allow industry to benefit from them nonetheless. Marver Bernstein (1955) and Anthony Downs (1967) argue that this is because the agencies that oversee the implementation of regulations lose public interest and support over time. Close relations with industry representatives and a loss of initial regulatory vigor leave these agencies relying upon the regulated industries for information and political support. (For a recent and more formal presentation of how interest groups use information advantages to influence public agency decisions, see Banks and Weingast 1992.)

Each of the above authors describes some form of what has been generically termed "agency capture," and they seek to explain why industrial interests often appear to capture the benefits of regulation for themselves. Reagan (1987) and others have countered that while this characterization of regulatory politics may sometimes be appropriate for economic regulation, it is inaccurate in describing social regulation (that is, regulations with the goal of protecting human health and safety).[2] Environmental regulations are excellent examples of social regulation. Though the problems associated with the need for social regulation can be explained in terms of market failures (e.g., negative externalities and information asymmetry), the market remedies of economic regulation are not appropriate here. Even Posner (1974) recognizes that his theory of regulation cannot account for the new forms of social regulation that impose unwanted costs upon industry. If one simply expands the arena of conflict to include the newly organized and motivated consumer and "public interest" groups, however, the analogy of a policy equilibrium is still relevant. Regulatory policy is now a compromise between industry and these new public interest groups, each seeking a unique set of benefits. Quite simply, in this expanded arena industrial interests do not always win.[3]

While there are numerous obstacles to agency capture in social regulation, there are those who still see capture as a very real possibility. James Q. Wilson (1980) characterizes social regulations as having widely distributed benefits and highly concentrated costs. Assuming that the costs and benefits of regulation are the main motivations for supporting or opposing its adoption, social regulations will almost always be opposed by a hard-core group of well-heeled, well-organized, and strongly motivated industrial interests. Supporters of these regulations (the recipients of the general but diffuse benefits), on the other hand, will need to be organized and galvanized by a policy entrepreneur, often with the help of a crisis event. Wilson expresses some surprise that regulations of this type are passed at all. If it takes a good deal of effort and resources to organize and motivate a dispersed constituency behind the enactment of social regulations, it is even more difficult to maintain this support afterward. In this sense then, Wilson sees some potential for agency capture, or at least agency inactivity, in social regulation over the long run.

Empirical studies of regulation have not been kind to the industry dominance perspective. Paul Sabatier (1975) found that air quality regulation in Chicago did not favor industry due to the presence of motivated and organized citizen's groups. Other scholars have found policy outputs discordant with industry interests in consumer protection (Pertschuk 1982), environmental protection (Kemp 1981; Lester et al. 1983), occupational safety and health (Kelman 1980; Scholz and Wei 1986), and financial regulation (Worsham 1991). Other studies have questioned the industry capture thesis with respect to public lands policy (Culhane 1981), insurance regulation (Meier 1988), and regulation in general (Meier 1985). Even economists have concluded that regulation often imposes costs upon industry without providing the benefits hypothesized by the industry dominance position (MacAvoy 1979; Viscusi 1984; Weidenbaum 1979).

While these studies have demonstrated that industrial interests do not always (or even often?) dominate regulatory policymaking, they do not provide evidence for the influence of countervailing public interest groups either. Regulation (and deregulation) has benefited consumers even when these consumers have not been organized (Derthick and Quirk 1985). In fact, many researchers have concluded that regulators and their political sovereigns, not organized groups, are the most important actors in the regulatory policy arena (Culhane 1981; Gormley 1979, 1986b; Mazmanian and Sabatier 1980; Moe 1982; Sabatier 1977; Welborn 1977; B. Wood 1988; Wood and Waterman 1991). This leads us to conclude that the politics of regulatory policymaking is more complex than can be described by simple industry dominance, or even by pluralist competition among various interests.

An Integrated Theory of Public Policy:
Modeling Policy Outputs

Twenty-five years ago, Robert Salisbury (1968) lamented the state of affairs within political science, where researchers had all but abandoned policy-oriented research in favor of studying "constitutional policy," or the rules of the game in the political system. Since that time, political scientists have approached the study of public policy with renewed vigor, usually using one of the three traditional models of policymaking discussed above. Unfortunately, each of the traditional theories of policy outputs has significant shortcomings: the economic model with respect to a theory or process of influence, the political model's artificial restriction on channels of influence, and the group politics model's depiction of the policy process as being either purely pluralist or dominated by industry. A more comprehensive and thoroughly integrated model of policy influence is clearly needed (for a concurring view, see Lester and Lombard 1990).

Political-Economic Characteristics

The first requirement in constructing an integrated theory of public policy is acknowledging that the general political and economic characteristics of a state have a tremendous amount of influence over the type of policies that state will adopt. These characteristics go under different names in the policy literature; Hofferbert (1974) calls them "socioeconomic resources and conditions," while Salisbury (1968) dubs them "system resources." Whatever they are called, state characteristics regarding the level of economic development, wealth, and the general tenor of political ideology within a state form a milieu of needs and boundaries of acceptability out of which policy options develop. The interaction of economics and ideology also produces a certain context or set of expectations against which the viability of policy options is judged.

The first set of independent variables in the integrated model of public policy reflects the economic and political characteristics of states. Economic resources and conditions have an impact upon public policy; wealth and economic development do matter. Public policy is generally responsive, and a state will not stringently regulate the noxious by-products of an industrialized economy if it has a low level of industrialization in the first place. Similarly, regulation costs money, so the wealth of a state can have some effect on the type of regulations that a state adopts and the resources available to regulators within that state. Finally, state political ideology helps determine what sorts of pollution control regulations are acceptable in a state (so, for example, conservative states are unlikely to be at the forefront in environmental protection).

Organized Interests

While wealth and political ideology may help set "boundaries of possible action" (Eulau and Prewitt 1973), these characteristics do not by themselves determine public policy. This is generally where the traditional economic model falls short. The combination of these characteristics naturally produces a number of different policy demands arising from advantaged and disadvantaged interests within society. These demands, however, must be articulated and pressed upon the decision-making system of government. Without being forcefully articulated, policy potential remains just that—potential. Salisbury has called this set of interests within the state a "demand pattern," or "the pattern of groups and individuals . . . articulating demands and pressing them upon the decisional system" (Salisbury 1968, 165). Groups and actors within this "demand pattern" in a state perform the crucial function of transforming the policy potential present in a state into political influence, and any government purporting to be representative should respond to social interests represented through these organized groups.[4]

The relevance of organized groups to a general theory of policymaking has been bolstered by the tremendous increase in the number and resources of political interest groups (Berry 1984; Cigler and Loomis 1990; Schlotzman and Tierney 1986). Moreover, organized groups have taken advantage of increased access to the political system as governmental institutions have become receptive to a wider variety of group demands (Heclo 1977; Melnick 1983; Sabatier 1977).

The political role of interest groups is especially important at the state level. There is a good deal of evidence that the diversification of organized interests at the federal level has yet to reach the states. In most states, those groups representing dominant economic interests are by far the most influential. The influence of these groups is particularly strong in regulatory policy, and in poorer and less industrialized states where countervailing interests are not well developed enough to provide opposition to the dominant industrial concerns (Ziegler and van Dahlen 1976). While state interest group communities diversified somewhat during the next seventeen years, state governments in general are still more susceptible to interest group pressures than is the federal government (Gray and Lowery 1993; Thomas and Hrebenar 1991; for empirical evidence, see Williams and Matheny 1984).

Regulatory capture is not the only possible state policy response to strong industrial interests, however. States with strong industrial sectors may enact *more* stringent regulations in an attempt to minimize the environmental impact of these industries. In some instances, researchers have found industrialized states aggressively regulating polluting industries to protect and enhance the state's value as a tourist destination (Eisinger and Gormley 1988). Lester et al. (1983) conclude that with regard to hazardous wastes, states are acting in a responsive and responsible manner by regulating polluting industries more stringently. In either case, these conclusions run against the grain of most regulatory theory, and fly in the face of the early state policy literature which claimed that states either lacked the political and economic resources to impose stringent regulations, or would sacrifice such regulations when competing against other states for industrial development (Rowland and Marz 1982; but see Thompson and Scicchitano 1985). While we may be able to find justifications for expecting both positive and negative relationships between the strength of a state's industrial interests and the quality of its air pollution control programs, the position taken here is that industry will seek out beneficial regulation (that is, some form of price and entry regulation) while avoiding regulation that imposes significant costs, such as environmental regulation (Meier 1988).

The second set of variables in the policy output model then represents the relevant organized interest groups in environmental policy. In pollution control policy, these groups usually represent affected industrial interests on the one side and environmental interests (broadly defined) on the other. While these two groups will be included in the integrated model, a strong case will be made for including energy-producing concerns in regulating air pollution, and for including mining and agricultural interests in the regulation of water quality.

The Political System

Like economic and political characteristics, the organized interests present within a state do not on their own create public policy. Economic and ideological concerns articulated by organized interests may prompt a state to adopt stronger or weaker pollution control regulations, but these concerns must be acted upon by a set of governmental intermediaries if they are to influence public policy. Government institutions embody the managerial and political capacities of state governments that are integral to policymaking. Moreover, the political system provides more than a neutral arena where organized groups reach a policy equilibrium. Political institutions within a state often have their own policy interests and goals, and one way in which they pursue these goals is by channeling and altering the pattern of interests entering the political system (Bosso 1987; Evans et al. 1985; Herring 1967; Schattschneider 1960). Members of the political system may also ignore group pressures and follow their own ideological dispositions in policy decisions (Kalt and Zupan 1984).

The third set of variables in the integrated policy output model represents the elements of a state's political system. The political system itself consists of political parties, governmental institutions, and the attitudes of the elite members of each. This set of institutions and elites within a state—a state's "decisional system" (Salisbury 1968)—eventually acts to form public policy.[5] For this reason, the integrated model includes an important role for political parties and the institutions of government in policymaking. Previous research provides the justification for including political system variables, and the tenets of democratic theory demand it.

Empirical Design

The impact of each set of variables in the policy output model must be assessed concurrently with that of the other variables. The majority of the research in comparative state policy studies has used the tool of multiple regression for this task. Since one major goal of this book is to demonstrate the theoretical *and empirical* superiority of the integrated model, it will be operationalized as a single multiple regression equation in order to facilitate direct comparisons with the traditional models.

Although the integrated model *can* be operationalized as a single regression equation, this empirical design is inappropriate for the integrated model of policy outputs developed here. Many politically relevant variables have both direct and indirect effects on policymaking, and multiple regression glosses over these indirect effects (Greenberg et al. 1977). A better methodological choice is to use a system of path analytic equations to model the process of policy influence. Path analysis, or causal modeling, not only allows us to identify the direct and indirect effects of our independent variables it also allows us to compare the relative impact of each independent variable on our dependent variable. This is something that multiple regression cannot do, and if this is attempted using single equation regression models, one can arrive at conclusions that are "simply wrong" (Lewis-Beck 1977, 565). A schematic representation of the integrated causal system producing state policy outputs is presented in figure 4.1.

Summary

In brief, in the integrated model of state policy outputs, public policy is made by institutions within the political system. Actors within this system, however, are heavily influenced by organized interests placing policy demands on the government. The political system also faces constraints on what it can and cannot do in the area of public policy—fiscal constraints stemming from the economic characteristics of the state and political-electoral constraints from the general ideological disposition of its citizens. Each of these constraints narrows the range of potential policy options in a state (Hofferbert 1974). An adequate model of public policymaking must include variables representing each of these important stages or sets of influences in the policy process. The integrated model sketched out here is far from the first of its kind (see Hofferbert 1974; Sabatier 1977; Salisbury 1968). This makes it all the more surprising that few researchers within political science have placed empirical demands upon these models, focusing instead upon the traditional models criticized earlier (yet see Erikson et al. 1989; Hofferbert and Urice 1985; Mazmanian and Sabatier 1980).

An Integrated Theory of Public Policy:
Modeling Policy Outcomes

Enacting a particular piece of legislation or designing a policy program is hardly the end point of the policy process. These activities only just begin to address social problems. A complete examination of public policy must not only explain the influences that underlie the formation of state pollution control policies, but evaluate the outcomes of these policies as well. Developing and testing a model

Figure 4.1. **A Model of Policy Outputs**

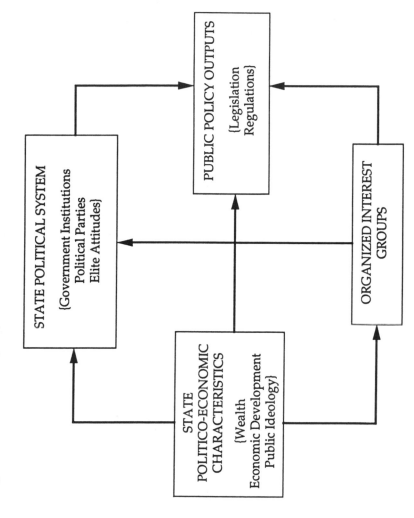

that explains only policy outputs, like the one above, stops short of this goal.

Policy outcomes have been defined as "the consequences for society, intended and unintended, that stem from governmental action and inaction" (Anderson 1990, 224); and as "the consequences of programs in human terms" (Nakamura and Smallwood 1980, 76). We can then think of policy outcomes as the *effects* or *impacts* of public policy. An evaluation of these outcomes helps us answer an important question: Is the policy attaining its stated goals? In the present study, policy outcomes are the effects pollution control regulations (and other regulatory efforts) have had on indicators of environmental quality. We seek here to answer specific questions: Have air pollution emissions been reduced? Have air and water quality improved? If so, can we account for the causes of these improvements? The act of problem solving is commonly used as a metaphor for describing the policy process, and an analysis of policy outcomes can tell us how well a particular policy solution is working.

Measuring Policy Outcomes

Research into the environmental outcomes of pollution control regulation brings us face-to-face with a very difficult problem: how do we measure environmental quality? Devising measures of change in environmental quality is exceptionally difficult (Goggin et al. 1990), and forces us to resolve trade-offs in three important areas—the objects of measurement, the method of measurement, and the assumptions behind the measurements.

Deciding on the objects of measurement in air quality is relatively easy since almost all regulatory efforts over the past twenty-five years have been aimed at reducing emissions and concentrations of six criteria pollutants. There are no analogs to these criteria pollutants in water quality control, however. Water quality can be measured using biochemical oxygen demand, dissolved oxygen, suspended sediments, suspended or dissolved solids, nutrient loads, pesticide residues, inorganic toxins, heavy metal ions, or countless other constituents. Each of these water quality measures has its own effect on human and ecosystem health, so using any one, or even a small subset, to represent water quality can lead to misrepresentations of water quality. We can try to make an end run around this galaxy of specific water constituents by using more general measures of water quality such as clarity, smell, conductivity, and whether or not waters support healthy native fish populations. The gains in information management associated with this strategy, however, are offset by losses in precision of measurement.

Second, choices have to made in the method of measuring environmental quality. Ideally, we would be able to take measurements from a comprehensive network of accurate and sensitive monitors. Determining changes in environmental quality in this fashion is very time-consuming and expensive, however, and puts real limits on the placement and timing of these measurements. Alternatively, we can measure environmental quality more subjectively using the expert judgments of pollution control engineers and program administrators. This method has the benefits of lower cost and increased flexibility in measurement, as well as allowing site-specific conditions that are difficult to quantify to enter into the evaluation of environmental quality. Again, however, this method gives up in objectivity and accuracy what it gains in cost savings and flexibility. Both methods of assessing changes in environmental quality are used regularly by government agencies and policy analysts.

Finally, we have to decide which assumptions underlie our measures of change in environmental quality. In broadest terms, we have a choice between "before-and-after" measures of change, and "with-and-without" measures of change (see Freeman 1990). In using a before-and-after measure of change, we simply measure pollutant levels before and after some event (e.g., the implementation of the 1972 FWPCA), and whatever differences we observe in environmental quality can be attributed to the event. As discussed below, however, factors other than regulation can affect changes in environmental quality. Increases in any number of economic indicators could lead to higher levels of pollution, and regulation may be able to do little more than hold the line against these increases. Thus, before-and-after measures of change in environmental quality may underestimate the effectiveness of regulation. Moreover, good measures of air and water quality were generally not available before 1970, and this makes using the before-and-after method of measuring changes in environmental quality very difficult.

The alternative to these before-and-after measures is a with-and-without measure of change. A with-and-without measure of change tries to control for influences on environmental quality other than those stemming from regulation. Here, predictions are made as to what present levels of air and water quality might be in the absence of regulation by estimating the relationships between economic factors and environmental quality at the beginning of the regulatory era and extrapolating these figures to the present. These *predicted* air and water quality levels are then compared with *actual* pollutant levels in the presence of regulation, and the difference between these predicted and actual levels is attributed to regulation. We see a trade-off here between errors in measuring change using before-and-after measures (which can lead to errors in impact assessment) and errors in estimating pollutant levels using with-and-without measures of change (which can also lead to errors in impact assessment).

The measures of change in environmental quality used in this book try to include the best of both worlds. Levels of change in environmental quality can be measured using actual data, much like the before-and-after approach, if we begin our measurements in the early to mid-1970s. Our measure of change in environmental quality then becomes the difference in pollutant levels between the 1970s and late 1980s. Borrowing from the with-and-without method of evaluating the environmental impacts of regulation, we then use both regulatory and nonregulatory variables to model these changes in air and water quality. The key to this process is how we account for the effects of regulation. Since we do not have good data for air and water quality before the imposition of federal regulation, a pure before-and-after impact assessment is out of the question. Environmental quality, however, is not affected simply by the presense or absence of regulation. Air and water pollution are also affected by differing *levels* of regulation. In fact, the *stringency* of regulations is more important than the simple presense or absence of regulation when it comes to policy outcomes (Kemp 1981). The strength of state pollution control programs provides us with a good measure of differing levels of pollution control regulation, and combining this measure of regulatory effort with our actual environmental quality data allows us to identify what effect stronger pollution control regulations have had on environmental quality over time (avoiding most of the shortcomings identified above in the process).

Policy Outcomes and the Research Setting

The study of policy outcomes is closely related to the study of policy implementation, since implementation is the crucial causal link between policy outputs and policy outcomes. While the naive belief that "a policy enacted is a problem solved" was cast aside long ago, research by political scientists often pays scant attention to the outcomes or impacts of public policy. The lion's share of research in public policy is directed toward explaining how and why particular policies are adopted (descriptive policy studies) or the impacts procedural changes have upon policymaking (i.e., institutional policy analysis; see Gormley 1987). Even in implementation studies, a good deal of the research remains process-oriented (Elmore 1979; Hull and Hjern 1987; Lester et al. 1987; Linder and Peters 1987; Nakamura and Smallwood 1980) or focuses upon quantifiable bureaucratic "outputs" (i.e. numbers of enforcement actions, clients served, and so on; see Desai 1989; Scholz and Wei 1986; Thompson and Scicchitano 1985; B. Wood 1991, 1992; Wood and Waterman 1991).

This review should not lead us to believe that political scientists have offered nothing in the way of policy outcome analysis, for this is not the case. We can find examples of important outcome evaluations in urban redevelopment policy (Derthick 1972; Pressman and Wildavsky 1973), social welfare policy (Copeland and Meier 1987; Murray 1984), and education policy (Coleman et al. 1966; Meier et al. 1989; NIE 1977), to name only a few. The majority of this research, however, has found little connection between the policy goals embodied in legislation and the observed effects of these policies (see Copeland and Meier 1987 for a good example to the contrary). Furthermore, few studies have examined the outcomes of regulatory policies.

When political scientists have focused upon regulation, they have a history of believing that effective regulation is very unlikely, if not impossible (Bernstein 1955; Edelman 1964; Huntington 1952; Lowi 1979; see Meier 1985 for a good review; J. Wilson 1980). Lewis-Beck and Alford (1980), however, demonstrated that strong regulatory programs and adequate funding and enforcement of these programs resulted in substantial social benefits in coal mining safety. Sabatier and Mazmanian (1983) also demonstrated that clear regulatory statutes backed up with sufficient resources and political support have been effective in coastal zone management. Nonetheless, a general note of pessimism remains regarding the effectiveness of regulation, and this pessimism is not unique to political scientists. In economics, there exists a cadre of researchers who contend that regulatory policies do not exhibit their desired and expected effects (Peltzman 1974; Posner 1974). In short, these researchers believe that regulation simply does not work. Conclusions along these lines have been arrived at in the areas of consumer product safety (Viscusi 1984), occupational safety and health (MacAvoy 1979), and state transportation regulation (Stigler 1971).

The state of research into environmental policy is hardly different. We have learned a great deal about the politics and processes behind the adoption of environmental regulations at the federal and state levels and the judicial and administrative implementation of environmental programs. We also know a good deal about the economic outcomes of environmental regulations (see chapter 1). Though there are a few notable exceptions (see my Introduction), when it comes to evaluating the environmental outcomes of pollution control regulations, political science research is mostly silent. This leaves us in the unenviable position of not being able to determine if pollution control efforts in the United States are having their desired effect. In order to answer this question, we must develop a model that allows us to evaluate the environmental outcomes of state pollution control regulations.

A Model of Policy Outcomes

Implementation is the crucial causal link between public policy and successful policy outcomes. This separation of policymaking and policy implementation has been viewed as artificial, since implementation is strongly influenced by the characteristics of the enabling legislation, and because important policy decisions are typically made by implementing agencies (Lipsky 1980; Nakamura and Smallwood 1980). Focusing on administrative implementation is useful, however, if we want to identify factors that contribute to program success once the policy ground rules have been laid (Mann 1982b). Moreover, at least some distinction between policymaking and policy implementation is necessary if the democratic ideals of responsibility and accountability are to have any meaning. Thus, in creating a model to evaluate the outcomes of public policy, we are essentially investigating the conditions necessary for effective policy implementation.

There are two widely recognized schools of thought on what makes for successful policy implementation (and thus successful policy outcomes), typically referred to as the "top-down" and "bottom-up" approaches. While both approaches are useful in their appropriate applications, the model of policy outcomes outlined below is generally representative of the top-down framework (see Mazmanian and Sabatier 1989). The top-down approach essentially seeks to identify what impact controllable political factors (and uncontrollable economic ones) have on the actions of agency officials, and thus on policy success. The top-down approach has been roundly criticized for relying excessively upon central authority figures and hierarchical control, and neglecting the contributions of lower-level bureaucrats and private actors in policy implementation (see Elmore 1979; Hjern 1982; Hull and Hjern 1987; Lipsky 1980). Moreover, these critics are skeptical of the utility of a top-down approach in policy areas that are often characterized by multiple statutes, multiple agencies, and the influence of numerous private actors. The competing bottom-up framework advocated by these scholars places primary emphasis on the strategic actions that clients and street-level bureaucrats employ to shape policy implementation to their advantage. The basic premise of bottom-up theorists is that if we want to know how to structure effective implementation (or identify impediments to successful implementation), we should focus our attention on the individuals who must apply these rules and regulations on a daily basis.

Blanket acceptance of these bottom-up critiques would result in a model of policy outcomes very different from the one outlined below. While the criticisms of Elmore, Hjern, and others have significant merit, they are of limited relevance for the analysis presented here. First of all, the bottom-up approach is most appropriate when attempting to structure an implementation process. That is not the goal here. Instead, we are primarily interested in assessing the effects of previously developed policies; a task for which the top-down framework is more appropriate (Sabatier 1986). Second, the conditions for effective implementation vary by policy type (Goggin et al. 1990; Ripley and Franklin 1986), and a top-down framework is more useful in the area of social regulatory policy (Ingram 1990). Finally, state pollution control regulations, characterized as they are by a few dominant statutes and strong lead agencies, are relatively more accessible using a top-down framework. In short, the top-down approach is more useful where there is a dominant public program in the policy area under consideration, and when we are primarily interested in the effectiveness of a program (Sabatier 1986).

Implementation researchers have identified a wide variety of factors that may influence program effectiveness in a top-down implementation framework. These factors can be operationalized within four general variable categories.

Internal Statutory Factors: Policy Outputs

A clear statute with unambiguously defined goals not only provides necessary direction for agency officials, it also provides the standards by which policy implementation can be evaluated (Van Horn 1979). A clear statute is not enough to ensure policy success, however. The statute must also provide the implementing agency with technical resources, policy tools, and sanctions for noncompliance that are adequate for the task at hand (Mazmanian and Sabatier 1989; Van Horn 1979). Finally, the potential for successful implementation is enhanced by a strong causal theory linking policy activities to program objectives, and by assigning policy implementation to agencies sympathetic to policy goals (Mazmanian and Sabatier 1989; Pressman and Wildavsky 1973). If most of these statutory conditions are met, the chances for effective implementation are improved.

Internal Political Factors: Bureaucratic Capacity and Support

Political institutions can exert a tremendous amount of influence over program success, and the character and resources of the bureaucracy responsible for policy implementation are particularly crucial to program success.[6] An agency and its affiliated clientele groups that are sympathetic and committed to program goals can be a boon to program effectiveness, while the opposition of either of these actors can prove to be an obstacle impossible to overcome. Similarly, an agency handicapped by inadequate financial resources will be an unlikely vehicle for effective policy implementation (Mazmanian and Sabatier 1989; Rourke 1984). It is important to note then that any state exercising a significant degree of control over environmental policy houses the implementation of that policy within a state agency designed specifically for this task. While the quality of these agencies varies across states, federal preemptive requirements assure that they are competent at some minimal level. Moreover, the EPA oversees implementation procedures in the states. The EPA's commitment to the goals embodied in environmental legislation and its "sense of mission" are well established. In addition, influential professional associations linking state environmental administrators with their federal counterparts help assure that the values of state bureaucrats are closer to those of federal administrators than to their colleagues in state government (Thompson and Scicchitano 1985; Walker 1969). Finally, Hebert and Wright (1982) demonstrate that state bureaucrats themselves are becoming much more professional. Thus, while all state environmental protection agencies may not be equally committed to environmental protection, previous research strongly suggests that state pollution control policies will be implemented by supportive bureaucratic personnel.

Less constant but no less critical elements of bureaucratic capacity and support are personnel resources and money. Even the most committed bureaucrats working within effective administrative structures need adequate budgetary resources to carry out their program responsibilities. Levels of funding and personnel also reflect the level of political support for pollution control provided by other internal political actors (e.g., state legislatures and political elites). States vary a great deal with respect to the levels of personnel and the fiscal resources invested in their environmental protection agencies, and any model of policy outcomes should take this variation into account.

Administrative "Outputs"

Statutory authority and money are not the only important elements of effective regulatory policy. State agencies and the federal EPA engage in a number of activities aimed at ensuring compliance with environmental regulations, and adequate inspections and aggressive or well-targeted enforcement can influence the probability of program success. Including these bureaucratic activity levels as explanatory variables reflects the deterrent influence of enforcement, as well as capturing the indirect influences of the many political factors that affect levels of state and federal enforcement efforts in the first place (Scholz and Wei 1986; B. Wood 1992).

External Environmental Factors

Statutory characteristics, political institutions, and administrative "outputs" are not the only influences upon public policy outcomes: external environmental factors often affect policy outcomes as well. Variations in overall economic conditions may affect public and governmental perceptions about the relative importance of policy goals (e.g., environmental protection versus an adequate energy supply), and thus shape implementation (Mazmanian and Sabatier 1989). In pollution control, the most salient economic changes are in levels of industrial activity, since a flourishing industrial sector produces more pollution. Other external factors such as the levels of fossil fuel consumption and technological development may also influence program efficacy, particularly in the area of pollution control. If we are to determine whether or not public policy has an impact upon environmental quality, we must control for these external environmental factors.

Outline for the Policy Outcome Model

The model for evaluating the environmental outcomes of pollution control regulations contains variables representing each of the factors identified in the above discussion. Internal statutory factors are represented by the strength and scope of a state's air and water pollution control programs. The influence of internal political factors is reflected in the budgets of state pollution control agencies. Administrative "outputs" are measured using state and federal environmental enforcement activities. Finally, relevant external environmental factors (e.g., changes in industrial output, agricultural activity, fossil fuel consumption, and so forth) are added to the outcome model in examining changes in air and water quality in the states of the United States. These four sets of factors—internal statutory, internal political, administrative "outputs," and external environmental—all interact to determine policy outcomes and the success of public policy. It is important to recognize that the dependent variable in the policy output

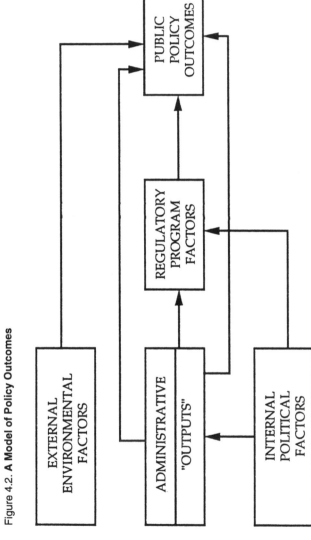

Figure 4.2. **A Model of Policy Outcomes**

model, regulatory program strength, becomes an independent variable in the outcome portion of the analysis. Policy outputs represent the crucial link between the two sections of the integrated policy model: between policy formation and policy implementation. Finally, a path analytic empirical design is used to operationalize the policy outcome model outlined above. As in the policy output model, a path analytic design allows us to estimate the direct and indirect effects of those variables affecting changes in environmental quality in the states (see figure 4.2).

Conclusion

This chapter has constructed a comprehensive, integrated theory of the policy process useful for explaining both policy outputs and policy outcomes. Subsequent chapters will subject this theory to a series of empirical tests in the area of state air and surface water pollution control regulation. While the models are tested using environmental policy, concluding that the models are useful only in this policy area would be a mistake. All of the hypothesized variables and linkages are common to public policy in general. As such, the models should have applicability for most mainstream policy applications within political science.

There are several strengths associated with the full integrated theory presented here. First, the theory represents a more realistic system of policymaking in which numerous actors, institutions, and conditions work in concert to influence public policy. Second, it explicitly provides for the linkage between policy outputs and policy outcomes around which much debate in policy research has been centered. Third, the causal model empirical design is sensitive to the nonlinear and interrelated nature of public policy, and recognizes that influences on public policy may have both direct and indirect components. Fourth, by operationalizing the hypothesized concepts as measurable variables, it demonstrates that such theories can be evaluated with actual data.

Notes

1. Sullivan (1972) suggests that economic factors can have an indirect impact upon policy through political institutions (his three-stage conditional model). The specific mechanisms are not outlined, however. Hofferbert (1974) believes that receding from a culture stressing self-sufficiency explains why economic variables influence welfare policies. Government intervention is necessary to coordinate and address high levels of mutual need in a complex society. This is not, however, an adequate explanation of how and why economic development influences public policy. Any theory linking wealth and industrialization to public policy must also address the awkward paradox stemming from the level of analysis used in state policy studies: why do wealthier and more industrialized states enact more expensive state welfare programs and regulations that are clearly not in the economic self-interest of the

entrepreneurs and wealthy citizens of that state (though see Piven and Cloward 1971).

2. Social regulation is unique for four reasons. First, the goals of social regulation are different from those of economic regulation. Social regulation has as its focus health and safety concerns, not prices or the market shares of firms. Because of this, increased competition—the panacea in economic regulation—is no solution in social regulation. Indeed, increased industrial competition may exacerbate the conditions requiring regulation in the first place. Second, social regulation usually applies across industry areas rather than to a single industry. Different industries with varying interests place competing pressures and demands upon regulators, allowing no one set of demands to be consistently served to the detriment of the others. Moreover, the personnel staffing social regulatory agencies generally identify very closely with the values embodied in the goals of the regulations (Goetze 1981; Hedge and Menzel 1985; Marcus 1980). In such an environment, regulators will not develop especially close ties with any individual industry, so agency capture is less likely.

Third, citizen interest and involvement in social regulation is typically high (though see Downs 1972), and citizen participation is sometimes required by statute (Gormley 1986a). Citizen interest is typically translated into an expression of interest by the political overseers of the regulatory agency. The agency can thus draw upon the public and politicians for political support, eliminating the need to fall back onto industry (yet see Pertschuk 1982). Indeed, when administrators at the EPA tried to develop closer ties with the regulated industries, they met with intense intra-agency resistance. Anne Gorsuch-Burford and Rita Lavelle experienced this firsthand when they attempted to give industry groups preferential access to agency decision makers and information during the first Reagan administration. Lastly, legislation establishing social regulations is almost always very specific with respect to statutory goals, the timetable for their attainment, and sometimes even the mechanisms to be employed in pursuit of these goals (e.g., the CAA of 1970 and 1977). There is less bureaucratic discretion in social regulation as compared with economic regulation.

3. This policy as interest group equilibrium theory has been carried into the deregulatory debate. According to Noll and Owen (1983), deregulatory questions are decided in an environment of interest representation and group pressures, and the characteristics of the interest groups in this process make the outputs of regulatory politics predictable. In this view, even social regulation sometimes creates and bestows benefits upon organized, self-interested, homogeneous groups. These groups (typically representing industry) rally to protect their benefits and the regulations that provide them. In this sense, it may be tougher to deregulate than to impose regulation in the first place.

4. In his argument, Salisbury claims that economic development and industrialization have led to more integrated demand patterns. This more integrated set of demand patterns, coupled with the decentralized decisional system found in the United States, meant that policy in the United States should become increasingly self-regulatory. Clearly, both of these contentions are wrong. The literature on interest group theory and the reality of group formation and activity has demonstrated that demand patterns become increasingly *dis*aggregated as societies become more developed. The claim to the contrary seems to be a remnant of the "end of ideology" train of thought so common during the early 1960s. In addition, the explosion in social regulation since the time of Salisbury's writing has conclusively disproved his claim that public policy would move increasingly toward the realm of self-regulation.

5. Salisbury includes political parties as group variables in the demand system section of the policy model. Keeping with past tradition in comparative state politics (and acknowledging that political parties are much more than simply interest groups), this re-

search employs parties as political variables—that is, as part of the decisional system influencing public policy.

6. Of course, state environmental bureaucracies are not the only important internal political factors in policy outcomes. These agencies are the most important political influence, however. Moreover, the influence of other internal political actors (e.g., state legislators and governors) is largely exercised through the policy output, agency budget, and agency enforcement action variables already included in the model.

5

The Politics of
State Air Quality Regulation

Chapter 4 presented a summary of three models commonly used to explain policy variation in the states: the economic and political models common in the comparative state politics literature, and the group influence model prevalent among regulatory policy theorists. I then evaluated each of these models from a theoretical standpoint in the area of environmental policymaking. Finally, chapter 4 developed an integrated model to explain policy variation across states. Chapter 5 empirically tests each of the three traditional models presented in chapter 4 in the area of state air pollution control regulation. In addition, variations in the strength of state air quality programs provide the initial forum for empirical validation of the integrated model of state policymaking developed in chapter 4. Given the empirical support for the economic (Dye 1966; Winters 1976), political (Erikson, Wright, and McIver 1989; Jennings 1979), and group influence models (Lowi 1979; Peltzman 1974; Stigler 1971), a comparison with these models is essential for evaluating the explanatory mettle of the integrated model. In short, this chapter tests theories of policy outputs in the area of state air pollution control regulation.

The Dependent Variable

Appropriate measures of state policy outputs are a continuing source of controversy in the comparative state politics literature (Lester et al. 1983). While significant progress has been made in this area (see Scholz and Wei 1986), the most commonly used measures of state policy outputs still represent expenditures. Expenditure figures are easily gathered, but they have been criticized as narrow and biased representations of policy activity (Fry and Winters 1970; Jacob and Vines 1971). In addition, it has been convincingly argued that economic output measures (i.e., expenditures) tend to bias comparative analysis in favor of economic input measures (i.e., socioeconomic independent variables; Lester et al.

1983; Munns 1975). The possibility exists, then, that the dominant role played by socioeconomic variables in comparative state policy analysis is a statistical artifact resulting from the type of dependent variable selected, rather than a true representation of the factors that determine state policy outputs.

In environmental policy, socioeconomic variables are more important in determining the level of spending on environmental programs than in determining the type of policy enacted (Lester 1980). Thus, not only are budgetary figures incomplete as measures of policy outputs, but socioeconomic explanations give a biased representation of the determinants of these outputs. The analysis by Williams and Matheny (1984) suffers from just such a problem. When analyzing variations in state expenditures for hazardous waste management programs, Williams and Matheny find that the influence of problem severity (their measure for policy responsiveness) is wiped out when total state budgetary levels are included as predictors of hazardous waste management expenditures. That overall state budgets help predict expenditures in hazardous waste programs is hardly surprising, and is clearly a statistical artifact of the sort mentioned by Munns (1975).

In order to evade the pitfalls associated with budgetary dependent variables, several non-fiscal measures of policy outputs have been devised (Fry and Winters 1970; Gray 1974; Sharkansky and Hofferbert 1969; Walker 1969). Though some researchers using non-fiscal policy output measures have produced results generally supportive of the "economics-determines-policy" conclusions of the economic development models, more recent attempts at using dependent variables of this type have deviated from this pattern (Lester et al. 1983; Scholz and Wei 1986; Wright et al. 1987).

Clearly, the strength of a state's air pollution control program cannot be adequately represented using expenditure figures. Nor can these programs be evaluated simply by looking for the presence or absence of legislation, since it is the stringency of regulations, not their presence or absence, that is of crucial importance in regulatory policy (Kemp 1981). The most comprehensive measures of state efforts in pollution control come from the Fund for Renewable Energy and the Environment (now Renew America; see also Lowry 1992). The evaluation matrix and rankings for state air pollution programs are taken from FREE's *State of the States: 1987* report (1987). States are ranked from weakest (one) to strongest (ten) with respect to their air pollution control programs (see table 5.1).[1]

The FREE rankings are specifically *not* an evaluation of environmental quality in the states, nor are they an evaluation of the effectiveness of state programs. The rankings simply evaluate the strength of each state's regulatory program. Alternately, the rankings can be viewed as a measure of how willing states have been to take advantage of the opportunities and incentives provided to meet or exceed federal minimum requirements in pollution control. The rankings themselves include the sanctions available to the appropriate agencies in each state; sanctions placed upon the state by the federal EPA; areas in which the state

Table 5.1

State Air Program Strength Scores

State	Score	State	Score
Alabama	3	Montana	2
Alaska	7	Nebraska	4
Arizona	7	Nevada	2
Arkansas	1	New Hampshire	6
California	10	New Jersey	9
Colorado	4	New Mexico	1
Connecticutt	9	New York	5
Delaware	1	North Carolina	8
Florida	7	North Dakota	1
Georgia	4	Ohio	8
Hawaii	4	Oklahoma	5
Idaho	2	Oregon	6
Illinois	7	Pennsylvania	8
Indiana	6	Rhode Island	6
Iowa	5	South Carolina	6
Kansas	2	South Dakota	1
Kentucky	7	Tennessee	3
Louisiana	5	Texas	7
Maine	3	Utah	3
Maryland	3	Vermont	3
Massachusetts	6	Virginia	8
Michigan	8	Washington	8
Minnesota	5	West Virginia	2
Mississippi	1	Wisconsin	9
Missouri	5	Wyoming	1

Source: FREE 1987.

exceeds federal requirements in pollution control, research, and development; the size of the state monitoring system; and the total air program budget in each state.[2]

Traditional Theories and State Air Quality Regulation

The Economic Model

The economic variables most commonly hypothesized to affect state policy outputs are wealth and industrialization. Per capita personal income in 1987 is used to represent the wealth of individuals in each state. Higher levels of per capita personal income should be associated with stronger air pollution regulations because wealthier states will be able to "afford" more regulation. Per capita state general fund expenditures in 1987 represent the wealth of state governments. The hypothesis here is that higher levels of state spending will be associated with

Table 5.2

Economic Model of State Policy Influence
(Dependent Variable = Strength of State Air
Pollution Control Programs)

Independent Variable	Initial		Revised	
	Beta	t-score	Beta	t-score
Per Capita Income	0.46	3.75***	0.52	4.74***
Per Capita Expenditures	0.14	1.09	—	—
Industrialization	0.43	3.78***	0.40	3.61***
	F-ratio = 12.39***		F-ratio = 17.91***	
	Adj. R^2 = .41		Adj. R^2 = .41	
	N = 50		N = 50	

***Statistically significant at $p < .01$.

stronger air pollution control programs. A state flush with revenue will likely enact more stringent regulations, since it is less costly (relatively speaking) for the state to do so (Williams and Matheny 1984).[3] The level of industrialization in a state is represented using the percentage of a state's gross state product (GSP) attributed to value added by manufacturing in 1986. The hypothesis associated with this variable is problematic. Traditionally, higher levels of industrialization have been associated with more liberal policies, and even with policy innovation, in the states. However, these industries are the targets of the costs associated with environmental regulations. If these industries have a strong degree of political influence, then higher levels of industrialization should be associated with weaker air pollution regulations. Because we are testing the traditional economic model of state policy outputs, for now we will adopt the traditional hypothesis of more industrialized states having more expansive programs.

Table 5.2 shows that economic variables are in fact related to stronger air pollution control programs. Higher levels of per capita personal income and industrialization are associated with stronger air quality regulations, though our other measure of wealth, per capita state expenditures, has no significant effect on air quality regulation. This suggests that overall state fiscal resources are not important in determining the strength of a state's air quality program. This variable is dropped from the final specification of the economic model.[4] Dropping per capita state expenditures from the analysis does not affect the model's explanatory power, and the coefficient estimates for both of our independent variables are statistically significant. According to the revised economic model, wealthier states both demand and can afford stronger air pollution control programs. Higher levels of industrialization also prompt states to increase their air pollution control efforts, though we really cannot tell at this stage whether this is due to the expanded policy demands of a more industrialized electorate.

The Political Model

Political scientists have been much more imaginative when developing political as opposed to economic variables in comparative policy research. Though dozens of different variables have been tried, they have, for the most part, been attempts at operationalizing the concepts of interparty competition, Democratic control of state legislatures, legislative apportionment, legislative professionalism, and state public opinion. We use three of these concepts as predictors of variations among states in the stringency of their pollution control regulations: legislative professionalism, interparty competition, and state public opinion.[5]

The first independent variable used in the political model represents the professionalism of a state's legislature. Theoretically, more professional state legislatures will be more responsive to citizen needs and more innovative in policymaking (Carmines 1974, Grumm 1971). With better-educated members, more resources, and more staff support, professional legislatures have the time and the capacity to examine issues in depth and thus develop more innovative and comprehensive policy solutions. These advantages of legislative professionalism should be of particular benefit in the complex and technical area of environmental protection, and should result in the adoption of stronger regulations. For example, improved legislative advisory capacities in science and technology typically associated with more professional state legislatures can be instrumental in formulating policy in the complex area of hazardous waste management (Bulanowski 1981). The variable itself is composed of factor scores from a set of characteristics thought to represent legislative professionalism.[6]

The second political independent variable represents the level of interparty competition in a state. The original contention that a high degree of interparty competition leads to more liberal state welfare programs is generally attributed to V.O. Key (1949). The assumption is that competition forces political parties to try and obtain the support of a large group of "have-nots" in the population, and social programs are the incentive offered to gather that support. While environmental groups and their members cannot be considered "have-nots" in an economic sense, environmental concerns have traditionally received less attention in state policy activities. In this sense then, environmental groups have long been policy "have-nots." While common throughout the literature, it is only recently that the influence of party competition has received much empirical support (Erikson, Wright, and McIver 1989; Jennings 1979; Meier 1987; but see Lester et al. 1983).[7]

Some of the most recent attempts at explaining state policy outputs have relied upon the concepts of state public opinion and elite attitudes as predictive variables. The hypothesis is very simple: state policy should reflect the attitudes and priorities of a state's citizenry and political elites. Operationalizing the concepts has been a bit more difficult, however. Ideally, the results of surveys examining ideological and environmental attitudes in each state over time would be available. Unfortunately, they are not. While there are numerous sources of public opinion data with regard to environmental policy and environmental protection, none of these uses the same question wording and they have not been gathered at regular time intervals (see chapter 1).

The first ideological variable is a measure of state public opinion (i.e., state opinion liberalism) developed by Wright, Erikson, and McIver (1985). These researchers construct an ideological measure on a liberal-conservative dimension by pooling several years of responses to CBS–*New York Times* polls. Unlike roll call measures, which evaluate elite opinion, this measure represents public opinion directly. The measure is constructed so that large negative values represent more liberal state electorates. Because of this, positive relationships between liberal public opinion and our dependent variable will be expressed by a negative coefficient. In later works, state public opinion is found to be a significant predictor of both state elite attitudes and state policy liberalism (Erikson et al. 1989).

The second ideological measure represents the ideology of state political elites. The measure itself is the average American Civil Liberties Union (ACLU), Americans for Democratic Action (ADA), and Committee on Political Education (COPE) scores for each party in a state's congressional delegation, weighted by the relative strength of each party in the state legislature. Each of these scores reflects a slightly different facet of liberalism, and their combined value is superior to any single score alone. All other things being equal, the more liberal a state's political elites, the stronger should be its air quality program.

The third ideological variable also measures state elite opinion. The variable is calculated by taking the average League of Conservation Voters (LCV) scores for each party in a state's congressional delegation and weighting them by the relative strength of each party in the state legislature. This variable is viewed as a refinement of the general elite ideology variable since it represents the level of environmental concern in a state directly. States having legislators with higher LCV scores should have stronger environmental programs.[8]

Using roll call measures such as these to represent the connection between state opinion liberalism and the ideology of state political elites, we must rely upon three assumptions. The first, and most crucial, is that these variables are reliable and valid measures of state ideology and public opinion. Holbrook-Provow and Poe (1987) conclude that such roll call–based measures are superior to other attempts at operationalizing this concept in terms of reliability and validity. The second assumption is that members of Congress reflect the wishes and sentiments of their constituencies in their voting behavior. The political science literature is replete with examples showing that this assumption is not far off the mark (Fenno 1978; Kingdon 1973; Miller and Stokes 1963). The last assumption is that the candidates elected to the state legislature by a state's citizens are not all that different from those elected to Congress.

The final ideological variable measures the general level of "policy liberalism" in a state. States that are more liberal in other policy areas are likely to have stronger air quality programs as well. Indeed, environmental concerns are some-times characterized as simply a different expression of a liberal penchant for regulating private industry. The liberalism measure used here is one developed by Wright, Erikson, and McIver (1985). The variable is a factor score derived from state policy activities in eight separate areas thought to reflect liberal con-cerns (interestingly, environmental programs are not included in this measure). Since states with more liberal policies load negatively on the liberalism factor, a positive relationship between policy liberalism and stronger environmental regu-lations will be represented by a negative coefficient. Because state public opin-ion is causally prior to both elite attitudes and policy liberalism (see Erikson et al. 1989) there are likely problems with collinearity and model specification when all three are used in a single multiple regression equation.

A convincing argument can be made that the political model tested above is incomplete, as it contains no variables representing the effect state bureaucracies can have upon air quality regulations. This omission is purposeful. It is most certainly not being argued that bureaucratic resources and expertise have no influence on public policy. Indeed, many fine examples in the literature show just the opposite—that bureaucratic agencies can and do have resources at their disposal to shape policy outputs and outcomes (Allison 1968; Lester et al. 1983; Meier 1993; Miller and Moe 1983; Rourke 1984; Warwick 1975). Bureaucratic variables are left out of the political model for altogether different reasons.

First of all, as a measure of program strength, the dependent variable evalu-ates the tools available in each state to regulate air pollution. It is specifically not an evaluation of how states use these tools or the progress states have made in improving air quality (traditionally thought of as bureaucratic functions). Sec-ond, air pollution control agency budget levels are included as one component of the dependent variable. If agency budgets were included as an independent vari-able, much of the observed relationship would likely be a statistical artifact from using budgetary independent variables to predict budgetary dependent variables. Third, state natural resource agencies have been found to be highly influenced by state legislatures and other political sovereigns on one hand, and clientele groups on the other (Brudney and Hebert 1987). Both of these influences are already represented in the integrated model. Lastly, bureaucratic variables will be in-cluded later when evaluating changes in environmental quality in the states. Changes in these indicators (policy outcomes rather than policy outputs) should reflect most strongly the influence of state agencies and the use to which they put the resources and regulatory tools available to them.[9]

The first item that stands out in the results from the political model is the strong association between legislative professionalism and the strength of a state's air pollution control program, as was predicted (see table 5.3). This sug-gests that legislative professionalism is particularly important in a complex and technical policy area such as environmental regulation. On the other hand, the measures of state ideology and policy liberalism perform miserably in this equa-

Table 5.3

Political Model of State Policy Influence
(Dependent Variable = Strength of State
Air Pollution Control Programs)

Independent Variable	Initial		Revised	
	Beta	t-score	Beta	t-score
Legislative Professionalism	0.50	4.03***	0.51	4.30***
Interparty Competition	0.19	1.29	0.17	1.51
State Opinion Liberalism	−0.18	−0.99	−0.21	−1.69*
Elite Liberalism	0.08	0.39	—	—
LCV Score	−0.08	−0.42	—	—
Policy Liberalism	−0.05	−0.30	—	—
	F-ratio = 5.59***		F-ratio = 11.78***	
	Adj. R^2 = .36		Adj. R^2 = .40	
	N = 50		N = 50	

*Statistically significant at $p < .10$.
***Statistically significant at $p < .01$.

tion. None have coefficients significantly different from zero. The initial conclusion would be that state public opinion has no direct influence on air quality
regulation, and that states having liberal policies in other areas are not exceptionally stringent in the environmental arena. We should be cautious in coming to
these conclusions at this stage in the analysis, however. The political model is
contaminated by collinearity. In fact, the correlation between our two elite opinion measures is 0.77, suggesting that these two variables do not measure different
concepts at all.[10] The interparty competition variable, while having a coefficient in
the correct direction, is not statistically significant. Clearly, however, it is not as
poor an explanatory variable as are the policy and state ideology measures.

The refined and restructured political model of air regulatory stringency includes variables representing legislative professionalism, interparty competition,
and state opinion liberalism. The reason for keeping the index of legislative
professionalism in the model should be obvious. Given the collinearity in the
original model, the true influence of the opinion liberalism variable is likely
underestimated. We can address this collinearity problem by examining the
causal ordering of our variables. State political elite attitudes and state policy
liberalism are both causally dependent upon state public opinion; thus, they may
be justifiably dropped from the analysis. Finally, interparty competition is kept
due to the strong theoretical rationale for its inclusion and its somewhat promising performance in the original model.

The refined political model clarifies to some degree the picture of political
variable influence. Legislative professionalism is still the most powerful predictor of regulatory program strength. States with more professional legislatures

enact stronger air pollution control programs, as expected. In addition, state opinion liberalism is significantly related to the strength of a state's air pollution control program. Freed from the muddying effects of collinearity, we can see that states with a more liberal electorate do in fact have stronger air quality regulations, all other things remaining equal. Finally, while the coefficient for interparty competition has been strengthened and is in the hypothesized direction, it is not statistically significant.[11]

The goodness-of-fit measures demonstrate that the revised political model performs on a par with the traditional economic model. In addition, a diagnosis of influential regression points suggests that these relationships may be in general underestimated.[12] All things considered, the political model accounting for variations in state air pollution control programs seems as persuasive as the economic model on statistical grounds, and superior to it on a theoretical basis. This is not a revolutionary development, however. From the outset, researchers have found political variables to be significant predictors of variation in state policy outputs. Even those scholars on the economic development side of the debate would concede this point. The crucial test of political variables comes when they are combined with economic variables. Economic development measures have traditionally eclipsed political institutions and conditions as predictors of state policy outputs when variables from the two models are combined. Before we move on to such a comparison, however, we must evaluate the power of the group influence model.

The Group Influence Model

One can hardly discuss determinants of variation in the area of environmental protection without discussing the role played by interest groups. Regulatory policy outputs, similar to policy outputs in other areas, have been characterized as reflections of the interests and power of the groups in each regulatory venue. The major theoretical thrust of most of these arguments is that dominant economic interests will, one way or another, turn regulation to their advantage. This contention, however, has been challenged on theoretical grounds in the area of social regulation (Reagan 1987) and on empirical grounds in natural resources management policy (Culhane 1981) and insurance regulation (Meier 1988). The primary groups competing for policy influence over air pollution regulations are those businesses most affected by these regulations, and environmental groups in the state.

The first industry strength variable is the value added by manufacturing of those industries most responsible for air pollution as a percentage of a state's gross state product in 1986.[13] Why is industry strength measured in this manner, rather than by using the number of firms in each state belonging to certain trade associations or business umbrella groups? The literature on interest groups suggests that to an increasing degree, corporations are eschewing reliance upon trade organizations and umbrella groups and are taking up the activity of lobbying themselves (Salisbury 1984; G. Wilson 1981). A second question might arise over the similarity of this measure to the industrialization variable used in the economic model. The present measure is considered superior to the industrialization measure for three reasons. First, as a more refined measure, it takes into account only those industries with a very large stake in air pollution regulation. Second, such a refinement or separation of business interests is consistent with much recent research questioning whether in fact business and industry speak with a unified voice on policy questions (Meier 1988; G. Wilson 1986). Third, the mechanism whereby this refined conception of industry strength affects public policy is explicitly spelled out, unlike in the economic model. Given these considerations, this variable is an accurate representation of potential industry strength. The hypothesis that industries act to avoid social regulations will be represented by a negative coefficient. The second industry strength variable is the value added by mining as a percentage of gross state product in 1986. The mining industry may have interests and influence over air pollution regulations separate from (but parallel to) those of manufacturing industries. Air quality regulations affect the mining industry both directly and indirectly by their impact on the major industrial customers of these industries. A negative relationship is hypothesized between mining industry strength and the quality of a state's air pollution control program.

The final industry strength measure is the percentage of each state's total energy budget received from the combustion of coal and petroleum products in 1987. This variable measures the degree to which each state is dependent upon fossil fuels. Electric utilities and other energy-generating concerns are responsible for over 70 percent of all sulfur dioxide emissions in the United States, and significant portions of nitrogen dioxide and particulate emissions as well. Although energy consumption plays a critical role in air pollution, energy interests are typically neglected by political scientists undertaking empirical environmental policy analysis (see Kemp 1981 for an exception). The hypothesis here is that heavy reliance upon fossil fuels will predispose a state to pass weaker air quality regulations.[14]

Environmental groups are also expected to play an important role in the creation of state air pollution policy. These groups experienced tremendous expansion in both numbers and memberships through the 1970s (Schlotzman and Tierney 1986). Moreover, groups like the Sierra Club, Friends of the Earth, and the Natural Resources Defense Council have had an impressive amount of influence on the content of environmental programs and their implementation at the federal level (Melnick 1983; Rosenbaum 1985; Wenner 1982; but see Williams and Matheny 1984). Given their impact at the national level, it is hypothesized that the stronger these environmental groups are in a state, the more stringent will be that state's air pollution regulations.[15] The measure itself is the number of Sierra Club, National Wildlife Federation, and Friends of the Earth members per 1,000 persons in each state.[16]

Table 5.4

Group Influence Model of State Policy Influence Control
(Dependent Variable = Strength of State Air Pollution Programs)

Independent Variable	Initial		Revised	
	Beta	t-score	Beta	t-score
Polluting Industry Strength	0.39	2.73***	0.44	3.44***
Environmental Group				
Strength	0.24	1.62	0.31	2.40**
Fossil Fuel Dependence	−0.33	−2.63**	−0.32	−2.60**
Mining Strength	−0.02	−0.16	—	—
	F-ratio = 5.07***		F-ratio = 7.96***	
	Adj. R^2 = .29		Adj. R^2 = .30	
	N = 50		N = 50	

**Statistically significant at $p < .05$.
***Statistically significant at $p < .01$.

The strength of the mining industry has no relation to the strength of a state's air quality program (see table 5.4). Each of the other independent variables in the group influence model significantly affect state air quality regulations, however. Specifically, states with large polluting industrial sectors have stronger air quality programs, and as expected, states with stronger environmental groups also have stronger air quality regulations. Finally, states that rely heavily upon fossil fuels for energy production do have markedly weaker air pollution control programs, all other things being equal. These results imply that state policymakers are responsive to the concerns of environmental groups in developing air quality programs. The flip side of this finding is that with the exception of energy-producing industries, states are not as responsive to industrial pressures for weak regulations as many regulatory theorists would have us believe. States that rely heavily upon fossil fuels have weaker air pollution control programs, but overall, policymaking in air pollution control can hardly be described by the "agency capture" theory of regulation (for concurring views, see Lowry 1992 and Svoboda 1992). Regression diagnostics show that the group influence model is free from collinearity and influential data problems.

The Integrated Model of Air Pollution Control

To this point, the analysis has found empirical support for all three traditional models of state policymaking in state air quality regulation. If statistical results were the only criterion used to determine the "best" of the three traditional models, the economic variable or "economics-determines-policy" model would be selected. Still, the economic model is only marginally better, statistically speaking, than the political model, while the group influence model is statistically significant in its own right. Social scientists rarely rely solely upon statistical considerations when evaluating competing models, and good social scientists never do. Sound theory always underlies a good model. Thus, the three traditional models must be compared on theoretical grounds as well. As we have seen, both the political variable and group influence models are superior to the economic model on theoretical grounds.[17] Institutionalists, however, would doubtless find the political variable model (or some derivative of it) most compelling, while pluralists and most regulatory theorists (principle-agent adherents aside) would select the group influence model. The result is that neither theoretical nor empirical evaluations prove any one traditional model to be superior to the others. A major contention of this analysis is that all of the traditional models provide a narrow and simplistic representation of the complex set of influences that interact in the milieu of the policy process. The economic model of policymaking lacks a convincing process whereby economic development is turned into policy influence; moreover, it restricts relevant policy demands and interests to those stemming from economic conditions. The political model rarely recognizes that factors other than governmental institutions and political parties can exert influence over state policy outputs. Finally, the group influence model makes no provision for the policy clout exercised by the institutions of state governments. The integrated model of state policy influence was developed to remedy the weaknesses in all three traditional models.

Independent Variables in the Integrated Model

Political-Economic Characteristics

The level of economic development, wealth, and the general tenor of political ideology within a state form a milieu of needs out of which policy options develop, and a certain context or set of expectations against which the viability of policy options is judged (Hofferbert 1974; Salisbury 1968). The first independent variable represents state wealth using per capita personal income in each state for 1987. The rationale for including a wealth measure should be clear: wealthier states will likely demand stronger regulations. Thus, it is hypothesized that higher levels of personal income will be associated with stronger pollution control programs. The second independent variable represents state political ideology. State policy should not only reflect the wealth of a state, but the attitudes and priorities of a state's citizenry and elites as well. The Erikson et al. (1989) opinion liberalism measure is used to represent state political ideology because state opinion liberalism is causally prior to the other commonly used ideological measures, elite liberalism and policy liberalism. The Erikson et al. measure is constructed so that a positive relationship between a liberal citizenry and stronger pollution control programs will be represented by a negative coefficient.

Organized Interests

The combination state wealth and public opinion naturally produces a number of different policy demands arising from advantaged and disadvantaged interests within society. These demands, however, must be articulated and pressed upon the decision-making system of government. This function is typically carried out by interest groups. The first interest group independent variable in the integrated model of state public policy represents the size of the polluting industry in each state. The position taken in the integrated model is that industry will seek out beneficial regulation (i.e., some forms of price and entry regulation) while seeking to avoid regulations that impose costs upon it, such as environmental regulation (Meier 1985). Industry strength is measured by using the value added by manufacturing (VAM) of the most polluting industries in a state as a percentage of GSP in 1986. The second "demand pattern" independent variable represents the percentage of each state's total energy consumption obtained from the combustion of coal and petroleum products in 1987. Rightly or wrongly, air quality concerns are often seen to conflict with energy supply concerns, so that states may trade off strong air pollution regulations in order to secure an adequate supply of energy. The hypothesis here is that heavy reliance upon fossil fuels will predispose a state to enact weaker air quality programs. Environmental groups are also expected to play an important role in the creation of state air pollution programs. Environmental interest group strength is again measured using the number of Sierra Club, National Wildlife Federation, and Friends of the Earth members per 1,000 persons in each state in 1987. It is hypothesized that the stronger these groups are in a state, the more stringent will be that state's air pollution control programs.[18]

The Political System

Finally, the state exerts its own interests both directly and by filtering external policy demands through governmental institutions. While economic and ideological concerns articulated by organized interests may prompt a state to adopt a particular type of policy, these concerns must be acted upon by a set of institutional intermediaries if they are to become public policy. The influence of a state's political system is represented using the professionalism of a state's legislature. In addition to being more responsive to citizens and more innovative in policymaking, professional legislatures are particularly beneficial in the complex and technical area of environmental regulation (see Bulanowski 1981). More professional legislatures then will quite likely work to develop stronger pollution control programs. Three other potential political system variables— state governors, state administrative agencies, and interparty competition—are left out of the integrated model operationalized here. Research into the influence of governors on state regulation (and environmental regulation in particular) suggests that this influence is inconsistent and highly idiosyncratic (Medler 1989; Teske 1991). While state administrative agencies are undoubtedly influential in state policy processes, it is argued that this influence will be most important in affecting policy outcomes (through implementation), rather than in affecting the components of the regulations themselves. Finally, environmental protection is not the type of policy that political parties typically use to try to win over marginal voters. In addition, ideology is more important than partisanship when it comes to determining elite political behavior in environmental policy (Calvert 1989).

A Causal Model of Policy Influence

As discussed in chapter 4, it is inappropriate to operationalize the integrated model using a single equation regression format. Following previous research, both the wealth and state public opinion variables are considered to be determined outside of the causal system. The strength of the polluting industries in a state is determined outside of the system as well. This does not mean that these variables themselves are not the result of some complex causal process. Undoubtedly they are. By entering these factors as exogenous variables, we are simply saying that the causal process that manufactured these variables is of little interest to us, and that these variables themselves are not influenced by other variables in the model (Asher 1983). The remaining three variables in the integrated model are entered as variables determined in large part within the causal system. The industrial sector is the largest single consumer of energy in the United States, so it is reasonable to assume that the level of fossil fuel dependence in a state is determined in part by the size of the polluting industries in that state. Fossil fuel dependence is thus entered as an endogenous variable. Legislative professionalism is entered as an endogenous variable as well. Wealth and state political ideology both help to determine the degree of legislative professionalism that is possible and/or desired in a state. Environmental interest groups are the final endogenous addition. Environmental interest group membership is largely confined to the middle and upper classes (though the same cannot be said about environmental concern), so wealthier states are likely to have more environmental group members. Moreover, statistical distinctions between generally liberal and specifically environmental elite attitudes are very difficult to make, though it is logical to assume that general state ideological attitudes are causally prior to specific environmental concerns and actions.

To begin with, the explanatory and predictive power of the integrated model exceeds that of any traditional model. In addition, both figure 5.1 and table 5.5 show that all three components of the integrated model are important in explaining variation in state air quality programs. All of the independent variables display coefficients in the expected direction, and three of these are statistically significant. Using the standardized regression coefficients, a cautious first inter-

118

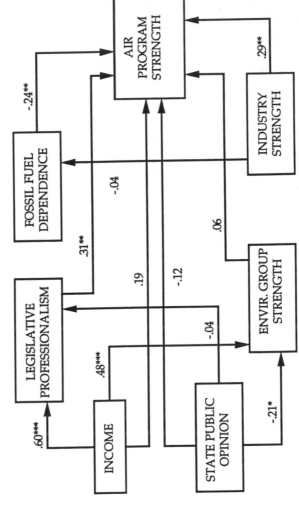

Figure 5.1. Integrated Causal Model of Air Quality Regulations

*Statistically significant at $p < .10$.
**Statistically significant at $p < .05$.
***Statistically significant at $p < .01$.

Table 5.5

Integrated Model of State Policy Influence
(Dependent Variable = Strength of State Air Pollution Control Programs)

Independent Variable	Beta	t-score
Per Capita Income	0.19	1.06
State Opinion Liberalism	−0.12	−0.87
Environmental Group Strength	0.06	0.38
Polluting Industry Strength	0.29	2.31**
Fossil Fuel Dependence	−0.24	−2.07**
Legislative Professionalism	0.30	2.09**

F-ratio = 8.39***
Adj. R^2 = .48
N = 50

**Statistically significant at $p < .05$.
***Statistically significant at $p < .01$.

pretation shows that the best single predictor of air program strength in the states is legislative professionalism (a political variable). More professional state legislatures enact stronger pollution control programs, as was predicted. Institutional characteristics and resources are very important to policymaking in the technical and highly salient area of air pollution control, as Bulanowski (1981) and Gormley (1986a) would lead us to believe.

The set of interests that make up a state's demand pattern are also quite important in policymaking. Polluting industry strength is a strong determinant of air quality programs, though this influence is of a positive nature. States with stronger polluting industries enact stronger air pollution control programs. This suggests that states attempt to counteract the effect these industries have on the environment by enacting stronger regulations. These results hardly portray state policymakers as captives of the dominant industrial interests within the state (though "capture" itself is really an administrative concept associated with implementation and cannot be evaluated using regulatory statutes alone). Rather than being "captured" by economically advantaged interests, state governments appear to be acting responsibly by enacting stronger and more comprehensive air quality programs where they are most needed. The other possible explanation for this positive relationship between industry strength and regulatory stringency is the exercise of symbolic politics. Here, states pass strict regulations that appear to address the problem of air pollution and satisfy citizen demands for action, while having little or no intention of implementing these regulations (Edelman 1964; Kemp 1981). These competing explanations for the positive relationship between industry strength and stronger air pollution regulations are examined in chapter 6.

While strong polluting industries prompt states to enact stronger air pollution regulations, states that rely heavily upon fossil fuels are predisposed to adopt weaker air pollution control programs. This suggests that state governments often act on the perceived trade-off between protecting air quality and securing an adequate supply of energy at an acceptable cost. This result also suggests that utilities and other power-generating concerns can exert a significant amount of influence in state politics, particularly over air quality regulation. Perhaps the most surprising result from the integrated model might be the weak influence of environmental interest groups. Recall, however, that most of the influence environmental groups have is a product of their association with the wealth and public ideology variables (i.e., most environmental group members are also members of the middle class, and it is difficult statistically to discern specifically environmental from generally liberal sensibilities). Thus, while these groups are important in environmental policymaking, their direct effect is minimal.

The coefficients for the variables representing wealth and state political ideology are problematic. Neither is statistically significant, indicating that we cannot conclude that either variable has an independent impact on state air pollution control regulation. This is odd, given the dominant role found for each of these variables in previous research (Dye 1966; Wright et al. 1987). While the variables are somewhat collinear, the magnitude of this correlation is not sufficient to explain these results. Wright and co-authors claim that income has traditionally been used as a surrogate for state public opinion in comparative state policy studies. They also demonstrate that the impact of income disappears when the opinion variable is introduced into a policy analytic model. For these reasons, dropping wealth from the analysis would seem justified. On the other hand, the position that economic or resource variables can *only* exert policy influence through public opinion is a misconception similar to believing that economic development needs no mechanism to exert policy influence. Furthermore, unlike the results obtained by Wright et al., income does not drop out of the integrated model in favor of state public opinion. Moreover, wealth obviously has important indirect effects that preclude it from being omitted from the model. The conclusion we can draw is that both of these exogenous variables are theoretically important, if not statistically significant, and omitting either one from the model would result in specification error.[19]

Effects Coefficients

The direct effect of independent variables on the strength of a state's air quality program is identical to the standardized coefficients presented in table 5.5. Standardized coefficients, however, do not allow us to compare the influence that each of our independent variables has upon the dependent variable (Lewis-Beck 1977). Obviously, we would like to be able to determine which of our independent variables has the greatest relative influence upon public policy. We can do this by making use of "effects coefficients" (i.e., the

Table 5.6

Effects Coefficients: Air Quality Regulation
(Dependent Variable = Strength of State Air Pollution Control Programs)

Independent Variable	Direct Effect[1]	Indirect Effect[1]	Total Effect[1]
Per Capita Income	0.19	0.21	0.40
State Opinion Liberalism	−0.12	−0.01	−0.13
Polluting Industry Strength	0.29	−0.01	0.28
Fossil Fuel Dependence	−0.24	—	−0.24
Environmental Group Strength	0.06	—	0.06
Legislative Professionalism	0.31	—	0.31

[1]Coefficients are rounded off to nearest .01.

total effect each independent variable has upon the dependent variable). These effects coefficients are presented in table 5.6.[20]

The effects coefficients show us that our initial conclusions regarding the relative strength of the independent variables in the integrated model were mistaken. Neglecting to include the indirect effects of our exogenous variables led us to underestimate the effect economic resources have in determining state policy. Wealth, instead of being statistically insignificant, turns out to be the single most influential factor behind strong state air quality programs. One should stress, however, that this conclusion is possible *only* if we explicitly state the causal mechanism for this influence. Wealth has little direct influence upon state policy. Rather, this influence is channeled through interest groups and through the institutions of state government. In addition, states with more professional legislatures and stronger polluting industries enact stronger air pollution control programs, suggesting that more professional state governments are acting responsibly in attempting to control the pollution produced by a large industrial sector. Furthermore, states heavily dependent upon fossil fuels respond to these energy demands by enacting weaker air quality programs. The conclusions stemming from the effects coefficients then are nearly the same as those obtained from a multiple regression model. Relying solely upon multiple regression, however, would obviously have led us to conclude erroneously that economic resources have little influence in state policymaking.

Finally, the lack of indirect effects stemming from the state public opinion variable is surprising. Previous research would lead us to believe that public opinion would be the most important factor affecting state policy outputs. This is clearly not the case with respect to air quality regulation. While public opinion has an impact, it is mainly direct. There are a couple of explanations for the poor performance of the opinion liberalism variable.

First, while public opinion may be of paramount importance in social welfare policy, resources, environmental need, and institutional influences may be more important in determining regulatory policy. These are the conclusions Salisbury (1968) arrives at when developing his integrated model of the policy process. Second, the opinion measure itself is based upon a Left–Right ideological spectrum that many consider to be irrelevant with respect to environmental issues, since environmental concerns often cut across traditional liberal-conservative boundaries (Inglehart 1977). The opinion liberalism measure may not capture the underlying philosophy of environmental concern, which has been described as "neither left nor right, but in front" (Capra and Spretnak 1984).

Conclusion

Several models purporting to explain differences in state policy outputs have been presented by researchers in political science. Each has its adherents (brandishing empirical evidence to support their claims) and detractors. The analysis presented here demonstrates that there is some support for each of the three traditional models. The analysis also highlights theoretical deficiencies in these models, however, and presents an alternative that is more theoretically complete and empirically sound. The economic, political, and group influence models on their own are insufficient when used to explain differences in air quality regulations across the states. The integrated model of policy influence provides a more satisfying picture of relevant policy influences in this area.

An analysis of cross-state variations in air pollution programs demonstrates the utility of the integrated model of policy outputs developed in chapter 4. State economic resources and public opinion are both important policy influences, working together to create a milieu out of which policy needs and possible remedies arise. Organized interests representing industrial and utility concerns also exert significant influence over state air pollution policy, but this influence is channeled through the institutions of state governments, which leave their own imprint on the final policy outputs. We can clearly see that each set of influences hypothesized by the integrated model of policy outputs has relevance in state air pollution control policy.

Is air pollution control policy identical to other policy areas, or is it somehow unique due to its subject matter? The answer to this question determines the utility of the integrated model in other areas of public policy. As in any policy area, there are winners and losers in air quality regulation. In addition, policy in this area is made within the same institutional framework and is subject to similar societal influences as other public policies. Perhaps, then, the analysis of environmental policy is not that different from other types of public policy; it simply receives less attention.

Notes

1. The rankings mean that the dependent variable in the analysis is really of ordinal measure, and a violation of the assumption of interval-level data that underlies multiple regression. However, use of these rankings can be justified on several grounds. First of all, a factor analysis of the variables in the FREE air pollution matrix produced a single factor with an eigenvalue of greater than 1. While such a composite interval measure would have been preferable to the rankings, these factor scores resulted in missing data for several states. Second, while other researchers in this area have used rankings ranging from 1 to 50, each state has had a unique rank (e.g., Lester et al. 1983). While the dependent variable in these articles acts more like an interval measure, it is in fact an ordinal measure as well (albeit with more variation). Moreover, this ranking results in a flat, unimodal distribution for the dependent variable—a violation of the normality assumption underlying regression analysis and arguably a more serious violation than my own. By contrast, the rankings based upon the ten-point scale do produce a normal curve in the distribution of the dependent variable. Third, there is likely a good deal of random measurement error in any instrument purporting to measure something such as "regulatory program strength." Measurement error of this type will serve to deflate the correlations between the dependent variable and independent variables, resulting in the underestimation of coefficients in significance tests (Berry and Feldman 1985). Finally, monte carlo simulations demonstrate that ordinal variables with this level of distinction act like true interval measures in regression analysis (Hanushek and Jackson 1977).

2. An objection might be raised to using this measure of state program strength: because FREE is an environmental interest group, their rankings may not be completely objective. After interviewing the individuals responsible for compiling the rankings, it became clear that FREE exhibits no regional or state-specific biases. Certainly, the FREE evaluations of state air quality programs may be a bit pessimistic, since any environmental interest group would like to see states doing more in this area. Since the rankings are not used to evaluate the *adequacy* of state programs, however, this is a moot point. Moreover, because whatever bias the FREE rankings might have is consistent across all states, the variable coefficients in the models will remain unbiased and efficient—that is, the model results will be unaffected.

3. I hypothesize that state expenditures may have some independent effect upon the stringency of a state's air pollution control regulations. The major influence of state spending in this area, however, is hypothesized to occur during policy implementation, and thus will have its impact on measures of environmental quality rather than measures of regulatory strength.

4. We can identify a second reason for dropping poorly performing variables in these preliminary analyses. Since one of the primary goals of this chapter is to compare the integrated model of policy influence with the three traditional models, it makes sense to maximize the empirical results of the traditional models in order to provide the integrated model with the stiffest possible competition. The coefficient estimate for per capita state expenditures provides an excellent example of the utility of regression diagnostic techniques (Belsley, Kuh, and Welsch 1980). Any time we have very volatile coefficient estimates, we should expect that a small number of data points are exerting a large influence over these estimates. Indeed, Alaska exerts enormous influence in this model, having a Hat-diagonal value of 0.846 (nearly six times the value of the next largest observation), Dffits = 1.73, and a value for Cook's D of 0.75. With Alaska dropped from the analysis, the coefficient estimate for state expenditures drops to −0.19, while the other coefficients remain largely unchanged.

5. Excluding Democratic legislative strength and legislative apportionment as predic-

tive variables should be explained. Chapter 1 demonstrated that ideology, not party affiliation, is the driving force behind legislators' environmental voting records. Thus, a measure of ideology replaces Democratic legislative strength in the political model. Legislative apportionment is excluded for an altogether different reason. The overrepresentation of rural constituencies in some states, and its hypothesized conservative effect on public policy, prevalent in the 1960s and before, has largely been rectified (Harrigan 1988; Van Horn 1989). Accepting this, there is little reason to include a legislative apportionment variable in the analysis.

6. Those characteristics of state legislatures believed to represent "legislative professionalism" and included in the creation of the professionalism index are: the length of the legislative session (in days), compensation levels of state legislators, the number of bills introduced in the 1985 legislative session, whether or not state legislators are provided with personal staff support, whether the state legislature has the power of legislative review over administrative rules, and whether or not the legislature utilizes computers for assessing the budgetary impact of legislation and the development of budgetary impact notes from this information (*Book of the States* 1988).

7. These data were collected for the years 1978–88. The index itself is simply the percentage of seats controlled by the majority party in both houses subtracted from 1. This results in an index ranging from zero (complete one-party dominance) to 0.5 (perfect competition). For a discussion of the idea that such indices largely miss the conceptual point, see Stonecash (1987). No attempt is made to distinguish party systems based on class divisions from those based on other foundations (Jennings 1979).

8. These data were collected for the years 1984–88. Assigning scores to certain states was a problem, since during this period two states (North Dakota and West Virginia) had no Republicans in their congressional delegations and three states (Alaska, New Hampshire, and Wyoming) had no Democrats. Values for these states were predicted using several variables highly correlated with the liberalism and environmental scores. Nebraska, with a unicameral and nonpartisan state legislature, was assigned the average value of the state's congressional delegation.

9. For skeptics of this approach, a variable representing state agency resources was included in the model (budgetary figures). This variable exhibited no statistical significance.

10. Collinearity is a condition in multiple regression where two or more of the independent variables are highly correlated with one another, violating the assumption of statistically independent explanatory variables. The degree of collinearity can be evaluated by either the variance inflation factor or the tolerance level. (For a clear discussion of collinearity and its effects on regression coefficients, see Hanushek and Jackson 1977 or Wonnacott and Wonnacott 1981.) Collinearity causes unbiased but inefficient coefficient estimators, resulting in a likely underestimation of t-statistics.

The tolerance levels for this equation are as follows: LCV score = .33, policy liberalism = .43, elite liberalism = .33, legislative professionalism = .85, party competition = .64, state opinion liberalism = .42.

11. The tolerance levels are as follows: legislative professionalism = .89, party competition = .93, state opinion liberalism = .84.

12. With Delaware dropped from the equation, the following results are obtained: legislative professionalism t = 4.49, party competition t = 2.00, state opinion liberalism t = −1.78, R^2 = .44. With New York dropped from the equation: legislative professionalism t = 5.28, party competition t = 1.84, state opinion liberalism t = −1.83, R^2 = .48.

13. The industries that are included in the Polluting Industry Strength variable are as follows (by SIC codes): Paper and Allied Products (26); Chemicals and Allied Products (28); Petroleum and Coal Products (29); Rubber and Miscellaneous Plastics Products (30);

Stone, Clay, and Glass Products (32); Primary Metal Industries (33); Transportation Equipment (37).

14. U.S. Department of Energy 1989. This variable is logged to correct for skewness.

15. National organizations are not the only environmental group influences at the state level. Independent state chapters of national federations (e.g., Clean Water Action) and homegrown state and local environmental groups are having an increasingly important impact on state policymaking (see chapter 1). Gathering membership data for these groups in all fifty states is nearly impossible, however. This variable was compiled by the author and is logged to correct for skewness.

16. A final potential influence on state air quality regulations is labor unions. The causal nature of their influence is complex and problematic. Regulations impose costs upon industry, costs which must either be passed on to the consumer through higher prices or, in a competitive market, internalized by the firm. One method of protecting profits while internalizing regulatory costs is to cut labor costs through layoffs or wage concessions. Thus, unions could be seen as opposing stringent air quality regulations. There are other possibilities, however. Insofar as both labor and environmental concerns are typically thought of as the province of liberal citizens and legislators, strong unions could be associated with more stringent air pollution regulations. More compelling is the "politics makes strange bedfellows" argument: unions will join with environmental groups in promoting stringent regulations when their normally divergent interests coincide (see Ackerman and Hassler 1981). Holloway (1979), however, finds that while unions do exert influence in policy areas of direct relevance to themselves (e.g., industrial policy), this influence becomes much less noticeable when unions attempt to become involved in "new liberal" policy areas such as pollution control regulation. A unionization variable was included in an initial specification of the interest group model, with negligible results.

17. Most political scientists would agree that economic considerations play a large role in determining citizen policy preferences and voting behavior. However, other considerations may be equally important, particularly in areas such as foreign policy, social welfare policy, and environmental protection policy. Indeed, there is little difference among different economic classes in their support for environmental protection policy (Ladd 1982).

18. It should be pointed out that Industrialization and Polluting Industry Strength are very similar variables; in fact, the latter is simply a subset of the former. The correlation coefficient for these two variables is .80, clearly presenting a confounding problem for the analysis. Since Polluting Industry Strength is a more refined measure, and since the theoretical underpinnings of the group influence model are superior to those of the economic model, this variable will be retained as the theoretically meaningful variable.

19. The integrated model has no problems with collinearity, though influence diagnostics show that the state of Delaware still seriously disrupts the analysis. With this state removed, the t-scores for all variable coefficients other than fossil fuel dependence increase by an average of 25 percent, as does the adjusted R^2.

20. The effect coefficient for any independent variable is simply the sum of its direct effect and its indirect effects. Indirect effects are calculated by multiplying the path coefficients (or beta weights) from the variable in question to any related endogenous intervening variable, and the path coefficient from this intervening variable to the dependent variable. For example, the indirect effect of Polluting Industry Strength on Program Strength is simply $(-.04 \times -.24) = .01$.

6

Environmental Outcomes of State Air Quality Regulation

While understanding the politics behind state pollution control programs is important in its own right, we would like to be able to evaluate the outcomes of these regulations as well. We have yet to answer the question, have air pollution control efforts made a difference? The rationale for assessing the results of public policies, or "policy outcomes," should be self-evident. Over the past twenty years, environmental protection has come to be viewed as a responsibility of government. With this in mind, we would expect environmental regulation to result in improvements in environmental quality. With respect to air quality regulations, we hope that these regulations would at least serve to reduce the emission of pollutants into the atmosphere. Ideally, we hope that these same regulatory efforts will improve ambient air quality as well. In evaluating the effectiveness of state air pollution control programs, we are operationalizing the policy outcome section of the integrated model of public policy developed in chapter 4.

Reductions in Air Pollution

Although air pollution control regulation has been fraught with conflict, delay, and missed deadlines, we have some evidence that this legislation has improved air quality. Since the passage of the CAA, emissions of five of the six criteria pollutants have been reduced. Sulfur dioxide emissions have decreased by 22 percent, suspended particulates by 64 percent, and lead by 95 percent. Similar reductions have been made in carbon monoxide emissions and in some sources of VOCs (see table 6.1). Nitrogen dioxide emissions have remained essentially constant over the past twenty years, but even this can be considered a small victory considering that GNP grew by over two-thirds during this same period. While the reductions have not been proportional or linear, atmospheric concentrations of these pollutants have declined as well. In terms of criteria pollutants, there is no doubt that the nation's air is cleaner than it was twenty-five years ago.[1]

Table 6.1

Changes in Air Pollution, Nationwide

Pollutant	Percent Change Pollutant Emissions (1970–86)	Percent Change Pollutant Concentrations (1976–86)
Sulfur Dioxide	−22	−37
Nitrogen Dioxide	+7	−14
TSP	−64	−23
VOC/Ozone[1]	−24	−20
Carbon Monoxide	−37	−38
Lead	−95	−81

[1]The emission figure is for volatile organic compounds, while the concentration figure is for ozone.
Source: Calculated from U.S. CEQ 1989.

The news regarding air quality is not all good, however. Nearly all urban areas in the nation exceed safe standards for atmospheric ozone, and a significant number of air quality regions exceed safe levels for carbon monoxide and sulfur dioxide as well (FREE 1987). All totaled, over 100 million people live in areas that routinely fail to live up to NAAQ standards for one or more pollutants (Smith 1992). Precipitation continues to become more acidic in several sections of the country, and these sections are expanding in size (U.S. CEQ 1989). Atmospheric levels of mercury have doubled this century, and many experts feel that gaseous mercury will become a public health problem in the twenty-first century *(New York Times* 1992b). Mercury is only one example of the ever-increasing amount of toxic air pollutants that continues to be spewed into the atmosphere. In 1989, the emission of toxic air pollutants topped 2.7 billion pounds (U.S. EPA 1991b). While the news is not all good, the federal government is not ignoring remaining air quality problems; the CAA amendments of 1990 contain programs that attempt to address these additional concerns (see chapter 2).

Air Quality and the Research Setting

Ironically, little research in environmental policy has told us what we most want to know with respect to environmental regulation: does it work? In air quality, government figures demonstrate that the nationwide emission levels of several criteria pollutants have declined substantially since the passage of the CAA. Ambient concentrations of these pollutants have declined as well (see table 6.1). Most policy observers go on to conclude that the CAA has been the cause of these improvements (see Schwarz 1988, for an example). Though air quality has improved by some measures, it does not automatically follow that environmental regulation has caused these improvements. Few of these studies attempt to evaluate changes in air quality while controlling for nonregulatory variables such as changes in economic activity, changes in economic infrastructure, or changes in energy consumption. This makes inferring a causal connection between regulation and these improvements problematic. All of these other factors may have just as great an impact on environmental quality as does regulation. Indeed, several economists are skeptical about the effectiveness of regulations for these (and other) reasons (MacAvoy 1979; Yandle 1989).

There are a few notable exceptions to the systematic neglect of the environmental outcomes of pollution control regulations, and most of these conclude that these regulations have little if any environmental impact. For example, MacAvoy (1979) contends that reductions in lead, sulfur dioxide, and particulates are solely a function of changes in industrial and economic activity, and thus cannot be attributed to successful pollution control regulations. Other studies have concluded that investments in pollution control have little or no relationship to levels of atmospheric particulates (Broder n.d.) and that the effects pollutant control regulations have had on industrial pollution are dwarfed by the influence of economic factors (MacAvoy 1987). Again, it has been suggested that in the Netherlands, governmental regulations have had little effect on pollution reduction (Hanf 1982).

Are the outcomes of air pollution control efforts truly negligible? The studies recounted above suggest this conclusion, but each of these has nontrivial flaws. Both MacAvoy (1979 and 1987) and Broder are hampered by short time frames for their studies; environmental impact can only be identified over long periods of time, and none of these studies has data beyond 1981. Moreover, MacAvoy (1979) simply uses a dummy variable to measure the presence or absence of regulation. There is no measure of regulatory stringency or effort. Broder attempts to measure regulatory impact by examining levels of atmospheric particulates—the one criteria pollutant for which natural sources often exceed man-made contributions to concentration levels, and where the impacts of regulation would thus be the most difficult to identify. Finally, MacAvoy (1987) relies only upon industry-reported expenditures for pollution control to measure the effect of regulation on emission levels.

There is limited evidence that pollution control regulations can affect levels of air quality. Lundqvist (1980) argues that Swedish air pollution policies have been more effective than those in the United States, largely because of the process by which they have been developed. Knoepfel and Weidner (1982) contend that air pollution control regulations have significantly reduced sulfur dioxide emissions in Western Europe. Moreover, when assessing U.S. emissions regulations on new automobiles, White (1982) concluded that these regulations were responsible for significant decreases in nitrous oxide emissions (though they were less successful in reducing carbon dioxide emissions). In summary, few researchers have attempted to evaluate the environmental outcomes of air pollution control regulations, and the research that is available has either been done outside of the United States or has come to contradictory conclusions. This leaves us in the unenviable position of being unable to determine whether air pollution control efforts in the United States are having their desired effect.

Controlling Pollutant Emissions

In order to evaluate the effect of state pollution control regulations on air quality, we must first develop a measure of air quality. Changes in sulfur dioxide and nitrogen dioxide best represent changes in overall state air quality. Of the other criteria pollutants monitored by the EPA, lead emissions are determined almost exclusively by federally mandated reductions in the amount of lead in leaded gasoline. State regulation is a moot point here. Ozone and volatile organic compounds are largely restricted to cities, and thus may not be indicative of overall state air quality. Moreover, ozone is also produced by certain atmospheric conditions which confound any inferences made between reductions in emissions and improvements in air quality. The production of carbon monoxide is so diffuse that the impact of regulation upon CO emissions would likely be less noticeable than for the two selected pollutants. Finally, particulate emissions are heavily influenced by natural sources of this pollutant, and it is difficult to separate the contribution of natural sources of particulates from the contribution of man-made sources.

Dependent Variables

The Clean Air Act requires the federal EPA, in conjunction with the states, to provide yearly figures on the emission levels of the six criteria pollutants. Since public policies rarely have immediate impacts, the effect of state air pollution regulations can only be evaluated over time. This is particularly true in the present analysis since we are evaluating the effects of different *levels* of regulation, rather than its presence or absence.

The dependent variables used here are the changes in emissions of sulfur dioxide and nitrous oxides in each state between the years 1973–75 and 1985–87. Values for the dependent variables are constructed by averaging the total sulfur dioxide and nitrous oxides emissions in each state for the years 1973–75 and the years 1985–87. The first average (1973–75) is then subtracted from the second (1985–87) to get the change in emissions for each pollutant between these two time periods. Three-year averages are used for the differencing, rather than single-year values, in order to smooth out the effect of particularly high or low emission levels associated with economic or other disturbances that might occur during a particular year.[2]

This averaged differencing technique for the dependent variable is a bit unusual in that it is not a purely cross-sectional design, nor is it purely longitudinal.

These research designs are not appropriate, however, since neither is able to pick up cross-state changes in pollutant emissions over time. The research questions posed here are tailor-made for a pooled time series design; however, the regulatory program strength variable that is central to the analysis is not available over time. This precludes the use of pooled time series analysis. A second approach for evaluating changes in emission levels might be to examine a series of interrupted ARIMA models for decreases in emission levels following the enactment of clean air regulations. This design is also unworkable, however, as the pre-regulation emissions data necessary for such an analysis are unavailable. Moreover, determining the effect of different levels of state regulatory effort would be exceedingly difficult using an ARIMA design. The differenced dependent variable is a reasonably valid measure of change, since we have confidence in the base emissions data themselves and because the emission trend lines for these pollutants exhibit no irregularities. Moreover, use of this averaged differencing method poses no apparent problems for the reliability or stability of our regression coefficients.[3] The averaged differencing technique outlined here is a capable and powerful measurement tool given the data limitations outlined above.

Given the construction of the dependent variable, a negative value for this variable means that pollutant emission levels in a state declined between the early 1970s and the mid-to-late 1980s. A positive value for this variable means that pollutant emissions increased during this time period. Correspondingly, negative coefficient estimates are interpreted as signaling that increases in the independent variable decreased emissions during the time frame in question, while a positive coefficient means that increases in the independent variable are associated with increases in pollutant emissions. Changes in pollutant emissions in each state are presented in table 6.2.

Independent Variables

Internal Statutory Factors

Internal statutory factors are represented by the strength of a state's air pollution control program. State air pollution control programs are ranked from weakest to strongest using the FREE rankings discussed in chapter 5. Remember that the FREE rankings are not an evaluation of environmental quality in the states, nor are they an evaluation of the effectiveness of state programs. The rankings simply evaluate the strength of a state's air pollution control program. This statutory variable represents the crucial link between the two portions of an integrated model of policy outputs and policy outcomes developed in chapter 4. The hypothesis here is that stronger pollution control programs will be associated with decreases in emission levels. This will be represented by a negative coefficient.

Table 6.2

Percent Change in State Pollutant Emissions, 1973–75 to 1985–87

	TSP	SO^2	NO^2		TSP	SO^2	NO^2
Alabama	−37	−27	9	Montana	−74	69	−12
Alaska	−29	70	156	Nebraska	−74	16	17
Arizona	10	−66	4	Nevada	−62	69	−12
Arkansas	−17	38	91	New Hampshire	105	−21	−31
California	56	−37	−12	New Jersey	−17	−48	−31
Colorado	26	14	35	New Mexico	−54	−30	37
Connecticut	111	−22	−29	New York	23	−30	−35
Delaware	−8	−44	26	North Carolina	−12	−7	−6
Florida	76	−24	−8	North Dakota	−69	97	87
Georgia	−10	78	28	Ohio	−83	−33	−17
Hawaii	−36	17	7	Oklahoma	−6	25	57
Idaho	37	−60	−21	Oregon	27	0	−10
Illinois	−49	−44	−22	Pennsylvania	−56	−39	−13
Indiana	−54	−18	−24	Rhode Island	102	−60	−36
Iowa	−71	−16	−8	South Carolina	−32	−6	−10
Kansas	−12	60	46	South Dakota	−38	89	4
Kentucky	−67	−48	−3	Tennessee	−48	−21	4
Louisiana	−52	−36	35	Texas	5	27	37
Maine	8	−37	−23	Utah	−24	38	40
Maryland	16	−53	−13	Vermont	63	−28	−11
Massachusetts	65	−14	−37	Virginia	−48	−44	−18
Michigan	−32	−56	−27	Washington	38	−33	−17
Minnesota	−1	−47	−33	West Virginia	−73	2	11
Mississippi	−42	79	18	Wisconsin	−49	−30	−23
Missouri	−10	0	3	Wyoming	−75	78	133

Source: Compiled from U.S. EPA 1973–88, *National Emissions Report.*

Internal Political Factors

While agency budgets are an important component of program strength, they may affect emission levels independent of their association with overall program strength. To test for this, expenditure figures are included independently as internal political factors. The second independent variable then is the average constant-dollar amount (1982 = 100) each state spent on air pollution control in the years 1970–85.[4]

Some might question the use of aggregate expenditure figures here, rather than expenditures weighted by some function (i.e., size of the state, level of pollution in the state, and so forth). Use of aggregate figures, however, is justified. First, pollution control can be seen as an aggregate problem. Many capital and operating expenditures are constant regardless of the amount of pollution to be "cleaned up" (this fact drives many economists to their conclusion that such command and control regulations are inefficient). Some critical level of spending on pollution control must be attained before substantial benefits accrue (similar reasoning for using aggregate expenditure levels can be found in Williams and Matheny 1984). Second, relative state effort is less important in controlling air pollution than is state administrative capacity. A less populous state may spend more per capita on air pollution control than a more populous state, but these per capita figures do not reflect the lower absolute level of resources devoted to environmental protection. For example, New Mexico and North Dakota spend twice as much per capita for air programs as do Pennsylvania and Ohio, while Wyoming spends three times as much as these two states and more than California (FREE 1987). Reasoning that New Mexico, North Dakota, and Wyoming therefore have greater administrative capacity in air pollution control than California, Ohio, or Pennsylvania would be a mistake. Total expenditures, not per capita figures, pay for inspectors, audits, research and development, and other measures of bureaucratic capacity within a state (see Meier 1988 and B. Wood 1992 for similar arguments in state insurance regulation and federal environmental regulation, respectively). For these reasons, aggregate expenditure figures are used. Increases in expenditures (i.e., increased political support and bureaucratic capacity) are expected to result in reduced pollutant emissions, exhibited by a negative coefficient.

Administrative "Outputs"

Regulations mean little to recalcitrant actors unless they are backed with at least a plausible threat of incurring negative sanctions for noncompliance. In pollution control, most enforcement actions can be classified as monitoring activities, where officials monitor compliance with permits, examine pollution control equipment, and monitor effluent and emission levels. Few sanctions are associated with monitoring actions. The remainder of enforcement activities can be classified as abatement actions. In abatement actions, officials seek to induce or force a polluter to install equipment, reduce effluent or emission levels, and generally cease unlawful pollution activities. Sanctions are most often used against polluters who refuse to comply with abatement orders. While monitoring activities provide officials with the information necessary to begin abatement proceedings, the real teeth of enforcement are in the abatement actions themselves. A polluter's incentive to comply with pollution control regulations is directly related to the probability of being sanctioned for noncompliance (Downing 1984). Thus, we would expect the level of abatement activities to have a greater impact than monitoring actions on pollution emissions in a state.

Enforcement activities vary by the level of enforcement as well. For the most part, states focus their enforcement efforts on stationary sources of pollution, since these sources have historically been a state responsibility. States devote fewer resources to mobile source enforcement efforts, since these sources have historically been a federal responsibility (see chapters 2 and 3). States also have fewer resources to devote to enforcement than does the federal EPA. Further-more, state sanctions are typically less severe than sanctions imposed by federal regulators, and state inspectors are often more sympathetic to industry positions than are their federal counterparts (Hedge and Menzel 1985).

State air pollution abatement activities are fairly inconsistent. Sanctions, re-sources, regulatory fortitude, and abatement definitions vary greatly across state jurisdictions. The data suggest that these differences lead a few states to pad their enforcement statistics with insignificant abatement actions or sanctions that the state lacks the resources to carry out. For instance, between 1977 and 1985, South Carolina reported 3,745 abatement actions, while the comparable numbers for California, New York, and Michigan were 126, 383, and 93 respectively during this same period. South Carolina is not that much more aggressive in enforcing pollution control regulations than are California and New York; rather, numbers like these suggest that some states are engaging in symbolic enforce-ment activities, inflating enforcement numbers in order to satisfy citizens and EPA officials.[5]

State enforcement figures with these characteristics are unlikely to show a consistent impact on pollutant emissions across states and over time. Indeed, significant evidence suggests that enforcement actions in general have a minimal effect at best on regulatory compliance. The infrequency of inspections and uncertainty of sanctions, due in large part to a lack of resources, means that most compliance with pollution control regulation is voluntary (Downing and Kimball 1982; interview with EPA official 1989). If enforcement is to have an effect on compliance, and thus on the attainment of regulatory goals, it must be consistent, focused, and backed up with adequate resources. This does not describe air pollution enforcement efforts in all American states.

EPA abatement standards and activities, on the other hand, are fairly consis-tent across regions and across time, at least when compared with state enforce-ment actions. Faced with its large jurisdiction, the EPA rarely expends scarce enforcement resources in pursuit of relatively trivial noncompliance. EPA en-forcement activities are usually concentrated on the largest and most significant polluters. Finally, even states with good enforcement records often hand over their toughest and most important enforcement cases to the EPA. This means that in comparison with state enforcement efforts, EPA enforcement actions will be more consistent, more focused, and supported with greater resources—exactly the factors deemed necessary for effective enforcement. Thus, we might expect EPA abatement activities to have a greater effect on pollutant emissions than do state enforcement efforts.[6]

The third explanatory variable in the analysis reflects the number of EPA abatement activities in each state between 1977 and 1985. We would expect higher levels of federal enforcement to be associated with decreased pollution emissions. The fourth explanatory variable represents state abatement activities in each state from 1977 to 1985. If the claims made in the preceding paragraphs are correct, we would expect state enforcement actions to have less of an effect on pollutant emissions, particularly emissions from mobile sources.

External Environmental Factors

The fifth independent variable is the change in economic activity associated with the most polluting industries in each state. Emission levels are heavily dependent upon industrial activity. This could mean (and has been interpreted to mean) that changes in emissions can be adequately explained by changes in economic activity. The economic variable itself is the difference in constant-dollar (1982 = 100) value added by manufacturing (VAM) in the seven industrial categories most responsible for air pollution between the years 1973–75 and 1985–87.[7] The first VAM average (1973–75) is subtracted from the second (1985–87) to calculate the change in industrial activity. Again, range averages are used to smooth out year-specific economic fluctuations. A direct positive relationship is hypothesized between economic activity and emission levels so that the coefficient for this variable should be positive.

Nearly all criteria pollutants are by-products of the combustion of fossil fuels. To test for the effect changes in fuel consumption have on emission levels, a fuel consumption variable is added to each emission equation. Some energy sources, however (i.e., hydroelectric power, nuclear fission, natural gas), have virtually no impact on the criteria pollutants examined here. For an accurate representation of the fuel consumption–pollutant emission connection, fuel sources must be carefully matched to specific pollutants. The overwhelming majority of sulfur dioxide emissions comes from burning coal. The sulfur dioxide emission model thus contains a variable representing the change in coal consumption in each state, in trillions of BTUs, from 1973–75 to 1985–87. Nitrous oxides are produced in much higher temperature environments (e.g. automobile engines) than is sulfur dioxide, and most of these use petroleum products as a fuel source. The most accurate explanatory variable, then, is the total consumption of petroleum products in each state.[8] This variable, added to the nitrous oxide emission model, represents the change in petroleum product consumption in each state in trillions of BTUs from 1973–75 to 1985–87. A positive value for these variables will represent an increase in the consumption of that particular fuel in a state between 1973 and 1987, while a negative value represents decreased consumption. The hypothesis of a positive relationship between energy consumption and pollutant emissions will be represented by a positive coefficient.

Multiple Regression Results

Multiple regression analysis demonstrates that levels of industrial activity have a significant effect upon air pollutant emissions (see table 6.3). The economic

Table 6.3

Multiple Regression Results: Changes in Pollutant Emissions
(Dependent Variable = Changes in State Pollutant Emissions,
Tons/Year, 1973–75 to 1985–87)

Independent Variable	Sulfur Dioxide		Nitrous Oxides	
	Initial Coefficient	Revised Coefficient	Initial Coefficient	Revised Coefficient
Intercept	12,709	15,767	90,098	95,727
Regulatory Program Strength	−27,947*	−29,084**	−15,051**	−15,518***
Industrial Activity	68.6**	65.7***	−2.9	−5.6
EPA Abatements	−244.1**	−251.4***	−20.3	−26.8
State Abatements	−73.9*	−72.6*	13.96	—
State Air Expenditures	−4.5	—	−6.3	—
Fossil Fuel Consumption	568.1***	570.2***	432.1***	436.4***
F-ratio	10.50***	12.88***	21.73***	32.12***
Adj. R^2	.54	.55	.72	.72
N	49	49[a]	50	50

[a]Arizona is dropped from the analysis due to an exceptionally large Dffit that skewed the results for the rest of the model (see note 9).
 *Statistically significant at $p < .10$.
 **Statistically significant at $p < .05$.
 ***Statistically significant at $p < .01$.

change measure displays a significant positive coefficient in the sulfur dioxide model. Each thousand-dollar increase in value added manufacturing output leads to a sixty-six-ton increase in sulfur dioxide emissions, all other things remaining equal. In the nitrous oxide model, however, industrial activity does not appear to affect pollutant emissions. This is to be expected. Recall that a majority of nitrous oxides come from mobile sources, and the influence of these sources is not captured by the industrial classification variable used here. Since industry emits a minority of this pollutant, we would expect the industrial variable to exert less influence in this model. On the basis of these results, we have to conclude that much of the change in sulfur dioxide emissions from 1973 to 1987 can be attributed to changes in the productive output of polluting industries within a state. In the absence of additional information, these results support the economic skeptics of regulation; changes in pollutant emissions can be attributed in part to changes in industrial activity.

The remainder of the results, however, contradict the contention that regulation does not matter. The strength of a state's air pollution control program has a significant effect on both sulfur dioxide and nitrous oxide emissions in a state. All other things remaining equal, states with more stringent air quality programs are more successful at reducing emissions of these pollutants. As a state moves up one point on the regulatory program strength scale, annual sulfur dioxide emissions are reduced by 29,000 tons, and nitrous oxide emissions are reduced by over 15,000 tons. Regulation *does* in fact make a difference; public policies are having their desired effects upon environmental outcomes.

State spending on air programs has no independent impact on emission levels. For sulfur dioxide and nitrous oxides, higher levels of spending are associated with reductions in pollutant emissions, but this effect is not statistically significant. Why do state spending levels fare so poorly in these models? Quite likely because the influence of bureaucratic resources on air pollutant emissions is more accurately represented by variables already included in the models, most notably program strength. Because state spending has little independent impact on emission levels in the presence of the program strength variable, this variable is dropped from the final emission reduction regression models.

In both regression models, federal enforcement actions have a greater effect on reducing pollutant emissions than do state enforcement actions, as was predicted, and stronger EPA enforcement efforts do reduce sulfur dioxide emissions. State enforcement activity has no effect on nitrous oxide emissions, but state abatement actions appear to reduce sulfur dioxide emissions. Each EPA abatement action is associated with a 251-ton reduction in sulfur dioxide emissions, while each state action is associated with a 73-ton reduction in these emissions. Since empirical results have confirmed our original suspicions regarding the utility of the state enforcement variable in the nitrous oxide model, this variable is omitted in the revised set of emissions equations.

Significant findings are also associated with the fuel consumption variables. Coal consumption is an important factor in sulfur dioxide emissions, as was expected, and changes in petroleum consumption are especially influential in the nitrous oxide emissions model. As fossil fuel consumption increases by one trillion BTUs, sulfur dioxide emissions increase by 570 tons and nitrous oxide emissions increase by 436 tons, all other things remaining equal. We should not be surprised that increases in energy consumption raise pollution emissions. This result does, however, support the contention that substantive environmental variables are important when evaluating policy outcomes.[9]

Causal Modeling

Multiple regression is not the best empirical choice for evaluating policy outcomes. Many of the variables that influence policy outcomes are causally related to other variables in the model as well. For example, the number of federal enforcement actions in a state strongly influences the state's own efforts in enforcing environmental regulations (B. Wood 1992). In turn, these state enforcement efforts, in conjunction with state budgetary expenditures, affect the strength of a state's pollution control program. Since most heavily polluting industries are also energy intensive, a state's dependence upon fossil fuels may be affected by changes in industrial activity. Fossil fuel dependence can also be influenced by state regulations insofar as these regulations provide incentives or disincentives for the combustion of different types of fuel (Knoepfel and Weidner 1982). Single equation regression techniques do not allow us to measure these causal relationships or the indirect effects that these relationships have on the dependent variable. Moreover, the use of a single equation regression technique does not allow the researcher to compare the relative influence of his or her independent variables when these variables are causally related (Lewis-Beck 1977). For these reasons, the model is also operationalized as a set of path analytic equations.

Following the discussion above, federal enforcement efforts, state expenditures, and changes in industrial activity are all treated as exogenous variables. This does not mean that these variables themselves are not the product of some causal process; undoubtedly they are. By entering these factors as exogenous variables, we are simply saying that the causal process behind these variables is not critical to policy outcomes, and that these variables themselves are not caused by other variables in the model. The remaining three independent variables are assumed to be determined largely within the causal system (i.e., they are endogenous variables). Multiple regression analysis confirmed our suspicions that state expenditures and some state enforcement efforts have little influence on emission levels independent of their relationship to program strength; thus, the direct paths from these variables to changes in emission levels are omitted.[10]

The direct effects of the independent variables on emission reductions are identical to the standardized regression coefficients from the revised models in table 6.3. What the causal models provide is the ability to calculate and compare the total effect (i.e., effect coefficient) for each independent variable. These effects coefficients allow us to compare the relative influence each independent variable has on the dependent variable, and thus to identify the most influential independent variables in the models. The effects coefficients are presented in table 6.4.[11]

The path diagrams substantiate the assumptions made when constructing the causal models. Fossil fuel dependence is affected by both economic activity in a state and a state's pollution control program, which means that both of these independent variables indirectly affect pollutant emissions through their effect on fossil fuel consumption. In addition, the strength of a state's air pollution control program is determined in part by state expenditures and state enforcement efforts, though this variable is much more than simply the composite influence of these two factors. Multiple regression concludes that neither state expenditures nor the state enforcement variable (for nitrous oxides) affect pollutant emissions directly; however, the path models show us that they are important factors in the overall process of reducing pollutant emissions.

The effects coefficients reinforce the conclusions drawn from the single equa-

138

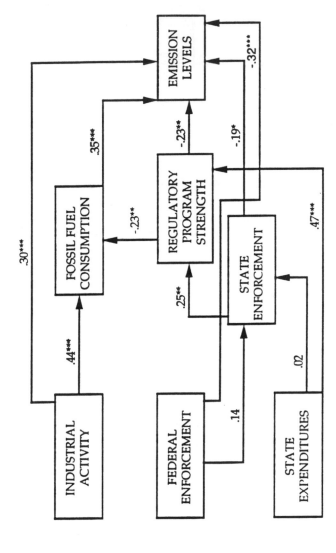

Figure 6.1. **Causal Model for Changes in Sulfur Dioxide Emissions**

*Statistically significant at $p < .10$.
**Statistically significant at $p < .05$.
***Statistically significant at $p < .01$.

Figure 6.2. **Causal Model for Changes in Nitrous Oxide Emissions**

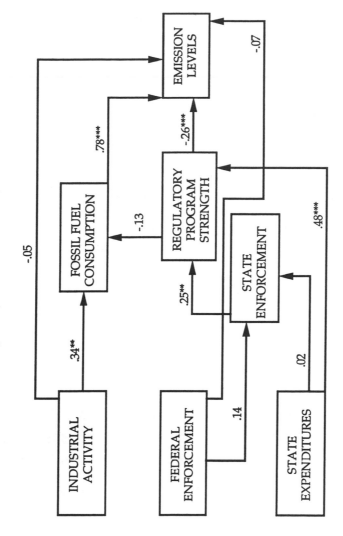

**Statistically significant at $p < .05$.
***Statistically significant at $p < .01$.

Table 6.4

Effects Coefficients: Changes in Pollutant Emissions
(Dependent Variable = Changes in State Pollutant Emissions, Tons/Year,
1973–75 to 1985–87)

Independent Variable	Sulfur Dioxide		Nitrous Oxides	
	Direct Effect[1]	Total Effect[1]	Direct Effect[1]	Total Effect[1]
Regulatory Program Strength	−0.23	−0.31	−0.26	−0.36
Industrial Activity	0.30	0.45	−0.05	0.21
EPA Abatements	−0.32	−0.36	−0.07	−0.08
State Abatements	−0.19	−0.27	—	−0.09
State Air Expenditures	—	−0.11	—	−0.17
Fossil Fuel Consumption	0.35	0.35	0.78	0.78

[1]Coefficients are rounded to the nearest .01.

tion regression models. While external environmental factors are important influences in pollutant emissions, they are not the only important factors. Changes in
industrial activity at the state level affect pollutant emissions, but the effect of
combined state air pollution control efforts exceeds the influence of industrial
activity on emission levels in both the sulfur dioxide and nitrous oxide models.
Federal enforcement actions are positively related to reductions in sulfur dioxide,
while fossil fuel (i.e., petroleum) consumption is of primary importance in determining changes in nitrous oxide emissions. Overall, all twelve of the total effects
coefficients reflect the hypothesized relationships between independent variables
and changes in state pollutant emissions.

Improving Air Quality

Energy consumption, industrial activity, and regulatory efforts all have significant effects on air pollutant emissions. Pollutant emission levels are not the same
as air quality, however. Whereas emissions are measured in thousands or millions of tons (i.e., absolute levels), air quality is typically measured using concentration levels (i.e., parts per million, or micrograms of a particular pollutant
present in a cubic meter of air). The primary and secondary national ambient air
quality standards (NAAQS) for the six criteria pollutants set by the EPA are all
concentration-based standards (see table 6.5). Concentrations of pollutants in the
atmosphere, not emission levels, create the adverse environmental and health
effects discussed in chapter 1. Concentration levels are thus a better measure of
air quality than are emission levels.

We often observe little relationship between area pollutant emissions and
concentrations of pollutants in the atmosphere for several reasons. First, pollu-

Table 6.5

Primary National Ambient Air Quality Standards (NAAQS)

Total Suspended Particulates (TSP)[a]	75 micrograms per cubic meter
	Annual maximum
Sulfur Dioxide (SO^2)	0.03 parts per million
	Annual maximum
	0.14 parts per million
	Daily maximum
Nitrogen Dioxide (NO^2)	0.053 parts per million
	Annual maximum
Carbon Monoxide (CO)	35 parts per million
	One-hour maximum
	9 parts per million
	Eight-hour maximum
Ozone (O^3)	0.12 parts per million
	Daily maximum
Lead (Pb)	1.5 micrograms per cubic meter
	Daily maximum

[a]In 1987, the TSP standard was changed to a standard for particulates smaller than 10 micrometers in diameter (the PM10 standard), since these smallest particles pose the greatest threat to human health. TSP measurements are used in the analysis presented here to maintain continuity with the measurements from the 1970s.
Source: U.S. Council on Environmental Quality 1983.

tants emitted in one state are often transported across state lines and register as increased ambient pollutant levels in neighboring states. In this way, pollutants from one state may affect air quality in several states. Second, myriad meteorological and atmospheric conditions determine if and how pollutant emissions are reflected in air quality measurements (for example, temperature inversions may cause significant air quality problems in metropolitan areas). Under these conditions, air quality deteriorates even though the emission of pollutants remains the same or decreases. Other weather conditions also affect the relationship between emission levels and air quality; high winds can blow pollutants away before they become a local air quality problem, rain effectively "washes" pollutants out of the atmosphere before they can accumulate to problem levels, and extremely humid conditions can bind certain pollutants together (e.g., particulates) taking them out of the atmosphere. In addition, temperature and sunlight directly affect whether certain pollution emissions (VOCs and nitric oxide) are catalyzed into criteria pollutants (ozone and nitrogen dioxide). Lastly, certain natural sources of pollution affect ambient air quality regardless of pollutant emissions from human activity.

For these and other reasons, the relationship between pollutant emissions and atmospheric concentrations of pollutants is fairly uncertain. Although attempting to remedy this by using complex atmospheric models, even the EPA is uncertain exactly how emissions affect ambient pollutant levels (U.S. EPA 1987). In social science research, Knoepfel and Weidner could find no relationship between sulfur dioxide emissions and ambient atmospheric concentrations of this pollutant, nor between regulatory efforts and ambient pollutant levels (Knoepfel and Weidner 1982). Thus, past research suggests that linking regulatory efforts and economic conditions to changes in ambient air quality levels will be a difficult task.

Dependent Variables

The CAA required the EPA to create a network of monitors to measure air quality levels across the country. In addition to these National Air Monitoring Stations (NAMS), most state environmental agencies have their own networks of State and Local Air Monitoring Stations (SLAMS). In conjunction with other associated monitoring stations, NAMS and SLAMS constitute a nationwide network of over 2,000 air quality monitoring facilities. The measurements taken at these facilities give by far the most comprehensive picture of air quality available. Measurements of air quality from NAMS and SLAMS within each state are used as the dependent variable in this part of the analysis.

In the early 1970s, pollutant concentration data from many of the SLAMS were of questionable quality. States did not have the necessary infrastructure or the necessary resources to produce consistently accurate pollution concentration measurements. The number of SLAMS and the quality of the data these SLAMS produced improved markedly after the mid-1970s, however (see Portney 1990a). In order to protect the validity of the data used here, early pollutant concentration measurements that are of poor or questionable quality have been purged from the analysis. Removing these observations has its cost; we lose seven cases in the sulfur dioxide model ($N = 43$) and thirteen cases in the nitrogen dioxide model ($N = 37$), but this is a cost we are willing to pay in order to protect the validity of the models' conclusions.

An important objection can be raised to using NAAQS measures to evaluate the effects of regulation on state air quality. This objection stems from the interstate nature of air pollution. Air pollution control regulations cannot affect air quality levels directly; they can only control the emission of pollutants within a state. State A may have a stringent pollution control program in place, but if neighboring state B does not, the spillover of pollutants from that neighboring state may raise ambient pollutant concentrations and mask the effects of air pollution regulations in state A. In short, the benefits of stringent pollution control regulations will not be confined within states, making the connection between regulatory activity and improvements in air quality problematic (recall Connecticut's refusal to enact stronger mobile source emission standards, mentioned in chapter 3). This interstate transfer of air pollutants becomes important when the EPA seeks to impose restrictions and sanctions in areas not meeting federal NAAQ standards.[12]

Four responses to this objection justify the use of NAAQS measures to represent state air quality. First, the most troublesome cross-boundary pollutant from a political standpoint, ozone, is not used to evaluate the effects of state regulation upon state air quality. Second, NAMS and SLAMS are typically located near centers of pollution emissions. Thus, they exhibit a bias toward local rather than interstate sources when measuring pollutant concentrations. The nature of NAMS and SLAMS also provide the third justification for using NAAQS measures. Sulfur dioxide and nitrogen dioxide are long-distance pollutants (for example, the majority of the acid-forming pollutants that fall on Minnesota and Wisconsin originate outside of these two states). While these two pollutants can travel great distances, they do so in the upper levels of the atmosphere where rain clouds form. NAAQS measures, on the other hand, are taken much closer to ground level, and the pollutants at ground level generally originate in the surrounding areas. (Because of these ground level monitors, however, NAAQS measurements often fail to detect deteriorations in air quality stemming from so-called tall stacks on electric utilities and smelters which in some cases emit pollutants more than a thousand feet above ground level.)

While these three conditions may be relevant justifications for using NAAQS measures in larger states, sulfur and nitrogen dioxides may cross borders and affect air quality in the smaller states of the East. While these states often have similar air quality regulations (FREE 1987), this does not solve the very real problem of associating changes in state air quality with state-level activities in these areas. This brings up the final justification for using NAAQS measurements to evaluate the connection between regulations and state air quality: they are the best data we have for the task. The cross-boundary problems of air pollution, while significant, do not invalidate NAAQ figures as measures of state air quality. If this were the case, we would have no objective basis for enforcing sanctions against violators of the NAAQ standards. The most serious problem in evaluating changes in air quality is not the cross-boundary nature of the problem, but the wide variety of factors that affect the conversion of emissions to measurable airborne pollutant levels.

The construction of the dependent variable representing state air quality is fairly complex. Those interested in the technical aspects of this construction will find them in the appendix. In brief, the dependent variable is the average percentage change in pollutant concentrations for all monitoring stations within a state between 1973–75 and 1986–88. Three-year averages are again used to smooth out yearly fluctuations in concentration levels. The first average (1973–75) is subtracted from the second (1986–88), and this difference is taken as a percentage of the average pollution concentration level during the earlier time period.[13] Percentages are used to represent changes in air quality, rather than raw changes in ambient concentrations, because they are easier to interpret and because these changes are most often represented in percentile figures (U.S. CEQ 1983, 1989; U.S. EPA 1987). The dependent variable is constructed so that a negative value will signify a reduction in ambient pollution concentrations (i.e., improved air quality) between these two time periods, and vice versa.[14]

Independent Variables

Internal Statutory Factors

Internal statutory factors are again represented by the strength of a state's air pollution control program. This variable is represented by the FREE scores, which rank states from weakest to strongest with respect to these programs. Stronger pollution control programs are expected to be associated with decreased pollutant concentration levels, or improvements in ambient air quality. This positive relationship will be represented by a negative coefficient. State pollution control program strength is entered as an endogenous variable in the causal models.

Internal Political Factors

State expenditures for pollution control represent internal political factors in the sulfur dioxide and nitrogen dioxide pollutant concentration models. Also, recall that many internal political factors are vicariously represented within state expenditures and within the program strength variable outlined above (see chapter 5). We again expect that larger state expenditures will be associated with improved air quality over time, and this relationship will be reflected in a negative coefficient estimate. State air pollution control expenditures are included as an exogenous variable in the causal models of air pollution concentrations.

Administrative "Outputs"

Administrative "outputs" are represented by the number of state and EPA CAA abatement activities undertaken in each state between 1977 and 1985. Remember that EPA abatement activities are more consistent and better supported than those at the state level, and thus are expected to have a more significant effect on improving air quality in the states. EPA abatement activities are included as an exogenous variable in the causal models, while the effect of state enforcement actions is accounted for by including this variable endogenously. Both types of enforcement actions should be associated with decreased pollution concentrations over time, reflected in a negative coefficient.

External Environmental Factors

In the pollutant emission models, changes in external economic activity and fuel consumption variables were represented as absolute figures (i.e., the absolute change in polluting industry VAM within each state, and the absolute change in trillions of BTUs consumed in each state). Absolute change measures were necessary since the dependent variables of interest were aggregate emission figures. The dependent variables in the present pollutant concentration models are not measured as raw changes in concentration levels (which are difficult for anyone other than an atmospheric scientist to assign meaning to), but are instead represented as percentage increases or decreases in ambient pollutant levels. In order to maintain logical consistency within the models, the economic activity and fuel consumption variables must be represented as percentage figures as well.

The first external environmental factor included in the ambient pollutant concentration models represents the percentage change in economic activity associated with the most polluting industries in each state from 1973–75 to 1985–87. The difference between the 1985–87 and 1973–75 figures is represented as a percentage of the 1973–75 VAM in these industries. The expected relationship between increased industrial activity and increased pollutant concentrations will be reflected in a positive coefficient estimate. The industrial activity variable is entered as an exogenous variable in the causal models.

The final explanatory variable in the air quality models represents the percentage change in fossil fuel consumption in a state from 1973–75 to 1985–87. For each fuel variable, the change in consumption within each state is presented as a percentage of the 1973–75 fuel consumption level.[15] Similar to the emissions models, changes in coal consumption are expected to have the greatest impact on sulfur dioxide levels and changes in oil consumption will influence nitrogen dioxide levels. Increases in fuel consumption within a state should result in increased ambient pollution levels and be represented by a positive coefficient. The fuel consumption variables are entered endogenously in the causal models. The results for the state ambient air quality models are presented in tables 6.6 and 6.7, and figures 6.3 and 6.4.

Results from the Pollutant Concentration Models

Accounting for changes in ambient air pollution concentrations is extremely difficult. Nevertheless, the models presented here demonstrate that air quality regulations have had a marked impact on reducing both sulfur dioxide and nitrogen dioxide pollution. The coefficients associated with the air program variable show that states with stronger pollution control programs have experienced, all other things being equal, larger reductions in the airborne concentrations of these pollutants. To be specific, in the revised models a one-point increase in the strength of a state's pollution control programs has led to a 5.9 percent reduction in sulfur dioxide concentrations and a 6.6 percent reduction in nitrogen dioxide concentrations since the mid-1970s, all other things being equal.

The other political variables are less successful in accounting for changes in state air pollution concentrations. Neither state nor federal enforcement activities have statistically significant effects on state pollutant levels. While the results

Table 6.6

Multiple Regression Results: Changes in Pollutant Concentrations
(Dependent Variable = Changes in State Ambient Pollutant Concentrations,
1973–75 to 1985–87)

Independent Variable	Sulfur Dioxide		Nitrogen Dioxide	
	Initial Coefficient	Revised Coefficient	Initial Coefficient	Revised Coefficient
Intercept	−27.7	−28.0	49.5	48.5
Regulatory Program Strength	−6.19***	−5.91***	−5.79*	−6.63**
Industrial Activity	0.36**	0.38**	−0.43*	−0.42*
EPA Abatements	0.01	0.01	−0.02	−0.01
State Abatements	0.002	—	0.01	—
State Air Expenditures	0.0005	—	−0.00005	—
Fossil Fuel Consumption	0.04	0.04	0.67*	0.59*
F-ratio	3.05**	4.78***	1.80	2.45*
Adj. R^2	.23	.27	.12	.14
N	43	43	37	37

*Statistically significant at $p < .10$.
**Statistically significant at $p < .05$.
***Statistically significant at $p < .01$.

Table 6.7

Effects Coefficients: Changes in Pollutant Concentrations
(Dependent Variable = Changes in State Pollutant Concentrations,
1973–75 to 1985–87)

Independent Variable	Sulfur Dioxide		Nitrous Oxides	
	Direct Effect[1]	Total Effect[1]	Direct Effect[1]	Total Effect[1]
Regulatory Program Strength	−0.49	−0.51	−0.37	−0.39
Industrial Activity	0.35	0.36	−0.32	−0.31
EPA Abatements	0.14	0.12	0.13	0.12
State Abatements	—	−0.23	—	−0.10
State Air Expenditures	—	−0.12	—	−0.18
Fossil Fuel Consumption	0.13	0.13	0.26	0.26

[1]Coefficients are rounded to the nearest .01.

from the emissions models would lead us to expect this result for nitrogen
dioxide, these results are at odds with those obtained in the sulfur dioxide model.
Here we see another example of how changes in air quality do not mirror

147

Figure 6.3. Causal Model for Changes in Sulfur Dioxide Concentrations

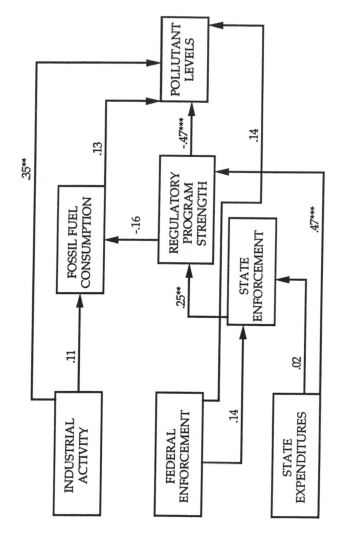

**Statistically significant at *p* < .05.
***Statistically significant at *p* < .01.

148

Figure 6.4. **Causal Model for Changes in Nitrogen Dioxide Concentrations**

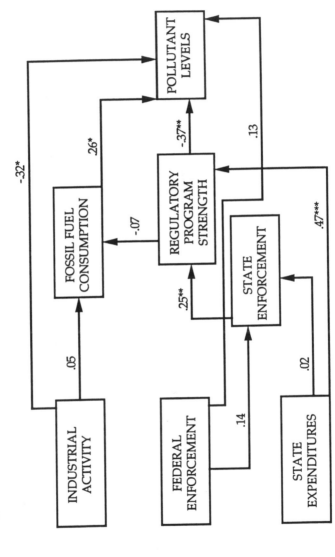

*Statistically significant at $p < .10$.
**Statistically significant at $p < .05$.
***Statistically significant at $p < .01$.

changes in pollutant emissions. Finally, state spending for air pollution control has no direct effect on changes in pollutant concentrations over time.

As we might expect, external environmental factors have a significant effect on changes in state air quality. The coefficient for the industrial activity variable shows that for each 1 percent increase in value added by manufacturing in the most polluting industries, atmospheric concentrations of sulfur dioxide increase about four-tenths of 1 percent. The effect of industrial activity does not carry over into the nitrogen dioxide model, however. Much like the nitrogen dioxide emission model, polluting industry activity has no negative effect on this measure of air quality. In fact, the nitrogen dioxide concentration model shows that increases in industrial output may actually be associated with lower concentrations of this pollutant. This result is a function of the construction of the economic activity variable. Once we remember that the majority of nitrogen dioxide comes from mobile sources not represented in the economic activity measure, this result is understandable, although its magnitude may be unexpected.

The second external environmental variables, changes in fossil fuel consumption, also exhibit significant relationships with air pollution concentrations. In both the sulfur dioxide and nitrogen dioxide models the fossil fuel coefficient is in the expected direction, though this relationship is statistically significant only in the nitrogen dioxide model. Each 1 percent increase in petroluem consumption leads to six-tenths of a percent increase in nitrogen dioxide concentrations, all other things being equal. Much like the pollutant emission models, increases in fossil fuel consumption lead to increases in ambient sulfur and nitrogen dioxide concentrations, and vice versa.

The path models demonstrate that while the indirect effects of our independent variables are smaller than they were in the emissions models, they are evident nonetheless. Of greater significance are the total effects coefficients from the sulfur dioxide and nitrogen dioxide models. The effects coefficients demonstrate that strong state air pollution control programs are the single most important factor in reducing the concentrations of these two pollutants. Far from dominating changes in air quality, the external environmental variables representing industrial activity and fossil fuel consumption take a back seat to the influence of state regulatory effort in pollution control. Once again, regulation makes a difference.

Overall, the summary statistical results from the air pollutant concentration models are weaker than those obtained when evaluating the changes in pollutant emissions over time. These results should not surprise us. As mentioned above, modeling changes in air pollutant concentrations is inherently difficult for a number of reasons. Dozens of factors affect ambient pollutant concentrations (weather conditions, natural sources of pollution, and so on), and most of these factors are unaffected by pollution control regulations. Indeed, given these difficulties and the paucity of results found by other researchers (e.g., Knoepfel and Weidner 1982), it is remarkable that the ambient pollutant concentration models perform as well as they do.[16]

Discussion

The results presented above suggest three related themes in the politics of air regulatory outcomes. The first theme is that regulation makes a difference. In the face of numerous controls and attempts to destabilize these results by introducing additional variables, the relationship between state air program strength and reduced sulfur dioxide and nitrous oxide emissions remains strong, consistent, and significant. Strong air quality programs result in decreased levels of pollutant emissions, even when controlling for substantive, economic, and other political variables. In addition to affecting pollution emissions, strong state air pollution control programs are instrumental in improving state air quality as well. In both the sulfur dioxide and nitrogen dioxide models, stronger state programs are associated with larger reductions in concentrations of these pollutants, even when controlling for other factors that affect air quality. In fact, the strength of a state's air quality program appears to be as important (sometimes more important) in reducing pollutant emissions and concentration levels as are changes in industrial activity in each state.

An argument might be made that stringent regulations retard economic activity, and thus the influence of regulation appears strong at the expense of the economic activity variable. We can discount this argument if we remember that while several empirical analyses have concluded that environmental regulations may have some statistically significant effect on reducing industrial activity, the level of this impact is *substantively* very small (Portney 1981; CBO 1985). Some might also argue that the fuel consumption variable is simply a surrogate for changes in economic activity, and thus that the impact of economic factors is much greater than is represented by the industrial activity variable alone. Changes in fuel consumption can be affected as much by regulation as by changes in economic activity, however (see Knoepfel and Weidner 1982). Moreover, these possibilities are controlled for by entering fuel consumption as an endogenous variable in the causal analysis.

The second theme is that enforcement matters, particularly in reducing pollutant emissions. Enforcement actions are more effective at controlling stationary sources of pollution (i.e., sulfur dioxide) than at controlling mobile pollution sources (i.e., nitrogen dioxide). Moreover, when enforcement actions are relatively consistent, focused, and well supported, as is the case with EPA abatement actions, they can contribute to reductions in pollutant emissions and thus to improvements in air quality. When enforcement actions are inconsistent or simply symbolic, however, they have less of an impact on pollutant emissions. Though states often protest against overzealous federal involvement in state policy activities under partial preemption, most state administrators readily admit the need for a strong federal presence in pollution control regulation. This federal presence serves two purposes. First, federal mandates and federal pressure provide state administrators with a lever that they can use to pry more money or stronger policy authority from state governors and legislatures. Second, state administrators view the federal enforcement presence as a "gorilla in the closet" that they can call upon for assistance in particularly difficult enforcement cases.

The greater effectiveness of federal enforcement actions brings to light a disturbing possibility. Almost without exception, federal enforcement activities at the state level declined through the 1980s, while state enforcement activities multiplied. This is no doubt a result of the budget cuts and reorganization suffered by EPA enforcement divisions during the Reagan administration, and Reagan's "new federalism" policies. While possible in some states, state enforcement actions cannot take the place of a strong federal presence in the enforcement arena. Following from the results presented here, any combination of reduced federal enforcement activities and an increased reliance upon the states may result in less effective pollution control programs and less progress in reducing air pollution emissions.[17]

The final theme is that changes in external environmental conditions, like industrial activity and fossil fuel use, play an important role in air quality. Government policies and enforcement efforts are not the only players in pollution control. Influences other than regulation account for changes in pollutant emissions and air quality, and thus help to determine whether or not policy goals are met. Moreover, many of these environmental influences are beyond the reach of regulatory control. This means that unless we are willing to enact and enforce regulations far more stringent and intrusive than those we already have, governmental efforts at controlling pollution will never be able to maximize the potential for pollution control and protection of environmental quality. Vastly stronger and more intrusive pollution control regulations are unlikely in the regulatory climate present in the United States. Indeed, we might question whether highly intrusive environmental regulations would be desirable even if they were possible. Such regulations might bring us uncomfortably close to life under the totalitarian regime of Ophuls's "Ecological Mandarins" (Ophuls 1977). While life in such a society might be more pleasant than life in a completely befouled environment, neither of these scenarios is very attractive.

Government directives are not the only solution to controlling and reducing environmental pollution, nor should we expect them to be. In order to maximize the potential for environmental protection, some combination of material and normative incentives is necessary in order to entice the private parties responsible for changes in industrial activity and fossil fuel combustion toward more environmentally benign activities. Government policies can provide not only the stick of regulatory sanction, but also the carrots of economic incentive and support for private initiatives in pollution control. Air pollution is not simply a governmental problem; it is a social problem, and finding a set of solutions will require the contribution and cooperation of all members of society.

Conclusion

This chapter has illustrated many of the problems that the environmental policy analyst must confront when attempting to study the outcomes of environmental policy. It also highlighted the limits placed upon this type of policy analysis by the complex and not fully understood processes connecting human activities with environmental quality. Nevertheless, I have shown that the environmental outcomes of air quality regulations can be systematically evaluated, with varying degrees of success. The first section of the analysis demonstrates that strong regulatory programs have significantly reduced the emission of air pollutants in the states. The fact that variations in regulatory program capacity directly affect pollutant emission levels is an important finding in its own right, for it is only by reducing emissions that air quality can be improved. The second section of the chapter focused upon changes in levels of ambient air pollutant concentrations in the states. While not as strong as those for the emissions models, these results show that strong state air pollution control efforts have reduced the concentrations of sulfur and nitrogen dioxides. While other factors such as fuel consumption and industrial activity are important, the conclusion to be drawn from this research is that in air pollution control, regulation *does* matter.

Notes

1. There is also evidence that pollution control programs in the United States and elsewhere have been having an impact on global pollution levels. For example, lead concentrations in the Greenland icecap have dropped significantly (7.5 percent) in the last twenty years *(New York Times* 1991).

2. There are two reasons why 1973–75 is selected as a starting point for measuring changes in emission levels. First, there was a lag of two or three years in implementing CAA regulations at the state level. Second, and more important, the EPA cautions that emissions data were of poor quality before the mid-1970s. Because of this, Portney (1990a) suggests that 1973–74 is a good place to begin measuring emission trends. The series stops in 1985–87 because these were the most recent data available in 1991.

3. Difficulties in using this averaged differencing approach are not identified by Blalock 1972; Achen 1982; Lewis-Beck 1980; Carmines and Zeller 1979; Berry and Feldman 1985; Wonnacott and Wonnacott 1987; Draper and Smith 1981; or Hanushek and Jackson 1977.

4. There are problems with using weighted measures of state expenditures. One has only to examine emission figures to realize that population has an uneven effect at best upon the level of criteria pollutants emitted in a state. Thus, weighting expenditure figures by population is nearly arbitrary, and not a good representation of state effort toward problem resolution. Another option would be to weight expenditure figures by emission levels. Because emissions are a function of industrial activity, however, this measure of state resources would be affected as much by economic fluctuations as by a state's commitment to air quality. The data here actually reflect expenditures from 1970 to 1980, and the years 1982 and 1985. Comparable data for the years 1981, 1983, and 1984 were unavailable, although given the nature of the budgetary process (Wildavsky 1984) it is

assumed that expenditures in these years would have little effect on the values of this variable (FREE 1987; U.S. Department of Commerce 1971–82).

5. I would like to recognize the contribution of B. Dan Wood and thank him for sharing his data base and his insights into the categorization scheme for enforcement actions used here.

6. The exception to this characterization of EPA enforcement actions occurred during the Gorsuch-Burford era at the EPA. From late 1981 to 1983, EPA enforcement divisions were reorganized several times and decimated by budget cuts. During this period, enforcement actions dropped off and were replaced (to the degree that they were replaced) by confidential agreements with polluters. Enforcement activity at the EPA returned to "normal" after Gorsuch-Burford was replaced by William Ruckleshaus in 1983.

7. These industrial classifications are: lumber and wood products; paper and allied products; chemicals and allied products; petroleum and coal products; rubber and miscellaneous products; stone, clay, and cement; primary metals; and transportation equipment.

8. The total petroleum product consumption variable also statistically outperforms alternative operationalizations of this concept (e.g., total gasoline consumption and total number of miles driven variables).

9. Heteroskedasticity tests for the models were negative. Tolerance levels for the models are as follows: Regulatory Program Strength = .76, .78; EPA Abatements = .80, .77; Industrial Activity = .77, .84; Fossil Fuel Consumption = .80, .81. Influence diagnostics showed the nitrous oxide model to be quite stable; however, because Arizona's coal consumption increased 2,700 percent during the period in question, this state seriously skews the analysis (Dffit = -1.8, Covariance Ratio = 0.05, Studentized Residual = -5.6). Arizona is dropped from the sulfur dioxide model.

10. Some readers may wonder if the strong positive relationship between regulatory program strength and emission reductions is a function of simultaneous causation (heavily polluting states may also have stronger pollution control programs) and scale effect (heavily polluting states usually experience larger absolute changes in emissions). I test for potential simultaneity by using a set of instrumental variables to obtain predicted values for regulatory program strength (see chapter 5 for the variables used). I then control for scale effects by using these instrumental values of regulatory program strength to predict *percentage* changes in sulfur dioxide and nitrous oxide emissions in the revised emission models. Stronger state air pollution programs are associated with decreased pollutant emissions in both the sulfur dioxide (beta = -0.38^{**}) and nitrous oxide (beta = -0.27^{*}) models. Moreover, when using changes in ambient air pollutant *concentrations* as instruments to predict changes in pollutant emissions, predicted changes in emission levels have no association with regulatory program strength.

This absence of simultaneity is understandable if we conceptualize the problem as distinguishing between responsive policy and effective policy. Policy is most responsive to absolute pollutant levels (i.e., the severity of the problem), and this relationship can be observed at one point in time (states with high emission levels will have strong programs). The impact of effective pollution control programs, however, can only be evaluated over time by looking at *changes* in pollutant levels (states with stronger programs will experience greater pollutant reductions). If this is the case, we should find a positive relationship between *absolute* pollution levels and program strength, and a negative relationship between *changes* in pollutant levels and program strength. When we regress absolute pollutant levels in the 1970s and 1980s on program strength, and regress program strength on changes in pollutant levels, we find these very relationships present at statistically significant levels.

11. The effect coefficient for any independent variable is simply the sum of its direct effect and its indirect effects. Indirect effects are calculated by multiplying the path coefficients (or beta weights) from the variable in question to any related endogenous intervening variable, and the path coefficient from this intervening variable to the dependent variable. For example, the indirect effect of Regulatory Program Strength on sulfur dioxide emission levels is simply $(-.23 \times .35) = -.08$.

12. For example, the city of Milwaukee meets the primary federal air quality standards for all pollutants except one—ozone. The state of Wisconsin and the city of Milwaukee stridently claim that they are doing a good job in controlling VOC emissions, which lead to high ozone concentrations, and blame the city's ozone problem on pollutants being blown up from Chicago and northern Illinois. Milwaukee feels it is unfair of the EPA to place sanctions on the city for a pollution problem not of its own making, and is presently suing Chicago in federal district court to get that city to impose an ozone control plan.

13. For example, if the average sulfur dioxide concentration in state X was 0.040 parts per million in 1973–75 and 0.030 parts per million in 1986–88, this difference (–0.010 ppm) would be taken as a percentage of the 1970s average concentration. This would allow us to say that sulfur dioxide concentrations in state X declined by 25 percent from 1973–75 to 1986–88.

14. Similar to pollutant emissions, changes in state ambient pollution concentrations vary a great deal. The average change in sulfur dioxide concentrations in the states during this time period was – 48 percent, with a standard deviation of 31 percent. The average change in nitrogen dioxide concentrations in the states during this time period was a 6 percent increase, with a standard deviation of 48 percent.

15. For example, if state A consumed 600 trillion BTUs of coal in 1973 and 800 trillion BTUs of coal in 1987, this difference (200 million BTUs) is taken as a percentage of the 1973 consumption level. This allows us to say that coal consumption in state A increased by 33 percent between 1973 and 1987.

16. In order to test the validity of the findings from the pollutant emissions and concentration models, the models were subjected to a critical empirical test. Both models were used to account for changes in a pollutant that is extremely difficult to control using regulation: atmospheric particulates (in many states, natural sources of this pollutant outweigh man-made sources). If the regulatory variables displayed a significant relationship to changes in particulate levels, we might suspect the validity of these variables in the sulfur dioxide and nitrogen dioxide models. In each case, however, state program strength showed no relationship to changes in atmospheric particulates. Regulation has little direct effect where we expect it to have little direct effect. Finally, the regulatory program strength variables remained significant predictors of changes in ambient pollutant concentrations even when including changes in pollution emissions as predictive variables. In addition to testifying to the stability of the regulatory program strength coefficients, these models showed a direct relationship between sulfur dioxide emissions and atmospheric sulfur dioxide concentrations, even when controlling for other factors. No relationship was found between nitrous oxide emissions and atmospheric concentrations of nitrogen dioxide (which is not unexpected, since meteorological conditions affect the formation of nitrogen dioxide).

17. A caveat is in order in light of these results. Alhough we have demonstrated that strong pollution control programs can make a difference in reducing air pollution, this should not be construed a supporting a contention that present regulatory efforts are adequate to address the environmental challenges facing society. We could just as easily extrapolate to the conclusion that if some present regulations are stringent enough, then more stringent regulatory programs will have an even greater impact. Regardless of the conclusion one draws, this analysis is explicitly *not* an evaluation of the *adequacy* of air quality regulation on the states.

7

The Politics of
State Water Quality Regulation

While air quality regulations are the most salient set of environmental protection activities, the majority of government and industry pollution control expenditures are targeted toward protecting and improving water quality (CBO 1988; see also chapter 1). The politics behind air quality regulations were systematically and quantitatively evaluated in chapter 5. The current chapter extends this line of investigation into the area of water quality regulation. In this discussion, special emphasis will be placed on the differences in regulating water quality versus air quality. The politics surrounding each set of regulations is quite different, due in large part to their respective federal enabling legislation. These differences lead us to a different set of expectations when analyzing water quality regulations in the states.

The Politics of Water Quality Regulation

The politics of water quality regulation are less contentious than those surrounding air quality regulation. Water quality regulation hardly has the "sacred cow" aura associated with air quality. In pollution control policy, the CWA and WQA are typically seen as supporting actors, though important ones, to the central clean air legislation. Water pollution control also has had a lower profile than either air pollution control or hazardous waste management. While several highly publicized events preceded the passage of the Clean Water Act, none of these were as directly associated with environmental catastrophe and human health as episodes like the hazardous waste contamination at Love Canal and Times Beach. Furthermore, the health threats associated with water pollution are not reported with the urgency of smog alerts and unhealthy air pollutant index days. In addition, the debate over clean water has never been cast in terms as stark as "clean air versus jobs" or "clean air versus an adequate supply of energy" which have characterized much of the debate in air quality regulation. Because of this, the topic of clean water is slightly less salient and definitely less disputatious by comparison.

Clean water legislation has long had a distributional (some would say pork barrel) facet not found in air quality regulation. Cities and municipalities are the largest producers of point source water pollution (EPA Administrator 1991). Before passage of the CWA, most cities deposited raw sewage directly into the ocean or public waterways, leading to serious water quality problems in these waterways. To remedy this, the architects of the Clean Water Act greatly expanded the municipal wastewater treatment construction grant program, whereby the federal government would pay for 75 percent of the costs of constructing municipal wastewater treatment facilities. (Recall, however, that this grant program was phased out by the 1987 WQA.)

The municipal wastewater treatment program quickly became the largest component of federal water quality protection efforts. In addition to addressing the serious problems of municipal effluent pollution, the construction grants program was a boon to members of Congress, industry, and municipal chambers of commerce. Construction grants funded large public works projects in members' districts, virtually assuring continued congressional support for clean water legislation. Industry has benefited as well, since municipal treatment plants that treat industrial effluent (i.e., most plants) in effect subsidize the cost of industrial waste disposal. Finally, by using federal funds to construct treatment plants larger than necessary, many municipalities were able to subsidize future growth and development. With the support of these groups, this major facet of water quality regulation experienced a minimal amount of conflict.

Aside from the construction grant program, we see much less direct legislative activity in water pollution policy. Because water quality regulation is a less salient and contentious issue, legislators have fewer incentives to become involved (Gormley 1986a). At the federal level, debate over water quality legislation lacks the sense of combat and test of wills typical of the Nixon–Muskie clashes in the early 1970s or the Dingell–Waxman battles of the late 1980s surrounding air quality legislation (for a concurring view, see Ingram and Mann 1984). At the state level, a good deal of literature contends that group pressures and administrative bargaining are more important in water quality regulation than in air quality regulation (Downing and Kimball 1982; Sylves 1982; Thomas 1976).

With a less contentious atmosphere, less political symbolism and salience, and less direct legislative involvement, we expect group pressures to play a more significant role in water quality regulation. We also expect that these groups would be more effective at the state level, given that state political environments are more receptive to interest group pressures (Kritz 1989; Thomas and Hrebenar 1990; Ziegler and van Dahlen 1976). These conditions, coupled with the distributional aspects of federal water quality legislation, suggest that "interest group politics" may characterize water quality regulation to a greater degree than is found in air quality regulation.

The Dependent Variable

In measuring the strength of a state's water pollution control program, we again rely upon rankings developed by FREE (FREE 1988; see Lowry 1992 for a similar use of FREE's water quality program rankings). These FREE rankings, however, do not display the same comprehensive picture of state water quality efforts provided for air quality. The FREE rankings are excellent with regard to state responsibilities under the NPDES system and state efforts at controlling nonpoint water pollution sources. Unfortunately, these rankings neglect other elements that are equally important to strong state water pollution control programs. In order to improve the state regulatory program measure, additional information was combined with the information that underlies the FREE rankings, creating a new set of rankings for the strength of state water pollution control programs.

The evaluation matrix used to create the measure of state water program strength borrows heavily from both the 1988 FREE rankings and the state water policy innovation index found in the *Green Index* (Hall and Kerr 1991). The FREE submatrices provide information regarding the level of state responsibility for the federal NPDES and municipal wastewater treatment grant program, the percentage of NPDES permitees in significant noncompliance with their permits, the number of EPA enforcement activities undertaken to back up the failure of state efforts under the CWA, and the scope and strength of the state's nonpoint source pollution control program. To the FREE rank score based on this data, I add one point for each of the following strengths or innovations in a state's water pollution control program: an approved industrial pretreatment program, a toxic water pollution control program, authority to regulate federal facilities under the CWA, a wetlands protection program, and a groundwater protection program (Hall and Kerr 1991).

The water pollution control program strength measure ranks states in ascending order from one (weakest) to thirteen (strongest) on the basis of the above information (see table 7.1 for complete state rankings). Similar to the air rankings, the water program rankings should not be interpreted as an evaluation of water quality in a particular state, or as a measure of state success in improving water quality. The rankings simply reflect the relative scope and strength of state water quality programs.

Traditional Models and State Water Quality Regulation

The Economic Model

The economic model is based on the assumption that states at a more advanced stage of development will have the need, demand structure, and resources necessary for more comprehensive public policies.[1] The substantive and political as-

Table 7.1

State Water Program Strength Scores

State	Score	State	Score
Alabama	5	Montana	8
Alaska	2	Nebraska	9
Arizona	5	Nevada	6
Arkansas	5	New Hampshire	6
California	8	New Jersey	11
Colorado	6	New Mexico	5
Connecticut	10	New York	10
Delaware	8	North Carolina	11
Florida	8	North Dakota	6
Georgia	10	Ohio	8
Hawaii	8	Oklahoma	6
Idaho	6	Oregon	11
Illinois	11	Pennsylvania	9
Indiana	7	Rhode Island	8
Iowa	9	South Carolina	7
Kansas	8	South Dakota	6
Kentucky	8	Tennessee	5
Louisiana	3	Texas	2
Maine	7	Utah	8
Maryland	11	Vermont	10
Massachusetts	6	Virginia	11
Michigan	11	Washington	7
Minnesota	12	West Virginia	5
Mississippi	7	Wisconsin	13
Missouri	8	Wyoming	9

Source: Compiled from FREE 1988; Hall and Kerr 1991, chapter 9.

pects of surface water regulation furnish no expectations that the economic model will perform any better here than when used to analyze air quality regulation. The variables used to operationalize the economic model for water quality regulation are the same as those used for air quality. The first variable, per capita personal income in 1987, represents personal wealth in each state. Wealthier states are supposed to be able to afford better regulation, and the economic model expects that higher levels of wealth will be associated with stronger water quality protection programs. The second variable measures per capita state general fund expenditures in 1987. States having more revenue sources or making greater use of these sources will likely use them to enact tougher water quality programs. The third variable, representing economic development or industrialization in a state, is measured using the percentage of gross state product attributed to value added by manufacturing in 1986. Even though the costs of regulation fall on these industries, economic model adherents claim that higher levels of industrialization will be associated with more comprehensive social

Table 7.2

Economic Model of State Policy Influence
(Dependent Variable = Strength of State Water
Pollution Control Programs)

Independent Variable	Initial		Revised	
	Beta	t-score	Beta	t-score
Per Capita Income	0.33	2.15**	0.42	3.34***
Per Capita Expenditures	0.17	1.12	—	—
Industrialization	0.26	2.07**	0.26	2.04**
	F-ratio = 5.95***		F-ratio = 8.25***	
	Adj. R^2 = .24		Adj. R^2 = .24	
	$N = 49^a$		$N = 49^a$	

[a]Alaska is dropped from the analysis due to an exceptionally large Dffit that skewed the results for the rest of the model (see note 2).
**Statistically significant at $p < .05$.
***Statistically significant at $p < .01$.

programs, and by extension, more stringent regulation. Since we are testing a traditional model, the traditional hypothesis of industrialization leading to more expansive regulatory schemes will be used here.

Table 7.2 demonstrates that economic factors are obviously important in determining the strength of state regulatory programs. Wealthier states enact stronger water pollution control programs. The other resource variable, per capita state expenditures, has no independent relationship with the strength of a state's water quality program. Poor statistical performance, coupled with the fact that individual wealth is a precondition for state government wealth, allows us to drop the state expenditure measure from the final version of the economic model. Finally, the coefficient for the level of state industrialization is positive and statistically significant. More industrialized states do develop stronger and more comprehensive water pollution control programs, as the theory behind the economic model predicts.[2] While both state wealth and level of economic development are important predictors of the strength of state water pollution control programs, we cannot yet conclude that these variables in fact determine the type of policy that a particular state will adopt. Before we can reach any conclusions in this area, we must first test the explanatory power of the other traditional models.

The Political Model

The political model contends that policy variation is a function of political institutions and ideology, and that these two factors work to shape policy outputs in the American states. The political model presented here uses the same set of independent variables as chapter 5, since the political institutions and ideological factors relevant in regulating water quality are no different from those in air quality.

The first variable in the political model is a measure of legislative professionalism. Increased amounts of time, resources, and support associated with more professional legislatures provide them with greater opportunities to be responsive and innovative in their policy deliberations. As a result, states with more professional legislatures should produce more comprehensive and stringent water pollution control programs. While this is certainly true in the case of air, recall that there is less legislative involvement in water pollution policy. This may result in legislative professionalism being less important in this policy area.

The second institutional variable is interparty competition. A high degree of interparty competition has traditionally been associated with increased policy activity in the states as political parties compete for votes by extending governmental benefits to a wider group of citizens. There are two reasons to expect that levels of party competition will have little effect upon water quality regulations, however. First, since the legislature is less involved in this policy area, the effect of party competition in the legislature will be diminished. Second, the distributional properties of the construction grant program have hardly been a topic of partisan debate. Both major political parties seek to increase state control over the grant program and to maximize the federal funds received for municipal construction projects. When trying to extract authority and funding from the federal government, intrastate cooperation is preferred over intrastate conflict.[3]

The political model for state water quality programs includes two variables representing the ideological dispositions that characterize a state. While the initial political model for state air quality programs used three measures of general state political ideology, our conclusions in chapter 5 made it clear that state opinion liberalism is causally prior to both state political elite ideology and state policy liberalism (see also Erikson et al. 1989). Thus, the political model of state water quality regulation uses only state opinion liberalism to represent general state political ideology. A more specific ideological measure is included by using the average League of Conservation Voters (LCV) score for each party in a state's congressional delegation. These scores are weighted by the relative strength of each party in each state's legislature. The LCV measure is a direct representation of the level of environmental concern expressed by a state's elected officials. If citizen and elite attitudes strongly influence state policy, states with higher LCV scores and more liberal political ideologies will have stronger water quality programs. The LCV measure is coded so that this hypothesized positive relationship between ideology and policy outputs is represented by a positive coefficient. The state opinion liberalism measure is coded so that a positive relationship between state opinion liberalism and stringent water quality regulations is reflected by a negative coefficient.

Table 7.3 shows that the performance of the political model does not meet the standard set by the economic model when accounting for variations in state

Table 7.3

Political Model of State Policy Influence
(Dependent Variable = Strength of State Water
Pollution Control Programs)

Independent Variable	Initial		Revised	
	Beta	t-score	Beta	t-score
Legislative Professionalism	0.13	0.91	0.13	0.92
Interparty Competition	0.08	0.61	—	—
State Opinion Liberalism	−0.14	−0.78	−0.15	−0.87
LCV Score	0.31	1.80*	0.32	1.89*

F-ratio = 3.54*
Adj. R^2 = .17
N = 50

F-ratio = 4.66**
Adj. R^2 = .18
N = 50

*Statistically significant at $p < .10$.
**Statistically significant at $p < .05$.

water quality programs. Only the League of Conservation Voters score of a state's congressional delegation is significantly related to the strength of a state's water quality programs. States with more environmentally inclined political elites have stronger state pollution control programs. While the legislative professionalism, interparty competition, and state opinion liberalism measures have coefficient estimates in the hypothesized direction, none are statistically significant. The summary statistics demonstrate that the political model tested here accounts for little of the variation in state water quality programs.[4]

Are political institutions and ideology really of little consequence for water quality policy? This question can be answered in a number of ways. First of all, remember that interparty competition was expected to be of little consequence in water quality regulation. Thus, we should not be surprised by the poor performance of this variable. Second, legislative professionalism was hypothesized to be of lesser importance than in air quality regulation, but perhaps not to the extent observed here. Before concluding that legislative professionalism and state opinion liberalism are of no importance in water quality regulation, however, we should remember that we are looking at only one facet of policy influence. One major thesis of this book is that the policy process is too complex to be represented by any of the traditional models in isolation, and that using any of these models exclusively can give misleading results.

The Group Influence Model

Interest groups are likely to be more influential in the regulation of water quality than in that of air quality. Less legislative involvement and a lower degree of public and political salience mean that the debate over water quality regulations will take place with less legislative oversight and public attention, increasing the prospects that water pollution control policy will be made in an arena of group conflict. This does not mean, however, that industry groups will control the content of water quality programs. Countervailing groups representing environmental concerns can play a powerful role in state environmental policy (Kritz 1989; Wenner 1982).

The demand pattern of groups having a direct interest in water quality regulation is slightly different than that in air quality. Two measures of polluting industry strength are used in the water policy group influence model. The first industry strength variable is the value added by manufacturing as a percentage of gross state product in 1986 produced by those industries most responsible for water pollution.[5] The second industry strength variable is the value of mining output in 1986 as a percentage of gross state product.[6] Mining interests are affected more directly by water pollution regulations than by air quality regulations, mainly because mining activities pose a greater threat to water resources than to air quality. State and federal requirements govern the discharge and disposal of mining wastewater, milling wastes, drilling sludges, and the control of acid mine drainage. As a result, the mining industry is a relevant force in state water quality regulation. Water pollution control unquestionably imposes costs on firms engaged in both manufacturing and mining. A negative coefficient estimate for these variables signals that states are responding to the concerns of strong industrial and mining groups by enacting less stringent water pollution control regulations. On the other hand, positive coefficients can be interpreted to mean that states respond to the increased environmental threat posed by large polluting sectors by developing stronger water quality programs.

Since the early 1970s, industry has found its regulatory priorities opposed by organized environmental groups pushing for stronger regulations and a stricter interpretation in their implementation. Environmental groups have been especially influential in the states in recent years (Kritz 1989). The measure of environmental group strength used here is the number of Sierra Club, National Wildlife Federation, and Friends of the Earth members per 1,000 persons in each state in 1987. If these groups are influential in water quality regulation, we should find stronger water programs in those states where these groups are the strongest, and this relationship will be reflected by a positive coefficient.[7]

The final set of organized interests in the model represents agriculture. Nonpoint pollutant sources account for 82 percent of the nitrogen, 84 percent of the phosphorus, 99 percent of the sediments, and much of the toxic chemicals reaching the nation's waters each year, and agriculture is the single largest source of nonpoint source pollution in the United States (ASIWPCA 1985; Conservation Foundation 1987). Few water quality regulations have focused on agriculture because of the decentralized nature of nonpoint source pollution problems. The regulation of nonpoint sources has increased in recent years, however, and these

Table 7.4

Group Influence Model of State Policy Influence
(Dependent Variable = Strength of State Water
Pollution Control Programs)

Independent Variable	Initial		Revised	
	Beta	t-score	Beta	t-score
Polluting Industry Strength	0.08	0.57	—	—
Environmental Group Strength	0.26	1.89*	0.23	1.84*
Mining Strength	–0.46	–3.02***	–0.51	–4.07***
Agricultural Strength	0.25	2.00*	0.26	2.13**
	F-ratio = 6.86***		F-ratio = 9.18***	
	Adj. R^2 = .32		Adj. R^2 = .33	
	N = 50		N = 50	

*Statistically significant at $p < .10$.
**Statistically significant at $p < .05$.
***Statistically significant at $p < .01$.

regulations are one characteristic of strong state water quality programs. This has brought agricultural interests into the regulatory fray. If agriculture were a typical industrial concern, it would oppose more stringent nonpoint source regulations. These new regulations have relatively little impact on the average farmer, however, entailing land use controls, soil conservation practices, and other programs already in place but not enforced or coordinated (ASIWPCA 1985). These regulations also impose few costs. In addition, in several areas farmers themselves have pushed for increased nonpoint controls as a response to deteriorating soil and water quality conditions (Heimlich and Langer 1986; Malone 1985). Anecdotal evidence and the available data suggest that many agricultural states are at the forefront in regulating nonpoint sources of water pollution (FREE 1988). The agricultural strength variable is measured as the average percentage of gross state product attributed to all crops and livestock in 1985 and 1986, and given the above considerations, we expect that this variable will exhibit a positive coefficient.[8]

Table 7.4 demonstrates that three of the four independent variables display coefficients in the expected direction. States with stronger environmental groups and a more important agricultural sector are more likely to have stronger water pollution control programs, all other things remaining equal. On the other hand, states heavily dependent upon the mining industry enact weaker water quality regulations. The biggest surprise in table 7.4 is the poor performance of the variable representing the strength of heavily polluting industries. Given the lack of empirical support for the "capture" thesis in regulatory policy, we expect that states having large polluting industries will not have weaker regulatory programs. In water pollution control, however, these states do not enact stronger regulations either (i.e., they are not responding positively to the increased environmental threat posed by these industries). This result is understandable if we look at the targets of regulation and the overall effects of water pollution control policy.

Nearly all efforts at improving surface water quality in the United States have focused upon controlling point sources of pollution using the NPDES. This emphasis has been somewhat successful, as the amount of water pollution attributable to point sources has dropped from over 50 percent in the early 1970s to 35 percent in 1987 (U.S. EPA 1988a; Rosenbaum 1991). Within this strategy of regulating point sources, controlling the effluent from industrial facilities is the success story of water pollution control (Magat and Viscusi 1990). Industrial facilities are consistently found to be in better compliance with their discharge permits than are municipal facilities (FREE 1988). Furthermore, industries increasingly discharge their wastes to a municipal treatment facility, rather than treating the wastes themselves and discharging effluent directly into a waterway (U.S. EPA 1990). As a result, state water pollution control administrators see industrial facilities as less of a threat to water quality than municipal treatment plants (ASIWPCA 1984). Overall, industrial dischargers are the major source of pollutants in only 9 percent of those streams not meeting their designated uses (U.S. EPA 1988a). States are not responding to the potential threat of polluting industries with stronger regulations because they see industrial threats to water quality as already being substantially controlled. Since industrial sources of water pollution are largely controlled and in compliance with federal and state regulations, the size of these polluting industries may not be a relevant factor in determining the strength of a state's water pollution program. For this reason, the industry strength variable is dropped from the revised group model of policy influence.

The revised model shows that the strength of the mining industry is the single most influential factor in determining the strength of state water pollution control programs. While states may not respond to pressure from manufacturing firms, states heavily dependent upon mining do respond with weaker water pollution control programs. State responsiveness to mining concerns can hardly be interpreted as making sound ecological sense, but before we can conclude that water quality regulations are controlled by mining interests, we have to examine the remaining independent variables.

As expected, the strength of the agricultural sector in a state exerts a significant positive influence over water quality regulations. States with agricultural economies enact stronger water quality protection programs. One could ask why producer strength in one sector, such as mining, leads to weaker regulatory programs while in a different sector, such as agriculture, producer strength results in a more expansive set of regulations being adopted. Both sectors are key targets of a new breed of regulation focusing upon nonpoint source pollution and water quality–based (as opposed to technology-based) permit standards. The best explanation for this situation is a combination of what James Q. Wilson (1980) calls "the politics of regulation," and plain old self-interested behavior.

.The costs of regulation in the mining industry are concentrated upon a relatively small number of operators and mine owners. These same costs of water quality regulation in agriculture, in addition to being less onerous, are spread out over a very large number of farmers and agribusiness concerns. While the benefits from regulation in both cases are widely dispersed, the *levels* of benefits are not equal. Agriculture is by far the largest source of pollutants entering the nation's waters, with mining activities placing a distant second (ASIWPCA 1985). In addition, the pollution problems associated with agriculture (e.g., pesticide and nutrient contamination, sedimentation) receive more attention than do those stemming from resource extraction. Both the real and perceived benefits of controlling agriculturally produced water pollutants are greater than those from controlling mining activities. According to Wilson, in a situation where the costs of proposed regulations are concentrated and the benefits are little recognized and dispersed (such as in mining), regulation itself will be very difficult. On the other hand, where the costs of regulations are more widely dispersed and the benefits more generally recognized (such as in agriculture), regulation becomes easier (J. Wilson 1980). In essence, agricultural states develop stronger water quality programs than mining states because the problem is larger and because it is easier and less costly to do so.

The second explanation for the positive response of agricultural states is derived from the farmer's self-interest. Both agriculture and mining use tremendous quantities of water. The quality of the water used, however, is generally irrelevant to the mine operator, but not to the farmer. Poor water quality can damage soils, reduce crop yields, increase acreage and irrigation maintenance, and contaminate the produce from the farmer's fields. In addition, water quality problems *from* farming often result in water quality problems *on* the farm, since the same water source is often tapped for both human and agricultural uses. For these reasons, farmers have supported stronger water quality regulations in several plains states (Floyd 1988; Ringquist 1993).

Environmental groups exert a positive influence over the stringency of state water pollution control programs. While this suggests that state governments are responsive to the environmental concerns of citizens expressed through these groups, remember that a similar finding was obtained in the group influence model in air quality regulation, only to be washed out in the full integrated model. As with all of the variables operationalized in the three traditional models, final judgment on their policy relevance must be reserved until they are placed into the integrated model of public policy. Finally, goodness-of-fit statistics for the group influence model are superior to those from either the final economic or political models.[9]

The Integrated Model of Water Pollution Control

Each of the three traditional models examines only one dimension of political influence over state public policy. While the group influence model emerges as empirically superior to the other traditional models when analyzing state water quality programs, final conclusions about the influence of certain factors cannot be drawn until each has been tested in the integrated model of policy influence. In remedying the deficiencies present in the simpler models of state policy outputs, the integrated model hypothesizes that state wealth and economic development may give rise to a certain set of policy demands and provide the wherewithal to address these demands. Policy demands are also influenced by public opinion, but in order to affect public policy these demands must be articulated and advanced by organized groups within society. Moreover, the activities of these groups are themselves channeled and altered by the institutions of state government before being embodied in the outputs of public policy. The integrated model for water pollution policy uses the following set of independent variables.

Independent Variables

First, wealth, general state political ideology, and the level of state environmental concern are hypothesized to be important in explaining water pollution control regulations in the states. These characteristics provide a context for political agenda setting and boundaries for possible policy actions in a state. Political-economic characteristics are represented by state per capita personal income, state opinion liberalism, and state legislative LCV scores, respectively. Second, representative governments should be responsive to social interests functionally represented through organized interest groups. Moreover, these interest groups should be especially influential in water quality regulation. In the integrated model of water quality regulation, organized interests are represented using the size of the mining industry, the importance of the agricultural sector, and the size of environmental interest groups in the states. Finally, states exert their own interests both directly, and by filtering external policy demands through governmental institutions. The influence of state political institutions is represented using the level of professionalism in state legislatures.

Five of the seven independent variables exhibit coefficients in the expected direction (see table 7.5). Still, discussion of the results associated with the income and LCV score variables is warranted. Traditional state policy theory leads us to expect that wealthier states would enact stronger water regulatory programs, but state wealth has no direct effect on the strength of state water quality programs. This is not unexpected, however. Recall that recent research concludes that wealth often acts as a surrogate for public opinion in state policy studies (Erikson et al. 1989). In the presence of variables that directly reflect public opinion and ideology, the direct effect of wealth disappears. A more substantive (but by no means definitive) explanation is that the wealthiest states do not, in fact, have the most stringent water pollution control programs. This distinction generally belongs to agricultural states and a few southern border states (e.g., North Carolina and Virginia). Contrary to the expectations of the

Table 7.5

Integrated Model of State Policy Influence
(Dependent Variable = Strength of State Water
Pollution Control Programs)

Independent Variable	Initial		Revised	
	Beta	t-score	Beta	t-score
Per Capita Income	−0.05	−0.20	—	—
State Opinion Liberalism	−0.19	−1.14	−0.22	−1.40
LCV Score	−0.09	−0.43	—	—
Environmental Group Strength	0.17	0.94	0.16	1.19
Mining Strength	−0.38	−1.96*	−0.42	−3.17***
Agricultural Strength	0.36	2.28**	0.36	2.82***
Legislative Professionalism	0.19	1.17	0.16	1.29

F-ratio = 4.66** F-ratio = 6.74***
Adj. R^2 = .34   Adj. R^2 = .37
N = 50 N = 50

*Statistically significant at $p < .10$.
**Statistically significant at $p < .05$.
***Statistically significant at $p < .01$.

economic model, wealth is simply not that important with respect to state water quality regulation. Wealth is removed from the final version of the single equation integrated model.

After displaying some promise in the traditional political model, the LCV score variable lapses into nonsignificance in the integrated model. The LCV variable, however, is at best an indirect measure of the level of environmental concern in a state. This concept is represented more directly by the environmentalism measure from the group influence model. A strong positive relationship is observed between the LCV variable and regulatory stringency in the absence of the more direct measure, but this relationship evaporates when controlling for the strength of environmental groups in a state. Due to these considerations, the LCV variable is dropped from the final integrated model.

The results presented for the final integrated model provide ample support for the utility of the integrated theory in analyzing state policy outputs. Table 7.5 shows that more professional legislatures, more liberal public opinion, stronger environmental groups, and a strong agricultural sector are all associated with stronger state water pollution control programs, though only the agricultural variable is statistically significant. As expected, legislative professionalism is less important in water quality regulation than it is in air quality regulation. On the other hand, a strong mining industry predisposes a state to adopt weaker surface-water quality regulations.[10]

Causal Modeling in Water Pollution Control

Following previous research, both wealth and state opinion liberalism are considered to be determined outside of the causal system. While wealth was a nonsignificant predictor of state program strength in the single equation integrated model, wealth does exert significant influence indirectly through endogenous variables in the causal model. The strength of the mining industry and the agricultural sector in a state are determined outside of the system as well. The remaining two variables in the integrated model are entered as variables determined in large part within the causal system. Both wealth and state political ideology help to determine the degree of legislative professionalism that is possible and/or desired in a state, so legislative professionalism is entered as an endogenous variable. Environmental interest groups are the final endogenous addition (for a more complete discussion regarding the selection of exogenous and endogenous variables, see chapter 5). The results from the integrated causal model are presented in figure 7.1. The effects coefficients for each independent variable are found in table 7.6.[11]

Several conclusions can be drawn from the integrated causal model. The first is that states respond positively to public opinion. We have good evidence that more liberal states have stronger water quality regulations, though again, this variable coefficient is not statistically significant. Second, state political institutions place their own imprint on state policy outputs. The legislative professionalism variable could have been dropped after its pathetic performance in the traditional political model. This variable is too important from a theoretical standpoint to delete on the basis of empirical results from a single sample, however. In addition, retaining this variable is necessary if we are to identify the indirect effect that state wealth has on the strength of state water pollution control programs. The importance of this variable, though admittedly marginal, would have been missed completely if we had let data and empirical results drive our theory and without the complex interaction of factors allowed by the integrated model.

Third, states respond to the policy interests of strong organized interest groups within each state. With respect to agricultural interests and environmental groups, this responsiveness leads to stronger water quality regulations. In responding to the mining industry, however, states weaken regulatory programs. These results suggest that a strong mining industry is able to lobby successfully for more lenient regulations even when stronger regulations are called for by the conditions that accrue from mining. By lightening the regulatory burden on the mining industry, then, states are not simply responding to interest group demands; they are also acting irresponsibly with respect to the threats to water quality present within the state.

Effects coefficients show that the single most important factor in determining what type of water quality protection program a state will adopt is the strength of

169

Figure 7.1. Integrated Causal Model of Water Quality Regulation

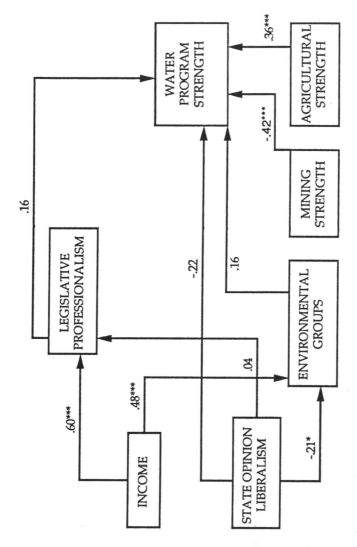

*Statistically significant at *p* < .10.
***Statistically significant at *p* < .01.

Table 7.6

Effects Coefficients: Water Quality Regulation
(Dependent Variable = Strength of State Water Pollution Control Programs)

Independent Variable	Direct Effect[1]	Indirect Effect[1]	Total Effect[1]
Per Capita Income	—	0.17	0.17
State Opinion Liberalism	−0.22	−0.03	−0.25
Mining Industry Strength	−0.42	—	−0.42
Environmental Group Strength	0.16	—	0.16
Agricultural Strength	0.36	—	0.36
Legislative Professionalism	0.16	—	0.16

[1]Coefficients are rounded to nearest .01.

the mining industry in that state. The least important independent variable (or policy influence) is the strength of environmental groups in the state, though the effects coefficients for state wealth and legislative professionalism are very nearly equal to the environmental group figure. With regard to state wealth, while resources are of paramount importance in regulating air quality, they are less important in a policy area characterized by fewer regulatory and political conflicts. The two most important influences in water quality policy represent organized interests. This supports the contention made earlier that the politics surrounding water quality regulation are closer to "interest group politics" than are those in air quality regulation. Finally, state opinion liberalism and political institutions have a positive impact upon the strength of water quality programs within a state.

Conclusion

The results from the integrated causal model for state water quality protection programs demonstrate the importance of including all components of the integrated model, even when preliminary investigation would lead us to focus only on those variables representing organized interest groups. No single traditional model of public policy sufficiently describes the politics of water quality regulation in the states. All three traditional models identify important dimensions of policy influence, but an adequate depiction of the process surrounding policy outputs in the American states must take into account each dimension and the relationships between them. While the goodness-of-fit measures from the integrated water pollution control model do not equal those obtained when analyzing air quality regulation, the integrated model once again compares favorably with the three traditional models in accounting for variation in state water quality programs.

Notes

1. See chapter 4 for a thorough critique of the economic model and the other two traditional models of policy influence.

2. $N = 49$ in the economic model for water quality regulation because the model excludes Alaska. Influence diagnostics showed that the state of Alaska seriously disrupted the analysis, even causing the coefficient for the state expenditure variable to flip signs. This is not all that surprising, considering the unusual levels of per capita wealth and state expenditures in Alaska. The influence diagnostics for Alaska were as follows: Studentized residual = 3.5, Hat diagonal = −.85, Dffit value = −5.00. Both the Hat diagonal and Dffit values were more than eight times the value of the next closest state.

3. Bureaucratic variables are again omitted from the political model of state policy influence. In order to test the proposition that bureaucratic variables are less important when analyzing policy outputs, a variable representing average state water program budgets was entered into the political model. It had no relationship with the measure of water program strength, displaying a correlation coefficient of −.04.

4. Because the independent variables presented here are identical to those used in the political model in chapter 5, the collinearity diagnostics and tolerances will be identical as well. The reader is referred to chapter 5 for the specific values.

5. These industrial classifications are food and kindred products, lumber and wood products, paper and allied products, chemicals and allied products, petroleum and coal products, leather and leather products, primary metal industries, fabricated metal products, and electric and electronic equipment.

6. This variable is logged to correct for skewness.

7. Compiled by the author. This variable is logged to correct for skewness.

8. U.S. Dept. of Commerce, Bureau of the Census 1976–91. This variable is logged to correct for skewness. A final potential group influence variable might be the strength of organized labor in each state. The heaviest burdens from water quality regulations fall on the mining, chemical, food processing, and metals industry (U.S. Dept. of Commerce, Bureau of Economic Analysis, 1992). These industries are also strongholds of organized labor. Since the costs imposed by regulation are often given as justification for layoffs and wage concessions, organized labor has an incentive to lobby against stronger water quality regulations. A variable measuring the level of unionization in each state was included in the group influence model to test for this influence. Union strength is not significantly related to changes in the dependent variable.

9. The tolerance values for the final group influence models are as follows: Mining Strength = .86, Environmental Groups = .87, and Agricultural Strength = .93. There are no observations in this model with suspicious Hat Diagonal, Cook's distance, or Dffit values.

10. The tolerance values for the final integrated model are as follows: Legislative Professionalism = .83, State Opinion Liberalism = .54, Mining Strength = .75, Environmental Groups = .71, and Agricultural Strength = .80.

11. Once again, the effect coefficient for any independent variable is simply the sum of its direct effects and its indirect effects. Direct effects are simply the path coefficients. Indirect effects are calculated by multiplying the path coefficients (or beta weights) from the variable in question to any related endogenous intervening variable, and the path coefficient from this intervening variable to the dependent variable.

8

Policy Outcomes in
Surface Water Regulation

Over $300 billion was spent on water pollution control in the United States between 1972 and 1986, with $69 billion of this being spent by the federal government on the municipal construction grants program alone (Conservation Foundation 1987). A reasonable question might be, what sort of return has this large public investment produced? In water policy, much like in air policy, little research focuses on environmental policy outcomes. Permitting and enforcement activities are related to environmental quality, however, and a few researchers have attempted to account for changes and variations in the number of NPDES permits issued, the size and average delay associated with permit backlogs, and rates of significant noncompliance with NPDES permits. The evidence suggests, moreover, that most water pollution control efforts actually focus on these procedural components of pollution control (e.g., permit compliance) rather than on improving water quality (Lowry 1992). Most research concludes that implementation in water pollution control is an extensive bargaining process between polluters and regulators over the conditions of regulation (Downing and Kimball 1982; Downing 1983).

Inferring environmental effects from research that focuses upon permit compliance is problematic. For example, noncompliance rates are not consistent across time or across types of facilities. In 1986, 35 percent of municipal facilities were in significant noncompliance with their permits. This figure is far higher than during the late 1970s or early 1980s, but this does not mean that municipal facilities were doing a much poorer job of preventing water pollution in 1986. Reporting requirements and noncompliance criteria were standardized and strengthened in 1986, causing a significant jump in noncompliance figures (U.S. EPA 1989b). Municipal noncompliance has been targeted in recent years by the EPA, and this targeting has resulted in a significant improvement in compliance rates among municipal treatment facilities. By 1988, municipal permit noncompliance rates had dropped to 13 percent, while industrial facilities had a 6 percent noncompliance rate (U.S. EPA 1990). The wide variation across states in how administrative actions are categorized, coupled with periodic redefinitions of just what significant noncompliance or permit violations entail, make drawing substantive conclusions about what these figures tell us extremely difficult.

For the most part, economists have engrossed themselves in assessing the efficiency and cost-effectiveness of water pollution control regulations (but see Magat and Viscusi 1990). Early on, both Schoenbaum (1972) and Freeman and Haveman (1972) argued that water quality regulations were grossly inefficient. Freeman and Haveman went so far as to conclude that the command and control regulations common in water policy, combined with the subsidization of industrial waste disposal through pollution control tax incentives and construction grants, virtually assured that these regulations would never reach their goal of cleaning up the nation's waters (Freeman and Haveman 1972). Other research has concluded that the costs of water quality regulation likely exceed its benefits (though it is recognized that costs are often overstated and the benefits underestimated; Freeman 1982).

Finally, research focusing on the institutional aspects of water pollution control has uncovered many unintended consequences of these regulations. For example, Gormley (1989) hypothesizes that the federal administrative requirements associated with partial preemption in pollution control have had the secondary consequence of forcing many states to improve the professionalism and administrative capacity of state government. In addition, the pursuit of increased economic efficiency through the privatization of municipal wastewater treatment programs has had the unintended consequences of undermining affirmative action goals and contributing to a loss of local government control over the delivery of municipal services (O'Toole 1989).

Each of the above types of research answers important policy questions. Political scientists, in seeking to identify procedural problems in implementation, hope to improve the transition from policy output to policy outcome. Economists, on the other hand, diligently try to make sure we are getting the most bang for the buck out of environmental regulations, and suggest alternatives that might improve this ratio. Neither branch of social science, however, has succeeded in tying public policies to improvements in environmental conditions. Neither has answered the question, does regulation matter?

Trends in Water Quality

Overall Water Quality Trends

One way the EPA evaluates overall changes in water quality is by examining treatment levels attained by permitees under the NPDES system and by estimating changes in pollutant effluent from these permitees. The number of municipal wastewater treatment plants achieving secondary treatment levels or better nearly doubled between 1977 and 1983 (U.S. CEQ 1983). In addition, since

1972 over 8000 municipal wastewater treatment projects have been completed (U.S. EPA 1989a). These increases have meant that the number of persons served by municipal wastewater treatment facilities having secondary treatment levels or better increased from 85 million in 1972 to 144 million in 1990. Much work remains to be done, however. Bringing all municipal treatment facilities into compliance with the 1987 WQA by 2008 is estimated to cost over $85 billion (U.S. EPA 1990).

Ten percent of all major facilities (municipal and industrial) are in significant noncompliance with their NPDES permits, but the proportion of permittees in significant noncompliance has been steadily decreasing (U.S. EPA 1990). Industrial facilities have been especially successful in reducing their discharge of pollutants into the nation's waterways. For example, Magat and Viscusi (1990) find that EPA enforcement efforts have significantly reduced the discharge of oxygen-demanding wastes from industrial facilities. The EPA estimates that since 1972, industrial discharges of suspended solids have been reduced by 80 percent, phosphates by 74 percent, and oxygen-demanding pollutants by 71 percent (U.S. CEQ 1989). Other estimates place decreases in industrial pollutant discharges at over 95 percent (EPA Administrator 1991). These decreases are a bit misleading, however. Since the mid-1970s, nearly half of all industrial polluters have stopped discharging their wastes directly into waterways, discharging them instead into municipal wastewater treatment systems. By 1990, only 27 percent of industrial oxygen-demanding wastes and 39 percent of industrial suspended solids were discharged directly into water bodies (EPA Administrator 1991).

Effluent figures for municipal wastewater treatment facilities show that even though the amount of oxygen-demanding pollutants entering these facilities increased between 1972 and 1982, the amount of wastes leaving these plants decreased by 46 percent. These figures should be considered in light of estimates from the Association of State and Interstate Water Pollution Control Administrators (ASIWPCA) suggesting that in the absence of environmental controls, wastes entering the nation's waterways through municipal treatment facilities would have increased 119 percent between 1972 and 1984 (ASIWPCA 1984).

The evidence is relatively strong that water pollution control regulations have significantly decreased the levels of point source pollutants entering the nation's waterways. We are less certain that these effluent reductions have resulted in improvements in water quality, however. Two studies have come to fairly optimistic conclusions regarding changes in surface water quality over time. In 1984, the ASIWPCA estimated that 64 percent of all stream miles in the United States fully supported their designated uses, and 22 percent partially support these uses. Only 5 percent of all stream miles have been confirmed as not supporting their designated uses (ASIWPCA 1984; U.S. CEQ 1989).[1] Moreover, the same survey results reported that over 13 percent of all stream miles in the nation had improved in water quality between 1972 and 1982, while 84 percent had remained the same and only 3 percent had degraded in quality (see table 8.1).[2] From these

Table 8.1

Changes in State Water Quality, 1972–82: Percentage of River and Stream Miles Assessed

State	Main-tained	Im-proved	De-graded	State	Main-tained	Im-proved	De-graded
Alabama	88	10	2	Montana	89	10	1
Alaska	0	0	100[a]	Nebraska	na	na	na
Arizona	88	12	0	Nevada	100	0	0
Arkansas	90	2	8	New Hampshire	57	41	2
California	93	7	0	New Jersey	39	48	13
Colorado	93	5	2	New Mexico	100	0	0
Connecticut	44	53	3	New York	79	21	0
Delaware	59	27	14	North Carolina	72	28	0
Florida	67	25	8	North Dakota	67	33	0
Georgia	98	2	0	Ohio	88	11	1
Hawaii	0	0	100[a]	Oklahoma	93	0	7
Idaho	56	12	32	Oregon	78	20	2
Illinois	64	35	1	Pennsylvania	98	2	0
Indiana	98	2	0	Rhode Island	91	9	0
Iowa	42	47	12	South Carolina	36	46	18
Kansas	53	20	27	South Dakota	92	8	0
Kentucky	85	10	5	Tennessee	78	20	2
Louisiana	na	na	na	Texas	21	59	19
Maine	42	58	0	Utah	56	34	10
Maryland	95	3	2	Vermont	96	3	1
Massachusetts	65	35	0	Virginia	na	na	na
Michigan	32	36	31	Washington	100	0	0
Minnesota	83	17	0	West Virginia	65	34	1
Mississippi	96	4	0	Wisconsin	98	2	0
Missouri	98	2	0	Wyoming	99	1	0

Note: Percentage of streams assessed ranges from 1 to 100.
[a]Based on an assessment of 1 percent or less of total stream miles.
Source: Compiled from ASIWPCA 1984.

figures, the ASIWPCA concluded, "The news is good. The water is cleaner" (ASIWPCA 1984). Similar conclusions were reached by the EPA in its biennial summary of state water quality reports (U.S. EPA 1983, 1987).

The ASIWPCA and EPA results are based largely upon subjective evaluations of water quality and changes in water quality. In several instances, neither measurement data nor professional evaluations were available for 1972, rendering the initial baselines against which changes were evaluated little more than educated guesses (U.S. GAO 1986a). According to the ASIWPCA, however, subjective expert evaluations of water quality are often equal to or superior to reliance upon chemical and biological measures alone. Expert judgments can take into account the mix of pollutants present in the body of water, as well as its physical characteristics, qualities that are difficult to evaluate using water monitoring data. Furthermore, the ASIWPCA claims that the waters evaluated in each state, while not a random sample, do emphasize those lakes and stream segments that are *most* affected by pollution. Because of this, the ASIWPCA data may more accurately reflect changes in water quality resulting from regulation. Finally, the ASIWPCA data cover a longer time period than any comparable evaluation of water quality. Nevertheless, at best the EPA figures should be interpreted with a good deal of caution, and the ASIWPCA figures with only slightly less.

More rigorous evaluations of changes in water quality have reached more ambiguous conclusions. For example, a joint study by the EPA and the U.S. Fish and Wildlife Service, based on a combination of objective and subjective measurements, found virtually no change in the water quality of the nation's rivers between 1977 and 1982 (U.S. GAO 1986a). In addition, a Resources for the Future (RFF) study concluded that estimated changes in water quality since the imposition of the Federal Water Pollution Control Act (FWPCA) have resulted in only minor improvements in water acreage suitable for sportfishing (Vaughan and Russell 1982). The authors of the study conclude that the majority of the benefits from these regulations came from improving the quality of fishing in waters that were already fishable.

Changes in Specific Water Constituents

A second Resources for the Future study attempted to estimate the effect of regulations on meeting water quality standards for four water quality constituents. In a classic example of "with-and-without" measurement of change, the RFF model estimated present levels of dissolved oxygen, biochemical oxygen demand, and pollutant loads for phosphorus and nitrogen based on point source pollutant inventories and estimates of nonpoint source pollutant loads in 1972. The model then predicted the values of the four water quality parameters identified above at 1,000 locations in the continental United States. These parameter values are predicted assuming no pollution controls beyond those required before the 1972 FWPCA, and again assuming all point sources were in compliance with the requirements of the 1972 FWPCA. The report concluded, somewhat surprisingly, that FWPCA controls had resulted in a 6 percent increase in the number of sites meeting the standard for dissolved oxygen (from 83 percent to 88 percent), a 10 percent increase in the number of sites meeting the biochemical oxygen demand standard (from 68 percent to 75 percent), and 19 and 7 percent increases in the number of sites meeting phosphorus and nitrogen standards (from 27 percent to 32 percent, and 30 percent to 32 percent, respectively) (Gianessi and Peskin 1981). Thus, while the model predicted improved levels of water quality, these improvements were small.

By far the most comprehensive evaluation of changes in water quality over time has been accomplished by the U.S. Geological Survey (USGS). Using a

Table 8.2

**Selected Water Quality Trends at USGS NASQUAN and
Bench-Mark Stations, 1974–81**

Constituent	Stations with Increasing Trends	Stations with Decreasing Trends	Stations with No Trend
Coliform Bacteria	25	112	463
Dissolved Oxygen	63	41	265
Nitrate, Total	116	27	240
Phosphorus, Total	43	50	288
Sodium	100	27	162
Sulfate (SO^4)	78	38	173
Suspended Sediment	43	39	194
Arsenic	62	11	220
Cadmium	48	6	231
Mercury	7	2	190
Zinc	18	32	238

Source: Adapted from Smith et al. 1987, table 1, p. 1608.

"before-and-after" type of analysis, researchers at the USGS computed nation-wide flow-adjusted trends for twenty-four measures of water quality at over 300 NASQUAN water quality monitoring stations between 1974 and 1981. The most significant improvements were associated with fecal bacteria counts, where stations displaying decreasing fecal bacteria counts exceeded stations displaying increasing counts by a 4.4:1 ratio. Still, 77 percent of the monitoring stations displayed no significant trend for bacteria. Significant improvements were also found in dissolved oxygen deficits, sediment loads, and phosphorous concentrations. Degraded water quality was most often attributed to nitrates, sodium, chloride, and heavy metals and waterborne toxic compounds (Smith and Alexander 1983).

Other more specific studies corroborate Smith and Alexander's results. While dissolved oxygen has increased and phosphorus levels have decreased in the middle Great Lakes in recent years, chloride and nitrate concentrations continue to increase (U.S. EPA 1989c). Toxic pollutant levels have improved in certain areas, however. For example, PCB levels in fish from the Hudson River have declined over 80 percent since 1978 (Faber 1992). Water quality regulation has only recently addressed the problems of toxic substances and heavy metals, so we should not be surprised that more progress has been made with regard to oxygen-demanding pollutants, bacteria, and nutrients. Overall, slightly more USGS stations reported increasing trends in pollutant concentrations than decreasing trends; however, the decreasing trends were at more significant levels (see table 8.2). The vast majority of National Stream Quality Accounting Network (NASQUAN) monitoring stations recorded no statistically significant trends in pollutant levels from 1974 to 1981 (Smith et al. 1987).

A separate analysis discovered that lead concentrations have decreased at nearly two-thirds of these same monitoring stations, while lead concentrations increased at only 6 percent of the stations (Alexander and Smith 1988). While these results appear to present decreases in lead concentrations as the success story of water pollution control, it is unlikely that these regulations had much to do with reductions in waterborne lead. The most plausible explanation for decreases in lead concentrations is the restrictions on lead in leaded gasoline that resulted from the Clean Air Act (Alexander and Smith 1988). Most of the lead finding its way into U.S. waters travels there through atmospheric deposition. This same method of pollutant transport is behind the heavy metal pollution problems in the Great Lakes. Thus, while reductions in lead concentrations in streams and rivers may not be a testimony to the effectiveness of FWPCA regulations, they do provide strong support for a more integrated environmental policy that pays particular attention to cross-media pollutants.

Major strides have been made toward reducing the amount of pollution reaching the nation's waters. There is some weak evidence that water quality has been improving as well. Many contend that simply holding the line on water quality in a decade (1972–82) where population grew by 11 percent and GNP increased by 25 percent is a significant accomplishment in its own right. Though this may be true, water quality has not come close to reaching the statutory goals set out in 1972. Interestingly, none of the analyses of water quality trends has explicitly tied improvements in these trends to water quality regulations. The ASIWPCA and EPA studies assume that regulation is responsible for water quality improvements, but this is never tested. The RFF studies only estimate the effects on water quality from hypothesized and uniform levels of regulatory effort. In comparison to the RFF study, the researchers at the USGS used actual measures of water quality constituents to track changes in water quality. While these USGS water quality trends have been roughly compared with regulatory activities, this is not the main purpose of the study (Smith et al. 1987). Regulation has only been conclusively tied to reductions in lead concentrations in rivers and streams, and these reductions have stemmed from clean air, not clean water, regulation (Alexander and Smith 1988).

To remedy this gap in knowledge, the GAO in 1986 released a study in which it painstakingly evaluated the effect of upgrading municipal treatment plants on effluent levels and stream water quality.[3] The GAO set up water quality monitoring stations downstream from four municipal wastewater treatment plants slated for major improvements in treatment technologies. These monitoring stations were able to measure concentrations of water pollutants immediately prior to and immediately after the installation of improved pollution control equipment at these plants. In all four case studies, the GAO concluded that improving municipal treatment facilities resulted in decreased pollutant effluent levels from these facilities. More importantly, three of the four case studies conclusively demonstrated that upgrading water treatment plants improved water quality down-stream from these plants. While effluent levels were also reduced at the fourth plant, increases from other pollution dischargers in the area offset the gains in water quality made at the municipal facility (U.S. GAO 1986b). Nevertheless, there was finally hard evidence that municipal wastewater treatment resulted in improved water quality—in essence, that regulation works.

Policy Outcomes in Water Quality Regulation

Though important, the results of the GAO study are not generalizable to entire state water quality programs. While regulation obviously matters at the micro level, the question still needs to be answered as to whether it matters at the macro (i.e., state) level. I will attempt to answer this question using the model developed and tested in the present chapter. Changes in water quality will be analyzed on a state-by-state basis. Specifically, the work presented here seeks to explain changes in state water quality since the passage of the FWPCA by evaluating these changes directly against changes in economic activity in each state, the strength of state water quality protection programs, and related administrative resources and activities.

Water quality is represented using a small number of specific water constituents, measured by highly sensitive monitors at fixed sites. This choice of specific constituents measured objectively makes the data collection and analysis more costly and difficult, but *concentrations* of specific pollutants cause the most harm to aquatic ecosystems, and the specificity and accuracy gained using this measurement strategy more than offsets the additional costs. Finally, I use a before-and-after technique to measure changes in water quality. We run the risk that this technique may underestimate the impact of regulation on water quality, but the models developed here remedy this potential shortcoming by controlling for the other non-natural and natural factors that can affect concentrations of water quality constituents (see below). The methodology is very similar to that used in chapter 6 to explain changes in state air quality over time.

Measures of Change in Water Quality

There are three networks of water quality monitors that measure concentrations of specific water constituents. The first is the EPA STORET data system. The data in the STORET system are poor measures of change in water quality, however. First of all, many of the monitors included in the STORET system are not fixed-site monitors. The EPA and state pollution control agencies move these monitors around as needed to measure water contamination at different sites. Many STORET monitors act as a kind of rapid deployment force to evaluate the nature and seriousness of water pollution episodes across the country. While obtaining data on water quality at specific accident sites is crucial if the EPA is to identify and control instances of acute water pollution, the mobile and temporary nature of these monitors makes it impossible to track changes in water quality at the same site over a long period of time.

Second, not only are many of the monitors temporary and mobile, but because they are set up to measure pollution from particular accident sites, they do not measure the same water quality constituents. For example, if two monitors are set up to identify changes in water quality, one downstream from a leaking landfill and one downstream from a petrochemical plant, these monitors will be calibrated to look for very different sets of pollutants. This makes tracking even changes in the same pollutants across areas very difficult. Finally, most of the monitoring sites that contribute data to the STORET system are not EPA sites. The majority of these sites are run by state and local governments, or by private industry. Because of this, there is little standardization of the type of monitor, the quality of the testing, and even the method by which similar water constituents are measured. In fact, the STORET system even contains data reflecting the "expert judgment" measurements of water quality discussed in chapter 4. For all of these reasons, if we want to measure long-term changes in a specific set of water quality constituents at permanently fixed sites, we must look for an alternative to the EPA STORET system.

An alternative is found in the two water quality monitoring networks administered by the U.S. Geological Survey. The USGS operates two large networks to monitor water quality in surface waters—the National Hydrologic Bench-Mark Network (Bench-Mark) and the National Stream Quality Accounting Network (NASQUAN). Both are nationwide networks that collect and analyze data on specific water quality constituents from fixed sites, but they were designed with different objectives in mind. Bench-Mark stations are located in small drainage basins in a variety of hydrologic, climatic, geologic, and geographic settings selected to be as close to their natural setting as possible, with little likelihood of significant development in the long-term future. Measurements from the Bench-Mark stations are used to track changes in water quality not associated with human use of the drainage basin (i.e., "natural" changes in water quality, though airborne contaminants can obviously affect water quality even in these basins). The original plan was to set up 100 Bench-Mark sites across the country, but this has proved impossible so far because of difficulties in finding 100 small drainage basins displaying the necessary characteristics (Smith and Alexander 1983).

The NASQUAN network was established in 1972 to provide data of the type needed to determine large-scale, long-term trends in the physical and chemical characteristics of the nation's surface waters. NASQUAN monitoring stations are located on larger rivers and streams to measure both the quality and quantity of water moving through "accounting units." The USGS has divided the country into 350 of these accounting units, and the long-term goal (almost realized) is to establish fixed monitors in each of these units. Almost all monitoring stations are located at the downstream end of accounting units. These stations monitor similar sets of water constituents at regular time intervals, though these intervals are not always equal for all constituents or across all sites. The characteristics of NASQUAN monitors allow us to evaluate changes in water quality over time on those rivers and streams most affected by human activities.

The Dependent Variables

Unlike the case of air quality, only pollutant concentrations are used to evaluate the effectiveness of state water pollution control programs (water pollutant emission or effluent figures for each state are unavailable over time). Stream monitors provide the best indication of overall water quality in a state because (a) most municipal and industrial sources discharge their effluent into rivers and streams, and (b) moving waters refresh and replenish themselves more rapidly, so changes in water quality should be reflected more quickly in rivers and streams. The characteristics of the NASQUAN system and the timing of water quality measurements at the monitoring stations mean that the NASQUAN network provides the data needed to calculate our measures of change in water quality. Data from the NASQUAN sites are used to calculate changes in the concentrations of dissolved oxygen (milligrams/liter), total dissolved solids (milligrams/liter), and phosphorus (milligrams/liter). Higher levels of dissolved oxygen represent higher levels of water quality, while higher levels of the other two constituents represent lower levels of water quality. These three water quality constituents are deliberately selected for a number of reasons.

If we are trying to discover what effects regulations have had on water quality, we ought to look at constituents of water quality that have been targeted by regulation. Heavy metals and other water toxins have only recently received much attention from water quality regulators, so measuring changes in water quality using these constituents makes little sense. On the other hand, total dissolved solids and phosphorus represent the type of pollutants that have been targeted by state and federal water quality regulations. Moreover, other traditional pollutants that contribute to dissolved oxygen levels (e.g., nitrate-nitrites, sediments, and so forth) have also been targeted by pollution control regulations for the past twenty years.

Dissolved oxygen, total dissolved solids, and phosphorus provide varying levels of generalization in measuring water quality and a variety of forums in which to investigate the effects of regulation on water quality. Dissolved oxygen is by far the most common constituent used to represent water quality. In fact, fish habitat zones themselves are determined in large part by the amount of dissolved oxygen present in the water. Relatedly, the majority of the pollutants targeted by traditional water quality regulations have some impact on dissolved oxygen levels. Thus, if we want an overall picture of the effects that regulations may have on water quality, dissolved oxygen is a good characteristic to measure. The total dissolved solids water quality constituent provides another commonly used measure of water quality. While not as ubiquitous as dissolved oxygen, dissolved solids levels do represent water degradation or improvement from a wide variety of specific pollutants.

The third and final water constituent, phosphorus concentrations, represents a very specific measure of change in water quality. As a single constituent affected by little besides human polluting activities, it provides an ideal marker for micro-level changes in water quality. Moreover, not only has phosphorus been the target of general water quality regulations, but several states have passed outright bans on the use of phosphorus in most commercial detergents. Public policies aimed at one specific pollutant are very rare (though lead restrictions in the CAA are a good example), particularly in water quality regulation. We might expect that if regulation is going to demonstrate an effect on any measure of water quality, it will be on phosphorus concentrations.

Our research design requires that we calculate one number to represent the average change in water quality in a state as measured by each constituent (that is, dissolved oxygen, total dissolved solids, and phosphorus). In order to do this, we make use of the averaged differencing technique discussed in chapter 6. We cannot simply calculate average constituent concentrations for each state, how-ever, because constituent concentrations are heavily dependent upon stream flow rates as well as pollutant loads. Before calculating average differences then, we must first standardize constituent concentration measurements by stream flow levels. The specifics of this process are found in the appendix. In short, we calculate the average flow adjusted concentration for each constituent in each state for the period 1973–75, and the average flow adjusted concentration for each constituent in each state for the period 1986–88. We then subtract the 1973–75 value from the 1986–88 value to get the average change in constituent concentrations in each state from 1973–75 to 1986–88. Finally, this difference is taken as a percentage of constituent concentrations in each state for the 1973–75 period. If water quality has improved in a state during this period, the dissolved oxygen variable will take on a positive value (seventies levels < eighties levels), while the dissolved solids and phosphorus variables will take on a negative value (seventies levels > eighties levels). Conversely, if water quality has declined in a state, the dissolved oxygen variable will take on a negative value (seventies levels > eighties levels), while the dissolved solids and phosphorus variables will take on a positive value (seventies levels < eighties levels). Changes in water quality constituents in the states are presented in table 8.3.

Independent Variables

Internal Statutory Factors

Internal statutory factors are represented by the strength and scope of a state's water pollution control program. State water pollution control programs are

Table 8.3

Changes in State Water Quality, 1973–75 to 1986–88:
Percent Change in Average Pollutant Concentrations

State	DOX[a]	DSL[a]	PHOS[a]	State	DOX	DSL	PHOS
Alabama	5	27	−28	Montana	2	26	−43
Alaska	na	na	−12	Nebraska	0	3	44
Arizona	na	na	na	Nevada	na	na	−31
Arkansas	6	−3	29	New Hampshire	na	na	na
California	5	−3	93	New Jersey	12	1	−46
Colorado	−2	41	12	New Mexico	−6	−14	−68
Connecticut	0	−7	−17	New York	11	−4	−71
Delaware	na	na	na	North Carolina	6	20	86
Florida	7	12	−14	North Dakota	−12	22	42
Georgia	5	32	18	Ohio	7	6	−14
Hawaii	na	na	−36	Oklahoma	−10	−13	−27
Idaho	13	25	−91	Oregon	na	7	−17
Illinois	21	37	−37	Pennsylvania	5	−8	na
Indiana	na	na	na	Rhode Island	na	na	na
Iowa	na	na	−14	South Carolina	−6	46	105
Kansas	26	8	48	South Dakota	na	na	−30
Kentucky	na	na	24	Tennessee	−9	19	−27
Louisiana	15	8	71	Texas	6	−35	−18
Maine	10	−40	−15	Utah	4	−3	−11
Maryland	25	−19	17	Vermont	na	na	na
Massachusetts	−1	20	−23	Virginia	28	28	68
Michigan	−4	40	−30	Washington	na	na	22
Minnesota	−4	19	−28	West Virginia	−4	na	−34
Mississippi	2	9	−21	Wisconsin	16	−13	−31
Missouri	22	2	−27	Wyoming	na	na	na

[a]Dissolved oxygen, total disolved solids, phosphorus.
Source: Compiled from USGS NASQUAN data base.

ranked from weakest to strongest based on the system used in chapter 7. Because certain elements of these rankings have no real potential for influencing the water quality constituents measured here, the rankings representing the strength and scope of a state's water pollution control program have been purged of those items representing toxic water control programs, groundwater pollution control programs, and wetlands protection programs. Removing these items from the water quality program matrix results in a program score that ranges from one (weakest programs) to ten (strongest programs). If stronger water pollution control programs are responsible for improvements in dissolved oxygen levels, this will be represented by a positive coefficient. Similarly, if stronger programs are associated with improvements in total dissolved solids and phosphorus concentrations, this will be reflected in a negative coefficient.

A final statutory variable is added to the last constituent concentration model.

Several states have instituted outright bans on the use of phosphates in detergents sold in the state. To account for this, a dummy variable coded one for each state banning phosphates and zero otherwise is included in the phosphorus model. If these phosphate bans have had the effect of reducing phosphorus concentrations in rivers and streams, this will be reflected by a negative coefficient.

Internal Political Factors

Internal political factors are represented by the average constant-dollar amount (1982 = 100) each state spent on water pollution control in the years 1972–81 (U.S. Department of Commerce, Bureau of the Census 1971–82). If expenditures are successful in improving water quality, we should find higher expenditure levels exhibiting a positive coefficient in the dissolved oxygen model and negative coefficient estimates in the dissolved solids and phosphorus models (for a complete discussion of the utility of using budgetary figures to represent internal political factors, see chapters 4 and 6). A third independent variable, representing the average constant-dollar amount (1982 = 100) each state received in federal municipal wastewater treatment construction grants from 1973 to 1987, is included in the water quality outcome model (U.S. Department of Commerce, Economics and Statistics Administration 1982–92; U.S. Department of the Treasury 1974–81). Municipal wastewater treatment grants have been the primary fiscal tool for controlling point sources of water pollution, and thus should be included in a model seeking to identify regulatory impacts on water quality. Again, if expenditures are successful at improving water quality, this variable should take on a positive coefficient in the dissolved oxygen model and a negative coefficient in the dissolved solids and phosphorus models.

Administrative "Outputs"

Administrative outputs are represented by the total number of federal abatement activities in enforcement (i.e., administrative orders, civil and criminal case referrals) in each state from 1974 to 1988.[4] Many states have primary NPDES enforcement authority, so using only federal enforcement activities does not provide a complete picture of enforcement efforts in water pollution control. The EPA did not begin centralizing data on state FWPCA enforcement actions until 1987, however, which makes obtaining a complete picture of enforcement activities in the states problematic. In water quality regulation, the federal EPA exercises significant enforcement authority in states with strong programs (e.g., New York, Massachusetts) and in states with weak programs and commitments (e.g., Texas, Louisiana). Moreover, federal enforcement actions are typically more significant and consistent than are state enforcement actions (Hedge and Menzel 1985; see also chapter 6). Thus, relying upon federal abatement actions does not introduce much bias into the models. If federal enforcement actions result in improved water quality, the enforcement variable will take on a positive coefficient in the dissolved oxygen model and negative coefficients in the dissolved solids and phosphorus models.

External Environmental Factors

As we saw in chapter 6, factors external to regulatory efforts can significantly affect air quality. In the same vein, levels of industrial production and activities that contribute to nonpoint source water pollution can significantly influence water quality levels in the states. Even though industrial point sources of effluent have long been targeted for cleanup under the CWA, changes in industrial activity in heavily polluting industries might still affect the concentration of certain water quality constituents, including those measured here. The industrial activity variable is the percentage difference in constant-dollar (1982 = 100) value added by manufacturing (VAM) in the seven industrial categories most responsible for water pollution between the years 1973–75 and 1985–87.[5] The first VAM average (1973–75) is subtracted from the second (1985–87), and this difference is taken as a percentage of the 1970s figure. Again, range averages are used to smooth out year-specific economic fluctuations. A direct negative relationship is hypothesized between industrial activity and water quality levels so that the coefficient for this variable should be negative in the dissolved oxygen model and positive in the dissolved solids and phosphorus models.

Industrial activity is not the only external factor affecting water quality. The majority of the contaminants reaching American waterways come from nonpoint sources of pollution. This is true for oxygen-demanding wastes as well as dissolved solids, phosphorus, pesticides, and certain heavy metals. Variables representing external environmental factors must then reflect the potential effects of these nonpoint sources. The second external environmental variable reflects the change in output in mining industries (a major nonpoint source polluter) in each state from 1973–75 to 1986–88 (U.S. Bureau of the Census 1974–90). This difference is represented as a percentage of the 1973–75 figure. A direct negative relationship is posited between mining output and trends in water quality.

The final external environmental variable reflects changes in the largest source of nonpoint water pollution, agricultural activity. With present farming techniques, the amount of land in production, not the output from that land, has the greatest effect on water quality. Increasing cropland acreage usually requires bringing more marginal land into production, and this marginal land is often highly erodible and contributes disproportionately to water quality problems. Conversely, taking this marginal land out of production contributes to improvements in water quality. For example, it has been estimated that idling 45 million acres of highly erodible land in the Conservation Reserve Program (CRP) has led to identifiable reductions in phosphorus, nitrogen, and sediment

Table 8.4

Multiple Regression Results: Changes in State Water Quality
(Dependant Variable = Changes in State Water Constituent
Concentrations, 1973–75 to 1986–88)

Independent Variables	Dissolved Oxygen		Dissolved Solids		Phosphorus	
	Initial Slope	Revised Slope	Initial Slope	Revised Slope	Initial Slope	Revised Slope
Intercept	3.74	5.50	−13.85	−9.22	−97.96***	−86.36***
Regulatory Program Strength	0.61	0.37	4.90*	4.29**	13.01***	12.10***
EPA Abatements	0.002	—	0.007	—	0.03	0.03
State Expenditures	0.0001	—	−0.001	−0.0007	0.009**	0.01***
Federal Grants	0.01	0.13	0.007	—	−0.17*	−0.21**
Industrial Output	−0.14	−0.13	−0.43	−0.45	0.41	—
Mining Output	−0.034	−0.033*	0.06*	0.06*	0.18**	0.08*
Agricultural Activity	−0.06	—	0.35	0.32*	0.14	—
Phosphate Ban	—	—	—	—	2.83	—
F-ratio	0.78	1.45	1.61	2.37*	3.18***	4.15***
Adj. R^2	.00	.05	.11	.17	.30	.29
N	35	35	35	35	42	42

*Statistically significant at $p < .10$.
**Statistically significant at $p < .05$.
***Statistically significant at $p < .01$.

loads in the nation's waters (Ribaudo 1989). Changes in agricultural activity are then measured by taking the average acreage of cropland in production in each state for 1973–75 and subtracting it from the average acreage of cropland in production in each state for 1986–88.[6] (This difference is represented as a percentage of the 1973–75 figure.) A direct negative relationship is posited between changes in agricultural activity and changes in water quality. The negative relationships between our two nonpoint source pollutant measures and changes in water quality will be represented by a negative coefficient in the dissolved oxygen model and positive coefficients in the dissolved solids and phosphorus models.

Multiple Regression Results

The overall results from the three water quality models are fairly weak (see table 8.4). The dissolved oxygen model is particularly disappointing, with only one variable expressing statistical significance and displaying little explanatory power in accounting for changes in dissolved oxygen concentrations. None of the models have even moderate problems with collinearity, however, and the few influential data points in the models pose no threat to the stability of the model results.

The three external environmental variables present relatively consistent results. Increases in industrial activity are associated with decreased dissolved oxygen levels and increased concentrations of phosphorus in the states, but the variable is not statistically significant in either model. Increases in polluting industry output are associated with lower levels of dissolved solids, but this result may not be as counterintuitive as it seems at first glance. Clean water regulations have been most successful at reducing discharges of dissolved solids from industrial facilities (ASIWPCA 1984; U.S. CEQ 1989). Thus, states experiencing relatively greater growth in these controlled industries may experience relatively better trends in dissolved solids concentrations than those states experiencing economic growth in other areas.

The two external nonpoint source variables also produce results consistent with our hypotheses. A 1 percent increase in mining output in the states leads to a 0.33 percent decrease in dissolved oxygen concentrations, a 0.06 percent increase in concentrations of dissolved solids, and a 0.08 percent increase in phosphorus concentrations, all other things remaining equal. Increases in agricultural activity (i.e., cropland under cultivation) may also lead to decreased dissolved oxygen levels and increases in dissolved solids and phosphorus loads in a state's waterways, although these effects are statistically significant only in the dissolved solids model. For each one percent increase in cropland under cultivation, a state has experienced an average 0.32 percent increase in dissolved solids concentrations, all other things equal. The results from these two variables demonstrate the influence that nonpoint sources of water pollution have on water quality in the states.

Regulatory efforts at improving water quality have met with no success, according to the results in table 8.4. Stronger state regulatory programs and higher levels of state spending for water pollution control have not resulted in improved water quality. Federal enforcement activities have not brought about improvements in water quality. Even states that have banned phosphorus in detergents cannot point to decreased phosphorus levels as an example of the success of these policies (although the coefficient is in the correct direction). The only statistically significant effect government efforts have had on overall water quality in the states comes from the federal municipal wastewater treatment grant program. For each additional million dollars the federal government spends annually for wastewater treatment facility construction in a state, phosphorus concentrations decline 0.21 percent, all other things remaining equal. Given the cost of the municipal wastewater treatment grant program, this seems like a very high price to pay for the observed improvements in phosphorus concentrations. Unlike the situation in air quality, it appears that regulation "does not work" in water pollution control. Much of this regulatory impotence is undoubtedly due to the problems in evaluating changes in water quality identified earlier, although we cannot escape the conclusion that water pollution control regulations are failing to live up to statutory expectations.

When estimating the relationships among the independent variables in the water quality model (see chapter 6 for how this was accomplished in air quality), we see expected results. Increases in federal spending for wastewater treatment facilities cause increases in state spending for pollution control, and higher state expenditures are one component of strong state water pollution control programs.[7] Furthermore, recall that the exogenous external environmental factors exhibit their expected relationships with changes in water quality in the states. The other results in table 8.4, however, demonstrate that the most important regulatory causal processes hypothesized by the integrated model of policy outcomes are not at work in water pollution control. The state regulatory strength and federal enforcement variables have no effect on changes in overall water quality in the states. Operationalizing the model as a set of path analytic equations thus makes little sense. The relationship between the independent variables and changes in water quality can be adequately represented by single multiple regression equations.

Discussion

The statistical results from the three water quality models are less than outstanding, even for the comparatively robust phosphorus model. Though disappointing, we must keep in mind that we are attempting to evaluate a complex natural process using only political and economic variables. Moreover, the levels of explanation in the dissolved solids and phosphorus models are consistent with the levels of explanation reached by water quality constituent models in hydrology and hydrogeology (see Smith and Alexander 1983). Since there is usually a strong stochastic element to most natural processes, natural systems are inherently very difficult to model. While these results do not give us a lot of confidence in our ability to account for changes in water quality levels in the states, we can learn a good deal about water quality regulation from the pattern of the results.

The coefficients for the regulatory strength variable deserve closer attention in the dissolved solids and phosphorus models. In both models, stronger regulatory programs are associated with significantly *higher* dissolved solids and phosphorus pollutant concentrations in a state. Moreover, higher levels of state expenditures are also associated with increased phosphorus concentrations. These results give the awkward impression that regulation might actually be counterproductive—that is, more ambitious regulatory activity results in lower levels of water quality.

Before reaching this conclusion, however, we should remember that ambient environmental conditions and implementation feedback are important to regulatory efforts in the states (Goggin et al. 1990; Lester and Bowman 1983; Mazmanian and Sabatier 1989). Public policy can be influenced as much by ambient environmental conditions as it itself influences these conditions. If water pollution control policy were simply ineffective, these variables would produce nondescript results. The strong and significant positive results in the dissolved solids and phosphorus models may demonstrate that states are in fact responding to problematic water quality trends with stronger regulatory efforts.

The counterintuitive results associated with the state regulatory strength and state expenditure variables are indicative of a process of *simultaneous causation*. State water quality regulations may affect water quality, but water quality levels may also affect the strength of state regulations (a causal model of water quality regulation would have an arrow running in each direction). We can address this simultaneity problem by finding a set of *instrumental variables* that are correlated with state regulatory program strength (but not with changes in water quality) and using these instruments to estimate the independent effect of state regulatory program strength on changes in state water quality (a similar procedure was used to test for and discount simultaneity in chapter 6; see, note 10). The variables used to account for state water program strength in chapter 7 are used as just such a set of instruments. When we use our instrumental prediction of the strength of a state's water quality program to predict changes in water quality, the strong positive relationship between regulatory program strength and increased water pollution disappears. Using this instrumental variable two-stage regression technique reaffirms that the strength of a state's water pollution control program has no effect on changes in water quality levels in the states, but it does show us that strong state programs are a response to poor water quality, as opposed to a cause of poor water quality.[8] If we cannot identify macro-level effects from water quality regulation, perhaps it is at least reassuring that state governments are attempting to combat increasingly serious water quality problems with expanded water quality protection programs.

Goodness-of-fit statistics and the strength of our independent variables improve as we move from the most general measure of water quality (dissolved oxygen) through a slightly less general measure (dissolved solids) to a very specific measure of water quality (phosphorus concentrations). The dissolved oxygen and dissolved solids variables are general measures of water quality in the sense that they reflect the effects of a wide variety of water quality constituents. While reflecting the influence of a large number of pollutants, dissolved oxygen and dissolved solids levels are themselves affected by a number of other factors, many of which are not affected by regulation (e.g., temperature, residual effects of stream flow, precipitation levels, runoff characteristics, and so forth). On the other hand, except in rare instances, human activities are the predominant source of phosphorus pollution. In short, human activities, regulatory and otherwise, have the greatest effect on water quality constituents like phosphorus. The fact that the strength of the statistical results from our models varies directly with the degree of human influence over the measure of water quality examined is wholly understandable, and might be seen as lending additional support to the validity of the models.

While the coefficients for the regulatory variables in the models do not demonstrate a strong regulatory effect on water quality, we cannot conclude that regulatory efforts are of no consequence in water pollution control. Overall water quality levels for a range of traditional pollutants have not improved significantly, but they have not degraded appreciably either, even with significant increases in population and GNP (Smith et al. 1987). Moreover, in several specific instances, water quality has improved significantly over the past twenty years (see U.S. EPA 1988a). Lake Erie has gone from being a cesspool to being one of the most productive sport fisheries in the country, and the Cuyahoga River no longer catches fire. PCB levels in Hudson River fish have declined 80 percent since the late 1970s (Faber 1992), and dissolved oxygen concentrations in the upper Mississippi River have improved in direct relation to the pollution control efforts of the cities of Minneapolis and St. Paul (MPCA 1990). Furthermore, recall that pollution controls have significantly reduced the amount of effluent reaching waterways from municipal and industrial facilities (Magat and Viscusi 1990), and that these reductions are reflected in improved levels of water quality immediately downstream from where these controls have been instituted (U.S. GAO 1986b).

When attempting to identify the effects of regulation on water quality at the macro level, however, regulatory effects are swamped by the contribution of pollutants from natural and uncontrolled nonpoint sources of pollution, and by natural variations in water quality. This is not surprising, given that over four-fifths of the pollutants affecting dissolved oxygen and dissolved solids concentrations come from largely uncontrolled nonpoint sources of pollution (Freeman 1990). We may be too optimistic in expecting water quality regulations that have historically targeted point sources of pollution to demonstrate a positive effect on changes in overall water quality levels that are themselves largely determined by nonpoint source pollutant loads.

Our results suggest that many states are not satisfied with their progress at protecting and improving water quality. While many might rest easier knowing that state governments are not sanguine about water quality problems, the results from the models cast serious doubt on the ability of traditional regulations to improve overall water quality. If states are attempting to combat problems with specific and easily identified water pollutants, such as phosphorus and fecal coliform bacteria, then more stringent point source controls and production bans may provide an answer. If, however, states are attempting to reverse declining trends in overall measures of water quality (e.g., dissolved oxygen, dissolved solids, nitrates and nitrites, and so on), more stringent point source controls are not the answer.

The results shown above suggest that we need to seriously consider significant changes in regulatory goals and regulatory structure in water pollution control. State responses to declining overall water quality conditions that emphasize traditional regulatory controls will produce only small improvements in water quality at steadily increasing costs. If state regulation is to have much substantive effect on overall water quality, these regulations need to emphasize nonpoint source pollution controls. We have seen some increase in nonpoint source control efforts, particularly in agricultural states (FREE 1988). In addition, the 1987 Water Quality Act requires all states to begin developing nonpoint source pollution control programs. These efforts at redirecting regulation toward nonpoint source pollution control should be encouraged and expanded.

The need for relying upon nonpoint source pollution controls in the future is indicative of the need for a much larger restructuring of environmental protection efforts that emphasize integrated cross-media or "holistic" approaches to environmental problems. For example, reducing the concentrations of toxic contaminants in the Great Lakes does not require more stringent water pollution controls being placed on the municipalities and industries that ring the lakes. The majority of the toxic pollutants that enter the Great Lakes ecosystem do so through airborne transfer and atmospheric deposition. In this example, the solution to water quality problems lies in air quality regulation (Irwin et al. 1984; see also Alexander and Smith 1988).

Most nonpoint source pollution does not stem from the consumptive use of water. In fact, most nonpoint source pollutants flow from land use, not water use, decisions. The effects of land use decisions in areas such as agriculture, silviculture, suburban development, and mining, however, are felt by aquatic ecosystems, not terrestrial ones. There is some evidence that nonpoint source pollution controls targeting these pollution sources can work. The EPA's pilot "Clean Lakes Program" has yielded significant improvements in water quality in several lakes by controlling urban and agricultural nonpoint source pollution (U.S. EPA 1990). This means that if regulations are to be successful in protecting and improving water quality, the carrots and sticks of these programs must be directed at affecting the land use decisions that lie at the heart of many water quality problems.

Conclusion

State regulatory efforts have not produced real improvements in general levels of water quality, though these efforts have reduced the level of effluent discharged into waterways and have improved water quality in specific areas. In the face of increasing economic and population pressures, water quality has not degraded appreciably either. Regulation must be given at least some credit for preventing water pollution from becoming worse. Nevertheless, we have to conclude that changes in water quality are affected much more by uncontrolled nonpoint sources of pollution and natural variations than by either traditional regulatory efforts or point sources of pollution. While regulation may not have identifiable effects on most measures of water quality, states are responding to worsening water quality conditions by expanding the strength and scope of their regulatory efforts. If these state policy responses are going to be successful in protecting and improving overall water quality, they should focus on coordinated cross-media controls on nonpoint sources of water pollution, rather than tightening controls on point sources of pollution.

Notes

1. The comparable figures for lake acreage are 84 percent fully supporting their designated uses, 10 percent partially supporting their uses, and 3 percent not supporting their uses; 3 percent of the lake acres were of unknown quality. For a water body to partially support its designated use, only a minimum amount of pollutants that seriously affect the most sensitive members of the aquatic community can be present. For full support of designated uses, there can be no biological effects of the chemical pollutants present.

2. The comparable figures for lake acres were 3.2 percent improved, 83.2 percent unchanged, and 13.6 percent degraded.

3. The argument has been made that the lack of a demonstrable connection between municipal wastewater treatment grants and improvements in water quality was one reason that the funding authority for the construction grant program was allowed to lapse in 1985, and also for the restructuring of the program in 1987 (U.S. GAO 1986b).

4. This data comes from the EPA's GREAT enforcement data storage and retrieval system in the Office of Water Enforcement and Compliance, and was obtained through a FOIA request. The EPA replaced the GREAT system with the STARS system in 1988.

5. These industrial classifications are food and kindred products, lumber and wood products, paper and allied products, chemicals and allied products, petroleum and coal products, leather and leather products, primary metal industries, fabricated metal products, and electric and electronic equipment.

6. USDA, National Agricultural Statistical Service, 1977, *Acreage.* A92.24/4–2:977; and USDA, National Agricultural Statistical Service, 1990, *Acreage.* A92.24/4–2:990. The crops included in these acreage figures are corn, sorghum, oats, barley, wheat, rice, soybeans, flaxseed, peanuts, sunflowers, cotton, dry edible beans, potatoes, sweet potatoes, and sugar beets.

7. The standardized coefficient for state expenditures regressed on federal grant expenditures is .76 with a t-score of 8.16. The standardized coefficient for state program strength regressed on state expenditures is .18 with a t-score of 1.28.

8. The relationships between the state program strength instrument and each measure of change in water quality in the revised water quality models are presented here in the format of coefficient (standardized coefficient) (t-score): for dissolved oxygen, 0.68 (.10) (0.49); for dissolved solids, 1.24 (.09) (0.41); for phosphorus 6.7 (0.26) (1.12). Using the instrument in place of the original state regulatory program strength variable slightly weakens the relationship between mining output and water quality in the phosphorus model. All other relationships between the independent variables and changes in water quality remain unaffected by the use of the instrument. Coefficients for the original state program strength variable are kept in table 8.4 to demonstrate the responsiveness of state policy to low levels of water quality.

9

Politics, Progress, and Prospects for Pollution Control

Pollution control policy is an area fraught with political complexity, scientific uncertainty, and technological unpredictability. The previous chapters have analyzed policy outputs and outcomes in the areas of air and water quality regulation. This final chapter summarizes some of the more important findings from this research and interprets them with respect to what they can tell us about the responsiveness of governmental institutions and the adequacy of governmental responses to environmental problems. Finally, the future prospects for pollution control and environmental policy are discussed in conjunction with state capacity for continued progress in environmental protection.

Outputs and Outcomes in Pollution Control

Policy Outputs

Analyzing policy outputs in state pollution control regulation reveals a complex process of policy influence. With respect to air quality, wealthier states with more liberal electorates and more professional legislatures enact more stringent regulations. States with strong polluting industries appear to be able to resist industry pressure and pass tougher air pollution control regulations, though the same fortitude is not displayed when it comes to resisting the demands of electric utilities. The energy–environment trade-off is readily observable in state pollution control policy, as states that are heavily dependent upon fossil fuels create significantly weaker air quality programs.

In water quality, both state wealth and the strength of political institutions are less important than in air quality regulation. The politics surrounding water pollution control exhibit a strong "interest group politics" element. States are able to resist pressures for lax regulations from heavily polluting industries, but this political backbone is lacking when it comes to resisting pressures from mining industries. States with strong mining industries respond to these political pressures by developing weaker water pollution control regulations. On the other hand, states respond to pollution potential and political pressure from strong agricultural sectors and environmental interest groups by strengthening their water pollution control programs.

The results of the foregoing analysis have demonstrated that each stage or section in the integrated model of policy outputs plays an important role in shaping public policy. The economic resources in a state and the political predispositions of that state's citizens are significant factors in shaping the policy demands and potential policy options in state pollution control. These state characteristics do not create public policy on their own, however. In each analysis, organized interest groups were of critical importance in pressing policy demands upon the institutions of government and in articulating more specific policy proposals. These groups form the link between policy potential and policy influence in the states of the United States. As the integrated theory suggests and as the empirical results from the integrated model demonstrate, group demands are not equal to public policy. In both air and water pollution control, governmental institutions are important in shaping the final outputs of the policy process. The analysis of policy outputs has also demonstrated the utility of causal modeling in policy research. Operationalized as a system of path analytic equations, the integrated model of policy outputs reveals a series of intertwined relationships between the variables that lie behind public policy, and displays results that would have been misinterpreted or missed altogether by single equation explanations.

The Responsiveness of Government

An examination of the influences behind state environmental policy tells us something about the responsiveness of state governments. States certainly appear to be responsive to influences and policy demands outside of political institutions. Do state policymakers only react to the economic situation in each state? No. State wealth has little influence on water quality policy, and while wealth is important in air quality regulation, it is not dominant. Policymaking at the state level is not as economically deterministic as some have made it out to be. State governments are also responsive to the desires of the citizenry, as reflected in the results for the state opinion liberalism variable in each integrated model. Especially in water, but also in air, states with more liberal electorates enact more expansive pollution control programs.

Finally, what of the influence of organized groups? One often hears economists, political scientists, journalists, as well as hairdressers and construction workers decrying the fact the policymaking and the wheels of government have been captured by "special interests." Leaving aside the obvious justifications for the legitimacy of group influence in a large and dispersed democracy, we can examine whether or not "special interests" have captured policymaking in pollution control. The results here suggest that this is not the case. While states do respond to demands for lax regulation from utilities and other large fossil fuel consuming concerns (in air pollution control) and the mining industry (in water pollution control), we also find the states responding with more stringent regulations where environmental groups and agricultural interests are particularly powerful. Indeed, in a direct reversal of the traditional "capture" hypothesis, states enact *more* stringent air quality regulations where polluting industries are especially strong. Here, state governments are perhaps acting less responsively and more responsibly. While organized interests may be dominant in a few states, in general state governments react to a whole host of pressures when forming pollution control policy.

Policy Outcomes

An analysis of policy outcomes helps us to answer the question, does the policy work? By extension, such an analysis also tells us something about the factors that affect successful policy outcomes. Whereas studying policy outputs helps to evaluate the *responsiveness* of state governments and political institutions, studying policy outcomes can give us hints as to the *adequacy* of these institutions and their policy responses.

Changes in economic activity and industrial production directly affect environmental quality. This is not surprising, since nearly all the targets of pollution control regulations are residuals of industrial production or personal consumption. This finding empirically drives home the point that pollution control is always going to be at odds with economic institutions in their present configurations. We should note, however, that it is not industrial activity *per se* that degrades air quality, but the combustion of fossil fuels that accompanies that activity. This suggests that by altering production processes and the fuel sources used, the competition between industrial production and environmental quality does not have to be a zero-sum game. Similarly, mining activities, not polluting industry production, are most strongly associated with degraded water quality. The mining industries present a smaller, less intimidating, and perhaps more manageable target for regulatory influence.

Of greater interest is the effect that regulation and regulatory activities have on levels of environmental quality. The evidence is clear that strong air quality programs significantly reduce sulfur dioxide and nitrous oxide emissions. While the results are slightly weaker, strong pollution control programs are associated with decreased atmospheric concentrations of these criteria pollutants as well. In short, stronger state regulatory programs do result in better air quality, even when controlling for other nonregulatory factors. While water quality regulations have reduced pollutant effluents, taken in total, state water quality regulations do not display the same positive policy outcomes as air quality programs. Even where water pollution control regulations are not having their intended effects, and water quality problems are getting worse, states are at least responding by increasing their regulatory efforts. Overall, these results provide enough evidence to conclude that in pollution control, regulation does matter.

The Adequacy of Governmental Responses

What about questions regarding the adequacy of state governments and their policy responses in environmental protection? The adequacy of institutions, regulations, and changes in environmental quality is not the subject of this book. Still, a few minor points related to these questions can be addressed here and will be returned to later in the chapter. At the national level, governmental responses in air and water protection seem to be having their intended effects. By nearly all measures, traditional air and water pollution are decreasing while air and (to a lesser extent) water quality are improving, sometimes dramatically (e.g., decreased levels of atmospheric lead and the "rebirth" of Lake Erie). While there is still much work to be done with respect to these first generation pollutants, the trend is positive. Not only regulation, but different *levels* of regulation make a difference in environmental quality. States with stronger air pollution control programs are rewarded for their efforts with better air quality. We should remember, however, that these positive effects of regulation are only evident for those pollutants that are easiest to control with traditional post-production control techniques. Governmental responses to second and third generation pollution problems such as acid rain, air toxins, heavy metals, and nonpoint water pollution have thus far been inadequate. While regulations may not always have a significant effect on environmental quality, the results suggest that they could.

Are governmental institutions and their policy responses up to the task of pollution control? There is some basis for guarded optimism. Have the improvements in environmental quality been adequate? From this author's point of view, the answer is an unqualified no. Only a very few measures of environmental quality have been touched upon here, and much progress remains to be made even with these. In addition, many threats to environmental quality have yet to be addressed by public policy. Guarded optimism regarding the potential for effective governmental responses in these areas should not be translated into complacency with present efforts. Finally, nowhere in the present set of pollution control regulations do we find recognition of the interconnectedness of the biosphere or the intrinsic value of an intact and healthy ecosystem. Until environmental policy embodies these concepts in addition to the concerns of human health and economic costs and benefits that are presently employed, improving and protecting environmental quality will remain a slow and difficult task characterized by uneven results.

Government Capacity and the Future of Pollution Control

Fiscal Capacity

Controlling pollution costs money—money for control equipment, inspectors, administrators, and for monitoring changes in environmental quality. Increased levels of pollution control that use the present approach to regulation will cost even more. Where will this money come from? Industry claims that pollution control costs are too onerous at present, and that requiring further expenditures could dangerously weaken its already precarious position in the economic marketplace. Such industry claims regarding the costs and consequences of regulatory requirements should be taken with a grain of salt, however. Capital expenditures by industry for pollution abatement equipment accounted for only 3 percent of all nonfarm business capital investment in 1990, and these costs have dropped significantly since 1975 (see chapter 1).[1] Most of the nations competing with American industries for world market shares in manufactured goods have more stringent pollution control regulations than the United States (for example, Germany and Japan), and there is no evidence that the costs of environmental regulation place U.S. firms at a competitive disadvantage (CBO 1985). Nevertheless, the industrial costs of environmental regulation are a legitimate concern.

In addition to potential financial limitations in industry, the present fiscal situation of burdensome budget deficits and political promises of holding the line on taxes (depending upon your income bracket) make the prospects of increased governmental expenditures for pollution control rather slim, at least at the federal level. States may continue to squeeze more resources for pollution control out of existing revenue sources, and some part of the federal "peace dividend" may fall the way of environmental protection. Even so, we have little reason to expect that the fiscal capacity of state governments will increase commensurate with the growing environmental threats these states must face. The serious budgetary difficulties that many states find themselves dealing with in the early 1990s suggest that even guarded optimism regarding further increases of state fiscal capacities may be misplaced. In the future, both the federal and state governments are going to be asked to do more in the area of environmental protection with less revenue, and the possibilities for this under the present system of regulation are small.

Administrative and Institutional Capacity

Some recent criticism by scholars of environmental policy and administration has focused upon the piecemeal nature of environmental regulation in the United States. Most legislation laying out the goals and methods of pollution control is medium-specific; the CAA focuses upon air pollution, the CWA and WQA are concerned with the sources of water pollution, RCRA and Superfund deal only with the management of hazardous waste, and so forth. There is very little coordination among these pieces of legislation, and this results in a fragmented approach to problem solving in the environmental area. This fragmentation is reflected and exacerbated in the structure of the agency charged with implementing these regulations, the EPA. There are separate offices within the EPA for air pollution and radiation, water pollution, solid and hazardous waste management, and pesticide regulation. The coordination among these offices is poor, and each administers its own enforcement and compliance programs and much of its own research and development.[2]

Fragmentation in policy and administration would pose no problem if pollutants restricted themselves to a single medium (i.e., if air pollutants stayed in the air). The fact is that many, or even most, pollutants travel across media (i.e., few pollutants pose exclusively first generation environmental problems). The oxides of sulfur and nitrogen that are emitted into the atmosphere eventually precipitate out and cause acidification problems in lakes and nutrient deficiencies in certain soil types (Regens and Rycroft 1988). The majority of the heavy metals and toxic pollutants contaminating the Great Lakes reach this ecosystem through atmospheric transport. Although hazardous wastes and pesticides usually contaminate soil, these compounds often leach into groundwater and surface water supplies, and can even cause local air pollution problems. Finally, this fragmentation extends across program areas as well. Energy, agricultural, and water resource development policies all have environmental consequences on a large scale, but with few exceptions the EPA is excluded from policy deliberations in these areas and is instead left to deal with the environmental consequences of these policies after the fact.

At the subnational level, nearly all state legislatures and most state administrative agencies are modeled after their federal counterparts. Because of this, we see considerable legislative, administrative, policy, and program fragmentation at the state level as well. The similarity between state and federal organizational structure and behavior means that the states suffer similar limitations on administrative and institutional capacity in the area of environmental protection. While the states have been more innovative than the federal government in integrating environmental decision making and administration, most of this integration has been undertaken for reasons of administrative efficiency rather than ecological rationality. These reforms must be expanded if they are to display significant environmental results (Council of State Governments 1975; Rabe 1986).

The cross-policy and cross-media effects of many pollutants require a greater degree of integration and coordination than is presently employed by governing institutions. Environmental policymaking is fragmented across several legislative committees, while the administration of policies having environmental impacts is spread across several agencies and fragmented within the environmental agencies themselves. What is lacking in environmental programs is recognition of the first law of ecology, "everything is connected to everything else" (Commoner 1972, 29). Until this concept becomes embodied in the process and institutions of environmental policy, state institutional capacity in this area will fail to reach its full potential, and the structure and results of the policies themselves will remain largely unchanged.

Political Capacity

We have ample evidence that most states have adequate political capacity as measured by their propensity to develop innovative pollution control programs (and adapt existing ones) to improve environmental protection within their borders. There are even suggestions that the federal government is following the states' lead in developing more innovative programs (Kamieniecki and Ferrall 1991; Kritz 1989). But what are the prospects for future progress in state and federal policymaking in the environmental area? At both levels, there are some reasons for optimism.

Over the past several years, the EPA has begun to use a few less conventional and less costly measures in administering environmental policy: the "bubble" concept and emissions banks in air pollution control, more autonomy for regional offices, and an increased reliance upon risk assessment in ordering its overall regulatory priorities.[3] The plan of the 1990 CAA to create a quasi market for tradable sulfur dioxide discharge permits suggests that we may increasingly find innovative approaches to pollution control in new federal legislation as well. For their part, the states appear willing to continue innovations in environmental protection. California is already considering new and more stringent regulations that may impinge upon certain elements of the "California life-style" (Brownstein 1989), while other states are considering experiments with economic alternatives to regulation like effluent fees and transferable discharge permits in an attempt to go beyond pollution control into pollution reduction. A fair appraisal would be that institutional and political capacity relevant to environmental policy may continue to improve, though the situation with respect to fiscal capacity is less clear. One question remains, however. Will this reform of current structures, institutions, and programs be enough?

The Limits of Pollution Control

Have efforts at controlling pollution and improving air and water quality been successful? Within the limits imposed by the uncertainty in all measures of environmental quality, the answer seems to be a qualified yes. While my research makes no claims in determining if these regulations have been successful *enough*, we can still ask questions about the effectiveness of these regulations in general. Are there limits to what pollution control regulation can accomplish? Are these regulations sufficient to protect and improve environmental quality?

Technical Limits

Pollution control regulations, even if successful, are not by themselves the answer to problems of environmental protection. There are a number of technical limits on how much pollution control activities can accomplish. The first of these are economic limits. Pollution control costs money, and the capital and operating expenses associated with pollution control increase exponentially with the degree of control desired. For example, reducing pollutant emissions or effluent levels by half may be relatively inexpensive, but a 75 percent or 90 percent reduction often costs many times more. In fact, reducing pollutant emissions by 99 percent can cost ten or more times as much as a 90 percent reduction (Downing 1984). Moreover, no political system will be able to ratchet down more stringent regulatory requirements indefinitely. Eventually, the costs of influencing the political system become smaller than the costs of regulatory compliance, and industry will choose the former action. Congress and state legislatures may continue to pass ever-more stringent regulations, but industry will simply ignore the increased requirements, and administrative agencies will not have the capacity or political resources to enforce them (see Melnick 1983; Yandle 1989). As the goals of these regulations become increasingly divorced from the economically and politically feasible means of attaining them, policy goals and requirements become "policy fictions" that both the regulators and the regulated routinely ignore (which can undermine the legitimacy of the regulations altogether; see Sagoff 1988). At some point then, further improvements in environmental quality from pollution control become economically unattainable.

A second technical limit on pollution control is provided by the technology of control itself. While great reductions are possible, no device can be 100 percent effective at removing pollution. Even technologies that are effective at removing pollutants are susceptible to tampering and mechanical failure, both of which can release enormous quantities of pollutants into the biosphere. Moreover, technologies for safely controlling and disposing of certain highly toxic pollutants (e.g., heavy metals and high-level radioactive waste) are simply not available. While technological solutions to these technological problems are possible, they are unlikely in the near future, and basing environmental protection strategies on the prospect of their development would be foolish. Lastly, by relying upon technological pollution control, we do nothing but buy time until the level of pollutants and the threat to environmental quality reaches pre-control levels. For example, a procedure that removes 75 percent of a particular pollutant is wonderfully effective, and if required in a particular industry, it would reduce emissions greatly. If, however, industrial production increases by a scant 3.5 percent per year (roughly equivalent to the growth rate of heavy manufacturing in the U.S. through the 1980s), the amount of pollution reaching the environment will reach pre-control levels in only forty years. If the yearly growth rate is 5 percent, this time period is reduced to twenty-eight years. After this, the enormous amount of capital and effort devoted to pollution control would only have allowed us to break even, that is, to maintain a level of environmental quality that was considered unacceptable in the first place.

A third technological limit placed upon pollution control stems from the physical law that matter can be neither created nor destroyed; it only changes form. (In the words of Barry Commoner's second law of ecology, "everything has to go somewhere"; see Commoner 1972, 36). When we "control" or "remove" pollutants in a process, we are really only shuffling them around; they have to go somewhere. The residue from the electrostatic precipitators and scrubbers used in air pollution control contains sulfuric acid, arsenic, and enough other toxic compounds that it must often be treated as hazardous waste. Initially, we disposed of this residue in waterways (turning air pollution into water pollution), and now we dispose of the residue in landfills (turning air pollution into land pollution). Similar transfers occur in water pollution control. The toxic sludge produced by municipal wastewater treatment plants is typically either dumped in the ocean, placed in landfills, or spread on rangeland as fertilizer. Some of these wastes can be recycled (for example, Milwaukee turns its wastewater sludge into the fertilizer Milorganite), but the vast majority of disposal techniques pose their own environmental threats. A persuasive argument can be made that the improvements in pollutant levels discussed in this book do not really reflect improvements in overall environmental quality. If air and water pollutants are simply removed from the air and the water to be disposed of on the land or in the ocean, can we really say that environmental quality has improved? Present pollution control policies, so this argument goes, have actually *displaced* rather than *resolved* environmental problems (see Dryzek 1987). While the results of this displacement may be better than the alternative of no control, these efforts are certainly not the solution to ecological degradation. Finally, many of the pollutants produced by routine methods of industrial production, electricity generation, and transportation persist for long periods of time. Pollutants that are "controlled" and "contained" may continue to pose threats to the environment for dozens of years (e.g., traditional landfill constituents), hundreds of years (e.g., toxic chemicals), or tens of thousands of years (e.g., high-level radioactive wastes). Without improved vigilance and containment methods, these pollutants will likely escape and contaminate the environments surrounding their resting places. Uncontrolled, contaminants such as PCBs and dioxins can cycle through the food chain for generations, while the chlorofluorocarbons we emit today will still be destroying ozone and contributing to global warming generations from now. Given the longevity and persistence of many pollutants, whether or not they are "controlled" depends largely upon one's frame of reference.

The slew of technical limits associated with the strategy of long-term reliance upon pollution control makes this approach to environmental protection insufficient. What are the alternatives? The generally agreed upon conclusion is that pollution *reduction*, rather than pollution control, is the most responsible and viable approach to environmental protection. While waste reduction has long been advocated by environmentalists, it has rarely been embodied as a policy goal. Reasons for this will be provided shortly.

Political Limits

Technical limits are not the only obstacles in the path of effective pollution control, or of transcending pollution controls in moving toward a more comprehensive approach to environmental policy. Additional limits are posed by political institutions and the distribution of political power in American society. These political limits are likely to be reached before the technical limits recounted above, and thus the political obstacles to pollution control are more realistic boundaries to what is possible in environmental protection.

The realities of the distribution of economic and political power in the United States make effective pollution control regulation extremely difficult. Some scholars claim that "market failures" (e.g., environmental externalities) are essential to a market economy because socializing some of the costs of production is the easiest way for businesses to maintain high profit margins (Williams and Matheny 1984). Industrial interests fiercely resist public interference (i.e., increased regulation) in the "private" business decisions that lead to these public externalities, and this resistance is often successful given the privileged position of business interests in the political system (Lester and O'M. Bowman 1983; Lindblom 1977; Mills 1956). Regulations aimed at pollution reduction instead of simply pollution control are especially difficult in this regard because they typically deal with alterations in production processes or the selection of raw material inputs, which are considered to be private internal business decisions. While some regulation of the residual outputs of productive processes (i.e., pollution control) is acceptable, truly effective environmental protection regulations aimed at reducing pollution at its source are nearly impossible to develop and implement due to the opposition of business interests and their influence in government (Williams and Matheny 1984). This process of economic influence, political manipulation, and intervention on behalf of large industrial concerns has already been identified during the twenty-year history of the EPA (Yandle 1989). While the solutions necessary to address many environmental problems are known, policymakers often lack the political will to make these difficult policy decisions for the reasons described above (Regens and Rycroft 1988; Smith 1992).

More than political realities and powerful interests frustrate truly effective environmental policy. The structure of political institutions provides a barrier as well. The fragmented nature of environmental policymaking and administration has already been discussed. One explanation for this fragmentation is that our political institutions are intentionally designed to deal with problems in piecemeal fashion. Political institutions and the social and physical sciences that underlie their foundations are characterized by a high degree of specialization and hierarchical organization. In these institutions, problem solving proceeds by dissecting large problems into smaller segments through analysis, with sequential experimentation on each piece of the problem in question in order to find a solution. Solutions to each piece of the problem are then aggregated to create a solution to the problem as a whole.

One of the defining characteristics of ecosystems, however, is that they are chock full of *emergent properties*—characteristics and functions that cannot be deduced from the constituent parts of ecosystems. This means that the emphasis on dissection and specialization that underlies our social and scientific decision-making systems works poorly in environmental protection, where "everything is connected to everything else." Treating only one aspect of environmental problems rarely results in a solution, and often ends up compounding the problem one intended to solve in the first place (e.g., pesticide applications causing one to be overrun with new pests, water development and reclamation projects that lead to soil salinization and increases in waterborne diseases, "secure" hazardous waste landfills that themselves become superfund sites). From this perspective, present fragmented political institutions are incapable of developing adequate responses to holistic environmental problems. Any successful approach to environmental policy then must begin by restructuring decision-making institutions and patterns of political communication (Dryzek 1987).[4]

Truly effective environmental policies must come from political institutions that can take a more holistic perspective on ecological problems, but integrated environmental management has long been a chimerical goal to environmental administrators. While many states have attempted some level of integration in their pollution control programs, more often than not these efforts have been spurred by concerns over regulatory relief, rather than improved environmental management. One hypothesized reason for the lack of progress toward integrated approaches to environmental problems is that we have yet to encounter an environmental crisis that requires this integration (Rabe 1986). Second and especially third generation environmental problems may provide just such a crisis. We see evidence of integrated responses to water pollution and toxic contamination problems at the state level (e.g., the interstate initiative to control nonpoint source water pollution in the Chesapeake Bay watershed), and in federal integrated environmental management projects in Philadelphia, Denver, Baltimore, and Santa Clara, California (Cohen and Weiskopf 1990). The EPA has also initiated a pollution reduction program. Progress has been slow on these projects, however, and future integrated pollution control efforts will have to learn from the successes and failures of these and other efforts at integrated environmental management.

New Problems in Environmental Protection

The results in this book demonstrate that federal and state efforts at controlling first generation air and water pollution have been relatively successful. All regulatory goals have not been met and many statutory deadlines have been missed, but all things considered, regulation has made a difference in improving air and water quality. Our understanding of the ecological threats facing the world has gone far beyond the reach of traditional air and water quality regulation, however. For the foreseeable future, second and especially third generation environmental problems will receive more public and governmental attention.

Primary among these third generation environmental problems is the specter of global warming (a warming of the earth's atmosphere due to increased levels of carbon dioxide, methane, and other greenhouse gasses). Global warming is a well-supported scientific theory, but not an established fact (remember, however, the same was said about acid rain and ozone depletion twenty years ago). If the predictions of many atmospheric scientists hold true, we can expect an average increase in global temperatures of between two and eight degrees centigrade by the middle of the next century. A temperature increase at the midpoint of this range would melt significant portions of the polar icecaps, flood low-lying coastal areas and islands that are the home to hundreds of millions of people, change weather patterns and vegetation zones, and rearrange entire biomes (Lyman 1990).

A second and more immediate third generation environmental threat is the depletion of the stratospheric ozone layer. Twenty-five years ago, it was hypothesized that normally inert chlorofluorocarbons could enter the stratosphere and troposphere, interact with sunlight, and destroy a significant percentage of the earth's protective layer of ozone. Ozone depletion in the stratosphere leads to increased levels of ultraviolet radiation at ground level, which in turn results in higher levels of skin cancer, eye cataracts, and the potential destruction of phytoplankton and zooplankton which underlie the entire oceanic food chain. Scientific theory has become estblished scientific fact. Not only is the stratospheric ozone layer "thinning," but it is doing so at twice the rate expected by most atmospheric scientists. In 1991, a NASA satellite over Antarctica recorded "dobson unit" measurements at *one-fifth* of their average level, corresponding to the lowest ozone levels on record (Malcom Brown 1991a). That same year, scientists for the first time found decreased ozone levels over temperate zones in both North and South America (Malcolm Brown 1991b). By 1993, ozone depletion in the northern hemisphere was ahead of even the most pessimistic protections (National Public Radio 1993).

Third generation environmental problems are not limited to global warming and ozone depletion. We can find dozens of others. Tropical deforestation continues to proceed at the alarming rate of one acre every second. If deforestation continues at its present rate, nearly all virgin rainforest will have vanished by 2010. Along with the forestland, we will lose over 25 percent of all known species of plant and animal life and a significant carbon "sink" that prevents carbon dioxide from accumulating in the atmosphere (everything is connected to everything else) (Tuchman 1991). Finally, first generation air and water pollution is increasing so dramatically in many developing countries that the sheer volume of these pollutants may have regional environmental effects. Astronauts on the space shuttle *Atlantis* commented that air pollution over the earth was by far the most easily identifiable sign of human activity visible from space *(New York Times* 1992a).

How will the United States respond to third generation environmental threats? Evidence from policy responses to first generation pollution gives some cause for optimism. Furthermore, the EPA and the states have not stood still regarding these pollutants and the administrative limitations on pollution control identified above. The EPA and other federal agencies are spending millions of dollars studying the causes of and potential solutions for third generation environmental problems. Much of this research is based on what is being learned in EPA's pollution prevention and integrated environmental management programs. Though the United States has been reluctant to participate in international agreements regarding third generation environmental problems (e.g., we refused to sign an acid rain agreement with Canada and refused to sign the global warming and species diversity treaties at the 1992 Earth Summit), we have been a leader in phasing out the use of chlorofluorocarbons faster than is required by our participation in the Montreal Protocol. By reversing Bush administration policy and agreeing to sign the greenhouse gas and biodiversity treaties, President Clinton and Vice President Gore have already strengthened the United States' participation in international environmental agreements, bringing us up to par with the commitments made by our Western industrialized partners. States are even addressing third generation environmental problems on their own. In an example of "thinking globally and acting locally" at the state level, several states have programs aimed at reducing chlorofluorocarbon and carbon dioxide emissions (B. Jones 1991; Sylvester 1990). Even with federal and state efforts, however, increased international cooperation is essential to making progress on third generation environmental problems.

Conclusion

We have seen that federal and especially state governments have had some success at reducing first generation environmental pollutants. We have also seen that a number of technical conditions limit the degree to which we can rely upon traditional pollution control regulations to solve environmental problems. In addition to these technical constraints, effective environmental protection policies, whether they are aimed at first, second, or third generation environmental problems, can be obstructed by the structure of political institutions and the distribution of political power in the United States (and internationally). The basic obstacles to effective environmental protection are social, however. True progress in environmental policy and environmental quality must stem from changes in societal norms and values. Eternal economic growth and especially increases in consumption are physically and logically impossible, yet each of these are core values as society is presently oriented. Unless these goals are altered, the *inevitable* result will be increasing resource scarcity, human suffering, environmental degradation, and perhaps the demise of liberal democracy and the unusual degree of personal freedom that comes with this political system (Ophuls 1977; Ophuls and Boyan 1992). The first step toward avoiding this unsavory set of circumstances is for mankind to learn to exist *within* the environment; as a part of the ecosystem, not separate from it and dominating it (Merchant 1980). Only by reorienting the status of humanity to be a member of the natural systems that surround us, and by recognizing our dependence upon these systems and the opportunities and limitations this entails, can we preserve both environmental integrity and a comfortable life-style for future generations.

At heart, the most important limits upon environmental policy and environmental protection are social ones. Governmental policies and programs in general reflect public opinion. Thus, comprehensive programs that adequately address holistic environmental problems will only arise in response to the development of a societal "ecological conscience." Developing this conscience requires a change in our norms, values, and perceptions of what is and is not necessary and practical, for

> the incremental, "practical" approach to environmental protection cannot hope to solve a systemic problem. The incremental approach will stop short of a solution that is inconsistent with the prevailing assumptions about economic and political feasibility. (Caldwell 1975, 12–13)

These changes in our norms and values will not come easily, nor can they be mandated, but policies that encourage shifts in our perceptions of what is involved in environmental protection will help. Changed norms and values will *lead* to institutional changes, and these changes will in turn produce improvements in institutional capacity, political capacity, public policy, and finally, environmental quality.

The Worldwatch Institute calls the 1990s the decisive decade for environmental change. Man's impact on the earth's environment is now on a scale with natural forces like volcanos, ice ages, asteroid impacts, and continental drift as agents of global change. The world has not succeeded in turning around a single environmental trend since the 1972 United Nations Conference on the Environment in Stockholm, and many experts feel that nothing short of an "environmental revolution" will avoid environmental catastrophe (L. Brown 1992). I have placed a great deal of emphasis on governmental capacity in protecting environmental quality; with respect to first generation environmental problems, the evaluation of state and national governmental capacity is fairly satisfactory. Governments cannot do everything, however. Nor would we want them to try. Changes in social norms, social values, and societal expectations for government and the economic sector all begin at the level of the individual. This means that in addressing ecological problems, one of the most important elements of governing capacity is the capacity we as individuals demonstrate for governing ourselves.

Notes

1. There are ample examples of businesses and industries "fudging" their figures on the technical and economic feasibility of regulatory compliance. For example, in response to the automobile emission requirements in the 1970 CAA, domestic automobile manufacturers claimed that the technology needed to meet these standards was unattainable. However, foreign automobiles had no problem meeting these same standards, and domestic manufacturers had already developed the catalytic converter technology required for larger American cars to meet the pollution standards. In a related example, in the 1970s the Chemical Manufacturers Association claimed that OSHA requirements for reducing worker exposure to vinyl chloride were technically unworkable, and would drive the vinyl chloride industry to financial ruin. The new production and control process developed to meet the standard was not only technically feasible, however; it also ended up saving the industry millions of dollars a year and improving its competitive position internationally (Reagan 1987). We also have to keep in mind that industry has significant political and tax incentives to overstate the costs of its investments in pollution control.

2. These conclusions were drawn after extensive observations and interviews with EPA officials during January 1989. This critique of fragmentation in environmental policy has also been recounted in the environmental policy literature (Rabe 1986).

3. Under the bubble concept, instead of regulating each different air pollution source in the same area, whether from the same industry or different industries, these can all be regulated as one large pollutant source. Any one of the constituent sources may exceed federal emission standards if comparable emission levels are reduced by a greater amount elsewhere within the "bubble." This allows industrial polluters greater latitude and discretion in determining where it is most economical to reduce pollutant emissions while holding emissions at or below the level they would be at without the bubble.

Emission banks allow industries to save, trade, or sell emission reductions in excess of those required by federal and state regulations. For example, if an industrial facility reduces nitrogen dioxide emissions by 50,000 tons per year more than is required by air quality regulations, the industry may "bank" these reductions and either sell them to another facility looking to expand in the same area (one that is not as efficient as the first industry in reducing emissions), or use them itself in a later expansion of the same plant. This is yet another way in which the EPA has been trying to encourage industries to reduce emissions more efficiently.

Finally, the EPA undertook a major risk assessment and risk management evaluation entitled *Unfinished Business,* in which the agency rated a number of environmental risks with respect to the probability of harm to humans and ecosystems. The results were somewhat surprising in that toxic waste dumps ranked very low on the list of risks, while less salient problems such as indoor air pollution ranked very high. A long-term goal of the EPA is to undertake more policy implementation and enforcement based upon these assessments of risk.

4. Dryzek refers to the basis for the present structure of political institutions and communication in policymaking as "Poppernian critical rationalism" after the "open society" ideal for communication and scientific problem solving championed by Sir Karl Popper. Dryzek takes this basis of communication and problem solving to task as being too hierarchical and fragmented. He offers an alternative basis for social problem solving and political communication based upon the critical theory of Jurgen Habbermas, and finds this to be superior in many respects, particularly when faced with problems of a holistic nature.

Appendix:
Calculating Changes in
State Air and Water Quality

Calculating Changes in Ambient Air Quality

Over one thousand air quality monitors measure air pollutant levels across the country. Not all monitors measure every criteria pollutant, however. Many monitors measure only one or two. In addition, several monitors measure non-criteria pollutants including heavy metals and toxic air pollutants. These measurements are taken on an hourly or daily basis, depending upon the monitor and the pollutant of interest. Because of the frequency of monitoring activity, individual monitors may take several hundred air quality measurements each year.

Calculating average ambient measures and air quality trends from this amount of data is an almost impossible task. Yet the EPA National Air Data Branch (NADB) compiles observations for each air quality monitor across the country. These monitor measurements are stored in the AIRS data bank and are published yearly as a several hundred–page set of summary tables called the *AMP Quick Look Report*. This summary data set contains frequency distributions for the ambient air quality measures taken for each pollutant at each monitoring site in the country. AIRS summary frequency distributions were obtained on computer tape from the NADB for the years 1973–75 and 1985–88.

In order to get a single value that represented concentration ratios for each pollutant within each state, the summary data sets themselves had to be reduced. An expected average concentration ratio was computed for each pollutant at each monitoring station using the frequency distribution provided for each site. The formula for this expected value is as follows:

$$E\,[x] = \Sigma_f\,(Px)$$

or

$$E\,[x] = .10(10x) + .20(30x) + .20(50x) + .20(70x) + .20(90x) +$$
$$.05(95x) + .04(99x) + .01(\text{Max2})$$

where

    $E\,[x]$ = the expected value or expected average concentration ratio for each site.

    $f\,(.10–.01)$= the relative frequency associated with a particular concentration ratio.

    $P\,(10–99)$ = the percentile rank associated with a particular concentration ratio.

    x = the ambient pollution concentration measure associated with the tenth percentile, the fiftieth percentile, etc.

    Max2   = the second highest pollutant concentration ratio observed at that monitoring station during the year.

This expected value contains a small positive bias with regard to the likely actual mean concentration ratio for each pollutant at each station, but this bias is consistent across stations and across time, so it makes no difference statistically. In addition, this bias was minimized by eliminating the single highest yearly pollutant concentration measure at each site.

    Once expected mean concentration ratios for each site had been calculated, these expected values themselves were averaged across all sites within a state for each pollutant. This means that measurements from monitors in highly polluted areas were combined with measurements from monitors in less polluted areas within a state, giving a true "average" value. Now, there is really no such thing as an "average" level of air quality within a state; certain areas are more polluted than others and these differences have real meaning for the people living in each area. However, since we are trying to assess *overall* air quality in a state, these differences have little relevance for the analysis presented here. Averaging expected values from each monitor in a state is a better representation of state air quality than is using only those monitors from the most polluted areas. If data from only the most polluted areas in each state were used, or if we used only the highest pollutant concentration levels, intrastate changes in industrial location and unpredictable atmospheric events would give us false impressions about consistent changes in state air quality levels.

    Next, the yearly pollutant averages for each state were combined for the years 1973–75 and 1985–87 (for particulates), or 1986–88 (for sulfur dioxide and nitrogen dioxide). The first average concentration value (1970s) was subtracted from the second (1980s) to get the average change in ambient air pollutant levels between these two time periods. A positive value for this difference means that pollution concentration levels have increased, on average, in the state, while a negative value shows that pollutant concentrations have declined. Finally, average changes in state pollutant levels are taken as a percentage change from average pollutant concentrations in 1973–75.

Calculating Changes in Ambient Water Quality

Background on NASQUAN

The U.S. Geological Survey (USGS) operates two nationwide networks to monitor water quality—the National Hydrologic Bench-Mark Network and the National Stream Quality Accounting Network (NASQUAN) (see chapter 8 for more information). The National Stream Quality Accounting Network was established in 1972 to provide the data needed to determine large-scale, long-term trends in the physical, chemical, and biological characteristics of the nation's waters. In short, the NASQUAN monitor network is used to track changes in water quality associated with human activities. Stations in the NASQUAN network are located to monitor stream flow from subregional drainage basins that collectively cover the entire land surface of the nation. Monitors at the NASQUAN stations measure stream flow rates, turbidity, conductivity, and concentrations of major inorganic constituents, nutrients, and trace metals.

As of 1990 there were nearly 350 NASQUAN sites located around the country. Station measurements are taken at regular intervals, although these intervals (i.e., weekly, monthly, quarterly) are not the same for all stations. Moreover, the same water quality characteristics are not measured during each interval, nor are identical characteristics measured across stations. NASQUAN stations measure literally hundreds of water quality parameters, often using different techniques to measure the same parameter. On the surface, this would seem to make calculating long-term water quality trends very difficult. Thankfully, nearly all stations regularly monitor a base set of water quality characteristics (e.g., dissolved oxygen, phosphorus, suspended sediment, nitrate-nitrite, dissolved solids, and so forth), allowing us to track concentrations of these constituents across stations and across time.

Considerations in Calculating Changes in Water Quality

Changes in water quality were measured using mean concentration levels for three common measures of water quality: dissolved oxygen, total dissolved solids, and phosphorus (see chapter 8 for information on these pollutants and why they were selected to represent water quality). All of these water constituents are measured in milligrams per liter of water. One cannot simply calculate mean concentration figures for sites within each state and compare these figures across time, however. NASQUAN sites are sampled at fixed time intervals without regard for variability in stream flow, and stream discharge has a significant effect on the concentration of these water quality constituents. Dissolved oxygen and substances introduced into the stream as a component of stream runoff, such as suspended sediments, will often show a positive relationship with stream flow. Conversely, many other chemical constituents may become diluted in increased stream flows and show a negative relationship with flow rates. The relationship between concentration ratios and flow rates may even exhibit both positive and negative responses over a range of flow levels. Consequently, identifying trends in the concentrations of these constituents can be very difficult because of the influence exerted by variations in stream flow.

In order to measure changes in water quality, all NASQUAN site measurements for the years 1973–1975 and 1986–1988 were obtained. Multiyear averages were then calculated and differenced to measure change in water quality over time (see below). Not all NASQUAN measurements could be used to calculate changes in water quality, however. Several new NASQUAN sites were added between 1975 and 1988, and these sites had to be eliminated from the analysis. In addition, NASQUAN monitors sited far downstream on major rivers were removed from the analysis, because attributing changes in pollutant levels at these sites to the regulatory efforts of any one state is exceedingly problematic. Twenty NASQUAN sites were excluded from the analysis in this fashion. Because all sites do not consistently measure the three constituents of interest, in several cases there were not enough observations to calculate representative mean concentration ratios. In order to assure the stability of the measures, any site with fewer than ten observations for stream flow or any of the three water quality constituents for either time period was deleted from the analysis. Finally, in order to weed out obvious errors in data entry, any sites reflecting changes in pollutant concentrations greater than 10,000 percent were excluded from the analysis.

Calculating Mean Concentrations: Dissolved Oxygen and Dissolved Solids

An adjustment for the flow-related effects identified above was accomplished by estimating the relationship between concentrations and flow rate using least squares regression. The relationship between concentration and flow levels is not always linear, however. The nature and form of this relationship varies with ecosystem type (i.e., across monitoring sites) and flow level (i.e., across time). The regression equations used to estimate flow-adjusted concentration levels must be sensitive to these variations.

For dissolved oxygen and dissolved solids, a general linear model was applied to the data

$$C = a + bf(Q)$$

where C is the estimated constituent concentration, Q is the stream flow, and $f(Q)$ may have one of the following four functional forms:

$$f(Q) = Q \qquad \text{(linear)}$$
$$f(Q) = \ln Q \qquad \text{(logarithmic)}$$
$$f(Q) = 1/(1 + BQ) \qquad \text{(hyperbolic)}$$
$$f(Q) = 1/Q \qquad \text{(inverse).}$$

Regressions were performed for each site during each time period using each of the four functional forms, and the functional form that maximized the R^2 value was selected for use in calculating the flow-adjusted concentration level. (Use of the maximized R^2 technique and these four functional forms is consistent with standard methodologies in hydrogeology; see R. Smith et al. 1982; Smith and Alexander 1983.) Flow-adjusted concentrations were calculated by applying the intercept and parameter estimate associated with the maximizing functional form at each site to the mean flow level for each site, for each time period. This provided a single best estimate for mean dissolved oxygen and mean total dissolved solids concentration levels at each site during each time period.

Calculating Mean Concentrations: Phosphorus

A similar adjustment for the flow-related effects associated with phosphorus concentrations was accomplished by estimating the relationship between concentration and flow rate using least squares regression. The relationship between phosphorus concentrations and flow levels is not linear, nor can it be estimated using a linear regression technique. Unlike dissolved oxygen and dissolved solids, the best estimate of the nature and form of this relationship rarely varies with ecosystem type or flow levels; this relationship is nearly always exponential in form (Smith and Alexander 1983). For phosphorus concentrations, the following nonlinear exponential model was applied to the data:

$$C = a + b1 \ln Q + b2 \, (\ln Q)^2$$

where C is the estimated concentration, Q is the stream flow rate, and $\ln Q$ is the natural logarithm of the discharge. Applying the intercept and parameter estimates from this model to the mean stream flow rates for each site allows us to calculate the best estimated flow-adjusted phosphorus concentration for each site.

Calculating Changes in Water Quality

In order to measure changes in water quality levels, data from the 1973–75 period had to be compared with data from the 1986–88 period. The flow-adjusted concentration levels for 1973–75 are based upon 11,000 observations at 277 sites. The flow-adjusted concentration levels for 1986–88 are based upon 13,000 observations at 311 sites. Flow-adjusted concentration levels during each time period for the three constituents were matched for each site, and then the mean concentration for 1973–75 was subtracted from the mean concentration level for 1986–88 for each constituent. The remainder represents the absolute change in mean constituent concentrations at each site over the period 1973–75 to 1986–88. Absolute changes can be deceiving with regard to many water quality constituents, however, since very large absolute changes for constituents like dissolved solids are possible at any one monitoring site, and these changes can wash out smaller changes at several other sites in a composite analysis. In order to standardize changes in these differences, the absolute difference in mean concentration levels at each site between 1973–75 and 1986–88 is represented as the percentage change from 1973–75 levels. Finally, the percentage mean concentration differences for all sites within the same state were combined to produce a single number representing the average percentage change in concentration levels for each constituent in each state. Matching and differencing mean concentration figures left us with 208 site observations in 35 states for dissolved oxygen, 211 site observations in 35 states for dissolved solids, and 253 site observations in 42 states for phosphorus.

Bibliography

Achen, Christopher. 1982. *Interpreting and Using Regression.* Sage University Paper Series on Quantitative Applications in the Social Sciences, series no. 07–029. Beverly Hills London: Sage.

Ackerman, Bruce A., and William T. Hassler. 1981. *Clean Coal/Dirty Air.* New Haven, CT: Yale University Press.

Adler, Jonathan. 1992. "Clean Fuels, Dirty Air." In *Environmental Politics: Public Costs, Private Rewards,* ed. Michael Greve and Fred Smith, Jr., pp. 19–45. New York: Praeger.

Advisory Commission on Intergovernmental Relations (ACIR). 1985. *The Question of State Government Capacity.* Washington, DC: ACIR.

———. 1991. *Significant Features of Fiscal Federalism.* Volume 2: *Revenues and Expenditures.* Washington, DC: ACIR.

Alexander, Richard, and Richard Smith. 1988. "Trends in Lead Concentrations in Major U.S. Rivers and their Relation to Historical Changes in Gasoline-Lead Consumption." *Water Resources Bulletin* 24:3, pp. 557–69.

Allison, Graham. 1968. "Conceptual Models and the Cuban Missile Crisis." *American Political Science Review* 62:3, pp. 689–718.

Anderson, James. 1990. *Public Policymaking: An Introduction.* Boston: Houghton Mifflin.

Appleton, Lynn M. 1985. "Explaining Laws' Making and Their Enforcement in the American States." *Social Science Quarterly* 66:4, pp. 839–53.

Asch, Peter, and Joseph Seneca. 1978. "Some Evidence on the Distribution of Air Quality." *Land Economics* 54, pp. 278–97.

Asher, Herbert. 1983. *Causal Modeling.* 2d ed. Sage University Paper Series on Quantitative Applications in the Social Sciences, series no. 07–003. Beverly Hills London: Sage.

Association of State and Interstate Water Pollution Control Administrators (ASIWPCA). 1984. *America's Clean Water: The State's Evaluation of Progress 1972–1982.* Washington, DC: ASIWPCA.

———. 1985. *America's Clean Water: The State's Evaluation of Progress 1985.* Washington, DC: ASIWPCA.

Bachrach, Peter, and Morton S. Baratz. 1962. "Two Faces of Power." *American Political Science Review* 56:4, pp. 947–52.

Banks, Jeffrey, and Barry Weingast. 1992. "The Political Control of Bureaucracies under Asymmetric Information." *American Journal of Political Science* 36:2, pp. 509–24.

Bardach, Eugene, and Robert Kagan. 1982. *Going by the Book: The Problem of Regulatory Unreasonableness.* Philadelphia, PA: Temple University Press.

Battaile, Janet. 1992. "Bush Overrides Agency on Pollution Restrictions." *New York Times,* May 17, sec. A.

Bauer, Raymond, Ithiel de Sola Pool, and Lewis A. Dexter. 1963. *American Business and Public Policy.* New York: Atherton Press.

Baumol, William, and Wallace Oates. 1975. *The Theory of Environmental Policy: Externalities, Public Outlays, and the Quality of Life.* Englewood Cliffs, NJ: Prentice Hall.

Belsley, David A., Edwin Kuh, and Roy E. Welsch. 1980. *Regression Diagnostics: Identifying Influential Data and Sources of Collinearity.* New York: John Wiley.

Bentley, Arthur. 1967. *The Process of Government,* ed. Peter Odegard. Cambridge, MA: Belknap Press of Harvard University Press. Original published in 1908.

Bernstein, Marver. 1955. *Regulating Business by Independent Commission.* Princeton, NJ: Princeton University Press.

Berry, Jeffrey. 1984. *The Interest Group Society.* Boston: Little, Brown.

Berry, William, and Stanley Feldman. 1985. *Multiple Regression in Practice.* Sage University Paper series on Quantitative Applications in the Social Sciences, series no. 07–050. Beverly Hills London: Sage.

Beyle, Thad, ed. 1988. *State Government: Congressional Quarterly's Guide to Current Issues and Activities, 1988–89.* Washington, DC: Congressional Quarterly Press.

Bishop, Catherine. 1991. "Death of a River Town." *New York Times,* December 29, sec. L.

Blalock, Hubert. 1972. *Social Statistics.* 2d ed. New York: McGraw-Hill.

Bobrow, Davis, and John Dryzek. 1987. *Policy Analysis by Design.* Pittsburgh, PA: University of Pittsburgh Press.

Book of the States. 1988. Lexington, KY: Council of State Governments.

Bosso, Christopher. 1987. *Pesticides and Politics: The Lifecycle of a Public Issue.* Pittsburgh: University of Pittsburgh Press.

Bowman, Ann O'M., and Richard Kearney. 1986. *The Resurgence of the States.* New York: Harper and Row.

———. 1988. "Dimensions of State Government Capability." *Western Political Quarterly* 41:2, pp. 341–62.

Brady, Gordon, and Blair Bower. 1982. "Effectiveness of the U.S. Regulatory Approach to Air Quality Management: Stationary Sources." *Policy Studies Journal* 11:1, pp. 66–76.

Braybrooke, David, and Charles Lindblom. 1963. *A Strategy of Decision.* New York: The Free Press.

Broder, Ivy. n.d. "Ambient Particulate Levels and Capital Expenditures: An Empirical Analysis." Photocopy. Department of Economics, American University, Washington, D.C.

Brown, Lester. 1978. *The Twenty-Ninth Day.* New York: W.W. Norton.

———, ed. 1989. *State of the World: 1989.* New York: W.W. Norton.

———. 1991. *Worldwatch Reader on Global Environmental Issues.* New York: W.W. Norton.

———. 1992. *State of the World: 1992.* New York: W.W. Norton.

Brown, Malcom. 1991a. "Lowest Ozone Levels on Record Found at South Pole." *New York Times,* October 10, sec. A.

———. 1991b. "Scientists Find Ozone Depletion over Temperate Zones." *New York Times,* October 22, sec. A.

Brown, Michael. 1980. *Laying Waste: The Poisoning of America by Toxic Chemicals.* New York: Washington Square Books.

Brownstein, Ronald. 1989. "Testing the Limits." *National Journal* (July 29), pp. 1916–20.

Bruce, John, John Clark, and John Kessel. 1991. "Advocacy Politics in Presidential Parties." *American Political Science Review* 85:4, pp. 1089–106.

Brudney, Jeff, and F. Ted Hebert. 1987. "State Agencies and Their Environments: Examining the Influence of Important External Actors." *Journal of Politics* 49:1, pp. 189–206.

Bulanowski, Gerard A. 1981. *The Impact of Science and Technology on the Decisionmaking Process in State Legislatures: The Issue of Solid and Hazardous Waste.* Denver, CO: National Conference of State Legislatures.

Bullard, Robert. 1990. *Dumping in Dixie: Race, Class, and Environmental Quality.* Boulder, CO: Westview Press.

Caldwell, Lynton. 1970. *Environment: A Challenge for Modern Society.* Garden City, NJ: The Natural History Press.

————. 1975. *Man and His Environment: Policy and Administration.* New York: Harper and Row.

————. 1990. *Between Two Worlds: Science, the Environmental Movement, and Policy Choice.* Cambridge: Cambridge University Press.

Calvert, Jerry W. 1979. "The Social and Ideological Bases of Support for Environmental Legislation: An Examination of Public Attitudes and Legislative Action." *Western Political Quarterly* 32:2, pp. 327–37.

————. 1989. "Party Politics and Environmental Policy." In *Environmental Politics and Policy,* ed. James Lester. Durham, NC: Duke University Press.

Capra, Fritjoh, and Charlene Spretnak. 1984. *Green Politics.* New York: Dutton.

Carmines, Edward G. 1974. "The Mediating Influence of State Legislatures on the Linkage between Interparty Competition and Welfare Policies." *American Political Science Review* 68:4, pp. 1118–24.

Carmines, Edward, and Richard Zeller. 1979. *Reliability and Validity Assessment.* Sage University Paper Series on Quantitative Applications in the Social Sciences, series no. 07–017. Beverly Hills London: Sage.

Carney, Leo. 1991. "Research Finds Ozone More Harmful than Previously Believed." *New York Times,* December 22, sec. NJ.

Carson, Rachel. 1962. *Silent Spring.* Boston: Houghton Mifflin.

Chamber of Commerce of the United States. 1981. *Environmental Quality Issues: The Relation of Federal Laws to State Programs.* Washington, DC: Chamber of Commerce.

Chubb, John. 1985. "The Political Economy of Federalism." *American Political Science Review* 79:4, pp. 994–1015.

Cigler, Allan J., and Burdett A. Loomis, eds. 1990. *Interest Group Politics.* 3d ed. Washington, DC: Congressional Quarterly Press.

Cnuddle, Charles, and Donald McCrone. 1966. "The Linkage between Constituency Attitudes and Congressional Voting Behavior." *American Political Science Review* 60:1, pp. 66–72.

Cohen, Steven, and Gary Weiskopf. 1990. "Beyond Incrementalism: Cross Media Environmental Management in the Environmental Protection Agency." In *Regulatory Federalism, Natural Resources, and Environmental Management,* ed. Michael Hamilton, pp. 47–65. Washington, DC: ASPA.

Coleman, James, Ernest Campbell, Carol Hobson, James McPartland, Alexander Mood, Frederic Weinfeld, and Robert York. 1966. *Equality of Educational Opportunity.* Washington, DC: GPO.

Commission for Racial Justice. 1987. *Toxic Wastes and Race in the United States.* New York: United Church of Christ.

Commoner, Barry. 1972. *The Closing Circle.* New York: Bantam.

Congressional Budget Office (CBO). 1985. *Environmental Regulation and Economic Efficiency.* Washington, DC: CBO.

————. 1988. "Environmental Federalism: Allocating Responsibilities for Environmental Protection." Staff Working Paper, September.

Conservation Foundation. 1987. *State of the Environment: A View toward the Nineties.* Washington, DC: Conservation Foundation.

Copeland, Gary, and Kenneth J. Meier. 1984. "Pass the Biscuits Pappy: Congressional Decision-Making and Federal Grants." *American Politics Quarterly* 12:1, pp. 3–21.

———. 1987. "Gaining Ground: The Impact of Medicaid and WIC on Infant Mortality." *American Politics Quarterly* 15:1.

Corson, Walter, ed. 1990. *The Global Ecology Handbook.* Boston: Beacon.

Council of State Governments. 1975. *Integration and Coordination of State Environmental Programs.* Lexington, KY: Council of State Governments.

———. 1986. *Innovations in Environment and Natural Resources.* Lexington, KY: Council of State Governments.

Crenson, Mathew. 1971. *The Un-Politics of Air Pollution: A Study in Non-Decision Making in the Cities.* Baltimore, MD: Johns Hopkins Press.

Crotty, Patricia McGee. 1987. "The New Federalism Game: Primacy Implementation of Environmental Policy." *Publius* (Spring), pp. 53–67.

Culhane, Paul. 1981. *Public Lands Policies.* Baltimore, MD: Johns Hopkins University Press.

Cushman, John. 1991. "EPA Proposes Rules on Utility Emission Trading." *New York Times,* October 30, sec. A.

Cyert, Richard, and James March. 1963. *A Behavioral Theory of the Firm.* Englewood Cliffs, NJ: Prentice Hall.

Dahl, Robert. 1956. *A Preface to Democratic Theory.* Chicago: University of Chicago Press.

Dales, J.H. 1968. *Pollution, Property, and Prices.* Toronto: University of Toronto Press.

Davis, Charles, and James Lester. 1987. "Decentralizing Federal Environmental Policy." *Western Political Quarterly* 40:3, pp. 555–65.

———. 1989. "Federalism and Environmental Policy." In *Environmental Politics and Policy,* ed. James Lester, pp. 57–86. Durham, NC: Duke University Press.

Dawson, Richard E., and James Robinson. 1963. "Inter-party Competition, Economic Variables, and Welfare Policies in the American States." *Journal of Politics* 25:2, pp. 265–89.

Derthick, Martha. 1972. *New Towns In-Town.* Washington, DC: Urban Institute.

———. 1985. "American Federalism: Madison's Middle Ground in the 1980s." *Public Administration Review* 47:1, pp. 66–74.

Derthick, Martha, and Paul Quirk. 1985. *The Politics of Deregulation.* Washington, DC: Brookings Institution.

Desai, Uday. 1989. "Assessing the Impacts of the Surface Mining Control and Reclamation Act." *Policy Studies Review* 9, pp. 98–108.

Dower, Roger. 1990. "Hazardous Wastes." In *Public Policies for Environmental Protection,* ed. Paul Portney, 151–194. Washington, DC: Resources for the Future.

Downing, Paul. 1983. "Bargaining in Pollution Control." *Policy Studies Journal* 11:4, pp. 577–86.

———. 1984. *Environmental Economics and Policy.* Boston: Little, Brown.

Downing, Paul, and James Kimball. 1982. "Enforcing Pollution Control Laws in the U.S." *Policy Studies Journal* 11:1, pp. 55–65.

Downs, Anthony. 1957. *An Economic Theory of Democracy.* New York: Harper and Row.

———. 1967. *Inside Bureaucracy.* Boston: Little, Brown.

———. 1972. "Up and Down with Ecology: The Issue-Attention Cycle." *The Public Interest* 28:3, pp. 38–50.

Draper, Norman, and Harry Smith. 1981. *Applied Regression Analysis.* 2d ed. New York: Wiley and Sons.

Dryzek, John. 1987. *Rational Ecology: Environment and Political Economy.* New York: Basil Blackwell.

Dunlap, Riley. 1987. "Public Opinion on the Environment in the Reagan Era." *Environment* 29:4, pp. 32–37.

————. 1989. "Public Opinion and Environmental Policy." In *Environmental Politics and Policy,* ed. James Lester, pp. 87–134. Durham, NC: Duke University Press.

Dunlap, Riley, and R.P. Gale. 1974. "Party Membership and Environmental Politics: A Legislative Roll Call Analysis." *Social Science Quarterly* 55:3, pp. 670–90.

Dunlap, Riley, and Rik Scarce. 1991. "Environmental Problems and Protection." *Public Opinion Quarterly* 55:4, pp. 651–72.

Dye, Thomas. 1966. *Politics, Economics, and the Public: Policy Outcomes in the American States.* Chicago: Rand McNally.

————. 1969. "Executive Power and Public Policy in the American States." *Western Political Quarterly* 22:4.

————. 1984. "Party and Policy in the States." *Journal of Politics* 46:4, pp. 1097–116.

"E Pluribus, Plures: Without Leadership from Washington, the States Set the Environmental Agenda for the Nation." *Newsweek* (November 13, 1989), pp. 70–72.

Easterbrook, Gregg. 1989. "Special Report: Cleaning Up." *Newsweek* (July 24), pp. 26–42.

Edelman, Murray. 1964. *The Symbolic Uses of Politics.* Urbana: University of Illinois Press.

Edner, Sheldon. 1976. "Intergovernmental Policy Development: The Importance of Problem Definition." In *Public Policy Making in a Federal System,* ed. Charles O. Jones and Robert Thomas, pp. 149–67. Beverly Hills: Sage.

Eisinger, Peter, and William Gormley, eds. 1988. *The Midwest Response to the New Federalism.* Madison: University of Wisconsin Press.

Elazar, Daniel. 1974. "The New Federalism: Can the States Be Trusted?" *The Public Interest* 35, pp. 89–102.

Elmore, R.F. 1979. "Backward Mapping: Implementation Research and Policy Decisions." *Political Science Quarterly* (Winter).

Emmert, Craig, and Carol Ann Traut. 1992. "Integrating Themes of Judicial Research: The California Supreme Court and the Death Penalty." Paper presented at the annual meeting of the Midwest Political Science Association, Chicago (April 8–11, 1992).

Engstrom, Richard, and Michael MacDonald. 1981. "The Election of Blacks to City Councils: Clarifying the Impact of Electoral Arrangements on the Seats/Population Relationship." *American Political Science Review* 75, pp. 344–54.

EPA Administrator. 1991. *Environmental Investments: The Cost of a Clean Environment.* Covelo, CA: Island Press.

Epstein, Samuel, Lester Brown, and Carl Pope. 1982. *Hazardous Waste in America.* San Francisco, CA: Sierra Club Books.

Erikson, Robert S., Gerald Wright, Jr., and John P. McIver. 1989. "Political Parties, Public Opinion, and State Policy in the United States." *American Political Science Review* 83:3, pp. 729–50.

Esposito, John. 1970. *Vanishing Air.* New York: Grossman.

Eulau, Heinz, and Kenneth Prewitt. 1973. *Labyrinths of Democracy.* Indianapolis, IN: Bobbs-Merrill.

Evans, Peter B., Dietrich Reuschemeyer, and Theda Skocpol, eds. 1985. *Bringing the State Back In.* New York: Cambridge University Press.

Faber, Harold. 1992. "Hudson Bass Running, But Off Limits to Fishermen." *New York Times,* April 12, sec. A.

Fenno, Richard F., Jr. 1978. *Homestyle: House Members in Their Districts.* Boston: Little, Brown.

Floyd, Dorinda. 1988. "Integration of Environmental and Agricultural Policy through the Implementation of the 1985 Farm Bill." Typescript, LaFollette Institute for Public Affairs, University of Wisconsin.

Freedman, Warren. 1987. *Federal Statutes on Environmental Protection.* Westport, CT: Quorum Books.

Freeman, A. Myrick. 1982. *Air and Water Pollution Control: A Benefit–Cost Assessment.*
New York: Wiley and Sons.

———. 1990. "Water Pollution Policy." In *Public Policies for Environmental Protection,* ed. Paul Portney, pp. 97–149. Washington, DC: Resources for the Future.

Freeman, A. Myrick, and Robert Haveman. 1972. "Clean Rhetoric and Dirty Water." *The Public Interest* 28, pp. 51–65.

French, Hilary. 1991. "You Are What You Breathe." In *Worldwatch Reader on Global Environmental Issues,* ed. Lester Brown, pp. 97–111. New York: W.W. Norton.

Fry, Brian, and Richard Winters. 1970. "The Politics of Redistribution." *American Political Science Review* 64:2, pp. 508–22.

Fund for Renewable Energy and the Environment (FREE). 1987. *The State of the States: 1987.* Washington, DC: FREE.

———. 1988. *The State of the States: 1988.* Washington, DC: FREE.

Game, Kingsley. 1979. "Controlling Air Pollution: Why Some States Try Harder." *Policy Studies Journal* 7, pp. 728–38.

Gianessi, Leonard, and Henry Peskin. 1981. "Analysis of National Water Pollution Control Policies." *Water Resources Research* 17:4, pp. 796–821.

Goetze, David. 1981. "The Shaping of Environmental Attitudes in Air Pollution Control Agencies." *Public Administration Review* 41, pp. 423–30.

Goggin, Malcolm, Ann O'M. Bowman, James Lester, and Lawrence O'Toole. 1990. *Implementation Theory and Practice: Toward a Third Generation.* Glenview, IL, and London: Scott, Foresman/Little, Brown.

Gormley, William. 1979. "A Test of the 'Revolving Door' Hypothesis at the FCC." *American Journal of Political Science* 23:4, pp. 665–83.

———. 1986a. "The Representation Revolution: Reforming State Regulation through Public Participation." *Administration and Society* 18:2, pp. 179–95.

———. 1986b. "Regulatory Issue Networks in a Federal System." *Polity* 18:4, pp. 595–620.

———. 1987. "Institutional Policy Analysis: A Critical Review." *Journal of Policy Analysis and Management* 6:2, pp. 153–69.

———. 1989. *Taming the Bureaucracy: Muscles, Prayers, and Other Strategies.* Princeton, NJ: Princeton University Press.

Gray, Virginia. 1974. "Innovation in the States: A Diffusion Study." *American Political Science Review* 67:4, pp. 1174–85.

Gray, Virginia, and Peter Eisinger. 1991. *American States and Cities.* New York: Harper Collins.

Gray, Virginia, and David Lowery. 1993. "The Diversity of State Interest Group Systems." *Political Research Quarterly* 46, pp. 81–98.

Greenberg, George, Jeffrey Miller, Lawrence Mohr, and Bruce Vladeck. 1977. "Developing Public Policy Theory: Perspectives from Empirical Research." *American Political Science Review* 71:4, pp. 1532–43.

Greenhouse, Linda. 1992. "Shield from Pollution Fines Is Upheld." *New York Times,* April 22, sec. A.

Greve, Michael. 1992. "Private Enforcement, Private Rewards." In *Environmental Politics: Public Costs, Private Rewards,* ed. Michael Greve and Fred Smith, Jr., pp. 105–27. New York: Praeger.

Greve, Michael, and Fred Smith, Jr. 1992. *Environmental Politics: Public Costs, Private Rewards.* New York: Praeger.

Grumm, J. 1971. "The Effects of Legislative Structure on Legislative Performance." In *State and Urban Politics,* ed. R.I. Hofferbert and I. Sharkansky. Boston: Little, Brown.

Haas, Peter, and Deil Wright. 1988. "The Changing Profile of State Administrators." In

State Government, ed. Thad Beyle, pp. 142–49. Washington, DC: Congressional Quarterly Press.

Hall, Bob, and Mary Kay Kerr. 1991. *The Green Index.* Washington, DC: Institute for Southern Studies.

Hanf, Kenneth. 1982. "The Implementation of Regulatory Policy: Implementation as Bargaining." *European Journal of Political Research* 10, pp. 159–72.

Hanley, Robert. 1992. "States Agree to Stronger Protection for Delaware River." *New York Times,* February 27, sec. B.

Hansen, Nancy Richardson, Hope Babcock, and Edwin Clark. 1988. *Controlling Nonpoint Source Water Pollution: A Citizen's Handbook.* Washington, DC: Conservation Foundation.

Hanushek, Eric A., and John E. Jackson. 1977. *Statistical Methods for Social Scientists.* Orlando, FL: Academic Press.

Harrigan, John. 1988. *Politics and Policy in States and Communities.* Glenview, IL: Scott, Foresman.

Hart, Stuart, and Gordon Enk. 1980. *Green Goals and Greenbacks: State Level Environmental Review Programs and Their Associated Costs.* Boulder, CO: Westview Press.

Haskell, Elizabeth, and Victoria Price. 1973. *State Environmental Management: Case Studies of Nine States.* New York: Praeger.

Hays, Samuel. 1987. *Beauty, Health, and Permanence: Environmental Politics in the United States, 1955–85.* Cambridge: Cambridge University Press.

Hebert, F. Ted, and Deil Wright. 1982. "State Administrators: How Representative? How Professional?" *State Government* 55:2, pp. 22–28.

Heclo, Hugh. 1977. *A Government of Strangers.* Washington, DC: The Brookings Institution.

Hedge, David, and Donald Menzel. 1985. "Loosening the Regulatory Rachet: A Grassroots View of Environmental Deregulation." *Policy Studies Journal* 13:3, pp. 599–606.

Hedge, David, Donald Menzel, and George Williams. 1988. "Regulatory Attitudes and Behavior: The Case of Surface Mining Regulations." *Western Political Quarterly* 41:2, pp. 323–38.

Hedge, David, Michael Scicchitano, and Patricia Metz. 1991. "The Principal–Agent Model and Regulatory Federalism." *Western Political Quarterly* 44:4, pp. 1055–80.

Heilbroner, Robert. 1974. *An Inquiry into the Human Prospect.* New York: W.W. Norton.

Heimlich, Ralph, and Linda Langer. 1986. "Swampbusting: Wetland Conversion and Farm Programs." *Agriculture Economic Report* no. 551. Washington, DC: U.S. Department of Agriculture, Economic Research Service.

Herring, Pendleton. 1967. *Public Administration and the Public Interest.* New York: Russell and Russell.

Hill, Kim Quaile, and Jan Leighley. 1992. "The Policy Consequences of Class Bias in State Electorates." *American Journal of Political Science* 36:2, pp. 351–65.

Hilts, Phillip. 1992. "President Bush Calls for Rapid Phase-Out of CFCs." *New York Times,* February 7, p. A–1.

Hjern, Benny. 1982. "Implementation Research: The Link Gone Missing." *Journal of Public Policy* 2:3, pp. 301–8.

Hofferbert, Richard. 1966. "The Relationship between Public Policy and Some Structural and Environmental Variables in the American States." *American Political Science Review* 60:1, pp. 73–82.

———. 1974. *The Study of Public Policy.* Indianapolis: Bobbs-Merrill.

Hofferbert, Richard, and John Urice. 1985. "Small Scale Policy: The Federal Stimulus versus Competing Explanations for State Funding for the Arts." *American Journal of Political Science* 29:2, pp. 308–29.

Holbrook-Provow, Thomas, and Steven C. Poe. 1987. "Measuring State Political Ideology." *American Politics Quarterly* 15:3, pp. 399–416.

Holloway, Harry. 1979. "Interest Groups in the Postpartisan Era: The Political Machine of the AFL-CIO." *Political Science Quarterly* 94:1, pp. 117–34.

Honadale, Beth. 1981. "A Capacity Building Framework: A Search for Concept and Purpose." *Public Administration Review* 41:5, pp. 577–89.

Hull, Christopher, and Benny Hjern. 1987. *Helping Small Firms Grow: An Implementation Approach:* London: Croom Helm.

Hunter, Susan, and Richard Waterman. 1992. "Determining an Agency's Regulatory Style: How Does the EPA Water Office Enforce the Law?" *Western Political Quarterly* 45, pp. 401–17.

Huntington, Samuel. 1952. "The Marasmus of the ICC: The Commission, the Railroads, and the Public Interest." *Yale Law Journal* 61.

Huth, Tom. 1992. "The Incredible Shrinking Swamp." *Conde Nast Traveler* (September), pp. 134–38, 184–91.

Inglehart, Ronald. 1977. *The Silent Revolution: Changing Values and Political Styles among Western Publics.* Princeton, NJ: Princeton University Press.

Ingram, Helen. 1990. "Implementation: A Review and Suggested Framework." In *Public Administration: The State of the Discipline,* ed. Naomi Lynn and Aaron Wildavsky, ch. 18. Chatham, NJ: Chatham House.

Ingram, Helen, and R. Kenneth Goodwin. 1985. *Public Policy and the Natural Environment.* Greenwich, CT: JAI Press.

Ingram, Helen, and Dean Mann. 1983. "Environmental Protection Policy." In *The Encyclopedia of Policy Studies,* ed. Stuart Nagel. Boulder, CO: Westview Press.

———. 1984. "Preserving the Clean Water Act: The Appearance of Environmental Victory." In *Environmental Policy in the 1980s,* ed. Norman Vig and Michael Kraft, pp. 251–72. Washington, DC: Congressional Quarterly Press.

———. 1989. "Interest Groups in Environmental Policy." In *Environmental Polics and Policy,* ed. James Lester. Durham, NC: Duke University Press.

Irwin, Frances, Edwin Clark II, and J. Clarence Davies. 1984. *Controlling Cross Media Pollutants.* Washington, DC: Conservation Foundation.

Jacob, Herbert, and Kenneth Vines. 1971. *Politics in the American States: A Comparative Perspective.* 2d ed. Boston: Little, Brown.

Jennings, Edward T., Jr. 1979. "Competition, Constituencies, and Welfare Policies in the American States." *American Political Science Review* 73:2, pp. 414–29.

Jessup, Deborah Hitchcock. 1990. *Guide to State Environmental Programs.* 2d ed. Washington, DC: Bureau of National Affairs.

Jewell, Malcolm. 1980. "The Neglected World of State Politics." *Journal of Politics* 44:3, pp. 638–57.

Johnston, George, David Freshwater, and Philip Favero. 1988. *Natural Resource and Environmental Policy Analysis: Cases in Applied Economics.* Boulder, CO: Westview Press.

Jones, Bradford. 1991. "State Responses to Global Climate Change." *Policy Studies Journal* 19:2, pp. 73–82.

Jones, Charles O. 1972. "From Gold to Garbage: A Bibliographic Essay on Politics and the Environment." *American Political Science Review* 66:2, pp. 588–95.

———. 1974. "Federal-State-Local Sharing in Air Pollution Control." *Publius* 4:1, pp. 69–84.

———. 1975. *Clean Air: The Policies and Politics of Pollution Control.* Pittsburgh, PA: University of Pittsburgh Press.

————. 1976. "Regulating the Environment." In *Politics in the American States*, ed. Herbert Jacobs and Kenneth Vines. Boston: Little, Brown.

Jones, Charles, and Robert Thomas, eds. 1976. *Public Policy Making in a Federal System*. Beverly Hills: Sage.

Kalt, Joseph, and M.A. Zupan. 1984. "Capture and Ideology in the Economic Theory of Politics." *American Economic Review* 74, pp. 279–300.

Kamieniecki, Sheldon, and Michael Ferrall. 1991. "Intergovernmental Relations and Clean Air Policy in Southern California." *Publius* (Summer), pp. 143–54.

Kelman, Steven. 1980. "Occupational Safety and Health Administration." In *The Politics of Regulation*, ed. James Q. Wilson, pp. 236–66. New York: Basic Books.

Kemp, Kathleen. 1981. "Symbolic and Strict Regulation in the American States." *Social Science Quarterly* 62:3, pp. 516–26.

Kettl, Donald. 1983. *The Regulation of American Federalism*. Baton Rouge, LA: LSU Press.

Key, V.O., Jr. 1949. *Southern Politics in State and Nation*. New York: Knopf/Vintage Books.

King, James. 1989. "Interparty Competition in the American States: An Index of Components." *Western Political Quarterly* 36:2, pp. 257–81.

Kingdon, John W. 1973. *Congressmen's Voting Decisions*. New York: Harper and Row.

————. 1984. *Agendas, Alternatives, and Public Policies*. Boston: Little, Brown.

Kneese, Allen. 1984. *Measuring the Benefits of Clean Air and Water*. Washington, DC: Resources for the Future.

Knoepfel, Peter, and Helmut Weidner. 1982. "Implementing Air Quality Control Programs in Europe: Some Results of a Comparative Study." *Policy Studies Journal* 11:1, pp. 103–15.

Kovacic, William. 1991. "The Reagan Judiciary and Environmental Policy: The Impact of Appointments to the Federal Courts of Appeals." *Boston College Environmental Affairs Law Review* 18:4, pp. 669–713.

Kraft, Michael. 1974. "Environmental Politics and American Government: A Review Essay." In *Environmental Politics*, ed. Stuart Nagel. New York: Praeger.

————. 1984. "A New Environmental Policy Agenda: The 1980 Presidential Campaign and Its Aftermath." In *Environmental Policy in the 1980s*, ed. Norman Vig and Michael Kraft. Washington, DC: Congressional Quarterly Press.

————. 1989. "Congress and Environmental Policy." In *Environmental Politics and Policy*, ed. James Lester. Durham, NC: Duke University Press.

————. 1990. "Environmental Gridlock: Searching for Consensus in Congress." In *Environmental Policy in the 1990s*, ed. Norman Vig and Michael Kraft. Washington, DC: Congressional Quarterly Press.

Kraft, Michael, Bruce Cleary, and Richard Tobin. 1988. "The Impact of New Federalism on State Environmental Policy: The Great Lakes States." In *The Midwest's Response to New Federalism*, ed. Peter Eisinger and William Gormley. Madison: University of Wisconsin Press.

Kritz, Margaret. 1989. "Ahead of the Feds." *National Journal* (December 9), pp. 2989–93.

Krupnick, Alan, Wesley Magat, and Winston Harrington. 1982. "Understanding Regulatory Decision-Making: An Econometric Approach." *Policy Studies Journal* 11:1, pp. 44–54.

Kuhn, Thomas. 1970. *The Structure of Scientific Revolutions*. 2d ed. Chicago: University of Chicago Press.

Ladd, Everett C. 1982. "Clearing the Air: Public Opinion and Public Policy on the Environment." *Public Opinion* 5:1, pp. 16–20.

Lakatos, Imre, and Alan Musgrave, eds. 1970. *Criticism and the Growth of Knowledge*. Cambridge: Cambridge University Press.

Landy, Marc, Marc Roberts, and Stephen R. Thomas. 1990. *The Environmental Protection Agency: Asking the Wrong Questions.* New York: Oxford University Press.

Larson, James. 1980. *Why Government Programs Fail: Improving Policy Implementation.* New York: Praeger.

Leary, Warren. 1992. "EPA Research Lags, Report Finds." *New York Times,* March 20, sec. A.

Lester, James P. 1980. "Partisanship and Environmental Policy: The Mediating Influence of Organizational Structures." *Environment and Behavior* 12, pp. 101–31.

———. 1985. "Reagan's New Federalism and State Environmental Policy." Paper delivered at the 1985 annual meeting of the Midwest Political Science Association.

———, ed. 1989. *Environmental Politics and Policy: Theories and Evidence.* Durham, NC: Duke University Press.

Lester, James, and Ann O'M. Bowman, eds. 1983. *The Politics of Hazardous Waste Management.* Durham, NC: Duke University Press.

Lester, James, Ann O'M. Bowman, Malcolm Goggin, and Lawrence O'Toole. 1987. "Public Policy Implementation: Evolution of the Field and Agenda for Future Research." *Policy Studies Review* 7:1, pp. 200–216.

Lester, James P., James L. Franke, Ann O'M. Bowman, and Kenneth W. Kramer. 1983. "Hazardous Wastes, Politics, and Public Policy: A Comparative State Analysis." *Western Political Quarterly* 36:2, pp. 257–81.

Lester, James, and Emmett Lombard. 1990. "The Comparative Analysis of State Environmental Policy." *Natural Resources Journal* 30:2, pp. 301–20.

Levine, Charles, and Paul Posner. 1981. "The Centralizing Effects of Austerity on the Intergovernmental System." *Political Science Quarterly* 96:1, pp. 67–87.

Levy, F.S., Arnold Meltzner, and Aaron Wildavsky. 1974. *Urban Outcomes.* Berkeley: University of California Press.

Lewis-Beck, Michael. 1977. "The Relative Importance of Socioeconomic and Political Variables for Public Policy." *American Political Science Review* 71:2, pp. 559–66.

———. 1980. *Applied Regression: An Introduction.* Sage University Series Paper on Quantitative Applications in the Social Sciences, series no. 07–022. Beverly Hills London: Sage.

Lewis-Beck, Michael, and John Alford. 1980. "Can Government Regulate Safety? The Coal Mine Example." *American Political Science Review* 74:3, pp. 745–56.

Lindblom, Charles E. 1977. *Politics and Markets: The World's Political Economic Systems.* New York: Basic Books.

Linder, Stephen, and B. Guy Peters. 1987. "A Design Perspective on Policy Implementation: The Falacies of Misplaced Prescription." *Policy Studies Review* 6, pp. 459–79.

Lineberry, Robert, and Edmund Fowler. 1967. "Reformism and Public Policies in American Cities." *American Political Science Review* 61, pp. 701–16.

Lipsky, Michael. 1980. *Street-Level Bureaucracy.* New York: Russell Sage.

Lovins, Amory. 1977. *Soft Energy Paths: Toward a Durable Peace.* New York: Harper and Row.

Lowi, Theodore. 1979. *The End of Liberalism: The Second Republic of the United States.* New York: W.W. Norton.

Lowry, William. 1992. *The Dimensions of Federalism: State Governments and Pollution Control Policies.* Durham, NC: Duke University Press.

Lundqvist, Lennart. 1980. *The Hare and the Tortoise: Clean Air Policies in the United States and Sweden.* Ann Arbor: University of Michigan Press.

Luoma, Jon. 1992. "New Effect of Pollutants: Hormone Mayhem." *New York Times,* March 24, sec. C.

Lyman, Francesca. 1990. *The Greenhouse Trap.* Boston: Beacon Press.

MacAvoy, Paul. 1979. *The Regulated Industries and the Economy.* New York: W.W. Norton.

———. 1987. "The Record of the EPA in Controlling Industrial Air Pollution." pp. 107–37. In *Energy, Markets and Regulation,* ed. R.L. Gordon, H.D. Jacoby, and M.B. Zimmerman. Cambridge, MA: Ballinger.

McCaull, Julian. 1976. "Discriminatory Air Pollution: If the Poor Don't Breathe." *Environment* 19, pp. 26–32.

McLaughlin, Milbrey. 1975. *Evaluation and Reform: ESEA Title I.* Cambridge, MA: Ballinger.

Magat, Wesley, and W. Kip Viscusi. 1990. "Effectiveness of the EPA's Regulatory Enforcement: The Case of Industrial Effluent Standards." *Journal of Law and Economics* 33, pp. 331–60.

Malone, Linda. 1985. "A Historical Essay on the Conservation Provisions of the 1985 Farm Bill: Sodbusting, Swampbusting, and Conservation Reserve." *University of Kansas Law Review* 34:1, pp. 573–83.

Mann, Dean, ed. 1982a. *Environmental Policy Implementation.* Lexington, MA: Lexington Books.

———. 1982b. *Environmental Policy Formation.* Lexington, MA: Lexington Books.

Marcus, Alfred. 1980. *Promise and Performance: Choosing and Implementing an Environmental Policy.* Westport, CT: Greenwood Press.

Marcus, Ruth. 1992. "Justices Make It Harder to Press Environmental Enforcement Cases." *Washington Post,* June 13, sec. A.

Mathtech, Inc. 1983. "Benefits and Net Benefits of Alternative Ambient Air Quality Standards for Particulate Matter." Report for the Economic Analysis Branch, Office of Air Quality Planning and Standards, U.S. Environmental Protection Agency. Washington, DC.

Mazmanian, Daniel, and Paul Sabatier. 1980. "A Multivariate Model of Policy Making." *American Journal of Political Science* 24:3, pp. 439–68.

———. 1989. *Implementation and Public Policy.* Lanham, MD: University Press of America.

Meadows, Donella, Dennis Meadows, Jorgen Randers, and William Behrems III. 1972. *Limits to Growth.* New York: Universe Books.

Medler, Jerry. 1989. "Governors and Environmental Policy." *Policy Studies Journal* 17:4, pp. 895–908.

Meier, Kenneth J. 1983a. "Consumerism or Protectionism: State Regulation of Occupations." Paper presented at the annual meeting of the American Political Science Association, Chicago, IL. September 1–4.

———. 1983b. "Political Economy and Cost–Benefit Analysis: Problems of Bias." In *The Political Economy of Public Policy,* ed. Alan Stone, pp. 143–62. Beverly Hills: Sage.

———. 1984. "The Limits of Cost–Benefit Analysis." In *Decision Making in the Public Sector,* ed. Lloyd Nigro, pp. 43–63. New York: Marcel Dekker.

———. 1985. *Regulation: Politics, Bureaucracy, and Economics.* New York: St. Martin's Press.

———. 1987. "The Political Economy of Consumer Protection: An Examination of State Legislation." *Western Political Quarterly* 40:2, pp. 343–59.

———. 1988. *The Political Economy of Regulation: The Case of Insurance.* Albany, NY: SUNY Press.

———. 1993. *Politics and the Bureaucracy: Policymaking in the Fourth Branch of Government.* 3d ed. Pacific Grove, CA: Brooks/Cole.

Meier, Kenneth, Joseph Stewart, and Robert E. England. 1989. *Race, Class, and Educa-*

tion: The Politics of Second Generation Discrimination. Madison: University of Wisconsin Press.

Mello, Robert. 1987. *Last Stand of the Red Spruce.* Washington, DC: Island Press.

Melnick, R. Shep. 1983. *Regulation and the Courts: The Case of the Clean Air Act.* Washington, DC: The Brookings Institution.

———. 1992. "Pollution Deadlines and the Coalition for Failure." In *Environmental Politics,* ed. Michael Greve and Fred Smith, Jr., pp. 59–103. New York: Praeger.

Menzel, Donald. 1983. "Redirecting the Implementation of a Law: The Reagan Administration and Coal Surface Mining Regulation."*Public Administration Review* 43, pp. 411–20.

Merchant, Carolyn. 1980. *The Death of Nature.* San Francisco: Harper and Row.

Mesarovic, Mihajlo, and Eduard Pestel. 1974. *Mankind at the Turning Point: The Second Report to the Club of Rome.* New York: Dutton.

Miller, Gary, and Terry Moe. 1983. "Bureaucrats, Legislators, and the Size of Government." *American Political Science Review* 77:2, pp. 297–322.

Miller, Warren E., and Donald Stokes. 1963. "Constituency Influence in Congress." *American Political Science Review* 57:1, pp. 45–56.

Mills, C. Wright. 1956. *The Power Elite.* New York: Oxford University Press.

Mills, Edwin, and Philip Graves. 1986. *The Economics of Environmental Quality.* 2d ed. New York: W.W. Norton.

Minnesota Pollution Control Agency (MPCA). 1990. "Mississippi River Water Quality Mirrors Metro Area History." *Minnesota Environment.* St. Paul, MN: MPCA.

———. 1991. *Acid Rain: Minnesota's Response.* St. Paul, MN: MPCA.

———. 1992. *Minnesota Pollution Control Agency.* St. Paul, MN: MPCA

Mitchell, Robert Cameron. 1984. "Public Opinion and Environmental Politics in the 1970s and 1980s." In *Environmental Policy in the 1980's: Reagan's New Agenda,* ed. Michael Kraft and Norman Vig. Washington, DC: Congressional Quarterly Press.

———. 1990. "Public Opinion and the Green Lobby: Poised for the 1990s?" In *Environmental Policy in the 1990s,* ed. Norman Vig and Michael Kraft. Washington, DC: Congressional Quarterly Press.

Moe, Terry. 1982. "Regulatory Performance and Presidential Administration." *American Journal of Political Science* 26:2, pp. 197–225.

Mohai, Paul. 1990. "Black Environmentalism." *Social Science Quarterly* 71:4, pp. 744–65.

Moorhouse, Sarah McCally. 1977. "The Governor as Political Leader." In *Politics in the American States: A Comparative Analysis,* ed. Herbert Jacob and Kenneth Vines. 3d ed. Boston: Little, Brown.

Mosher, Lawrence. 1982. "Reagan's Environmental Federalism: Are the States up to the Challenge?" *National Journal* 14:5, pp. 184–88.

Munns, Joyce M. 1975. "The Environment, Politics, and Policy Literature: A Critique and Reformulation." *Western Political Quarterly* 28:4, pp. 646–67.

Murray, Charles. 1984. *Losing Ground: American Social Policy 1950–1980.* New York: Basic Books.

Nakamura, Robert T., and Frank Smallwood. 1980. *The Politics of Policy Implementation.* New York: St. Martin's Press.

Nathan, Richard. 1989. "The Role of the States in American Federalism." In *The State of the States,* ed. Carl E. Van Horn, ch. 2, pp. 15–31. Washington, DC: Congressional Quarterly Press.

Nathan, Richard, and Fred Doolittle. 1983. *The Consequences of the Cuts: The Effects of the Reagan Domestic Program on State and Local Governments.* Princeton, NJ: Princeton Urban and Regional Research Center.

———. 1987. *Reagan and the States.* Princeton, NJ: Princeton University Press.

National Governors' Association (NGA). 1989. *Funding Environmental Programs: An Examination of Alternatives.* Washington, DC: NGA.

National Institute of Education (NIE). 1977. *Administration of Compensatory Education.* Washington, DC: GPO.

National Public Radio. 1993. "All Things Considered," April 22.

Navarro, Peter. 1981. "The 1977 Clean Air Act Amendments: Energy, Environmental, Economic, and Distributional Impacts." *Public Policy* 29:2, pp. 121–46.

New York Times. 1991. "Evidence Suggests Air Pollution Regulations Having Global Impact." October 15, sec. c.

———. 1992a. "Astronauts on Space Shuttle Test Device to Study Atmosphere." March 26, sec. A.

———. 1992b. "Mercury Levels Increasing in Atmosphere." February 18, sec. C.

Nice, David. 1983. "Representation in the States: Policymaking and Ideology." *Social Science Quarterly* 64:2, pp. 404–11.

———. 1987. *Federalism: The Politics of Intergovernmental Relations.* New York: St. Martin's Press.

Niskanen, William. 1971. *Bureaucracy and Representative Government.* Chicago: Aldine, Atherton.

Noll, Roger, and Bruce M. Owen. 1983. *The Political Economy of Deregulation: Interest Groups in the Regulatory Process.* Washington, DC: American Enterprise Institute.

O'Toole, Lawrence. 1985. *American Intergovernmental Relations.* Washington, DC: Congressional Quarterly Press.

———. 1989. "Goal Multiplicity in the Implementation Setting: Subtle Impacts and the Case of Waste Water Treatment Privatization." *Policy Studies Journal* 18:1, pp. 1–20.

Olson, Mancur. 1965. *The Logic of Collective Action.* Cambridge: Harvard University Press.

———. 1982. *The Rise and Decline of Nations.* New Haven, CT: Yale University Press.

Ophuls, William. 1977. *Ecology and the Politics of Scarcity.* San Francisco: W.H. Freeman.

Ophuls, William, and A. Stephen Boyan, Jr. 1992. *Ecology and the Politics of Scarcity Revisited: The Unraveling of the American Dream.* New York: W.H. Freeman.

Peltzman, Sam. 1974. "Toward a More General Theory of Regulation." *Journal of Law and Economics* 19, pp. 211–40.

Pertschuk, Michael. 1982. *Revolt against Regulation.* Berkeley: University of California Press.

Peterson, Paul, Barry Rabe, and Kenneth Wong. 1986. *When Federalism Works.* Washington, DC: The Brookings Institution.

Piven, Frances Fox, and Richard A. Cloward. 1971. *Regulating the Poor: The Functions of Public Welfare.* New York: Pantheon.

Plotnick, Robert D., and Richard F. Winters. 1985. "A Politico-Economic Theory of Income Redistribution." *American Political Science Review* 79:2, pp. 458–73.

Portney, Paul, ed. 1981. *Environmental Regulation and the U.S. Economy.* Baltimore, MD: Johns Hopkins Press.

———, ed. 1990a. *Public Policies for Environmental Protection.* Washington, DC: Resources for the Future.

———. 1990b. "Air Pollution Policy." In *Public Policies for Environmental Protection,* ed. Paul Portney, pp. 27–96.

Posner, Richard. 1974. "Theories of Economic Regulation." *Bell Journal of Economics and Management Science* 5:3, pp. 337–52.

Postel, Sandra. 1991. "Emerging Water Scarcities." In *Worldwatch Reader on Global Environmental Issues,* ed. Lester Brown, pp. 127–46. New York: W.W. Norton.

Pressman, Jeffrey, and Aaron Wildavsky. 1973. *Implementation.* Berkeley: University of California Press.

Public Interest Economic Foundation. 1984. "The Aggregate Benefits of Air Pollution Control." Prepared for the Office of Air Quality Planning and Standards, U.S. Environmental Protection Agency, Washington, DC.

Rabe, Barry. 1986. *Fragmentation and Integration in State Environmental Management.* Washington, DC: Conservation Foundation.

Reagan, Michael. 1987. *Regulation: The Politics of Policy.* Boston: Little, Brown.

Reeves, Mavis. 1981. *The Roles of State and Local Governments: Adapting Form to Function.* Washington, DC: U.S. Advisory Commission on Intergovernmental Relations.

Regens, James, and Robert Rycroft. 1988. *The Acid Rain Controversy.* Pittsburgh, PA: Pittsburgh University Press.

Rein, Martin, and Francine Rabinovitz. 1978. "Implementation: A Theoretical Perspective." In *American Politics and Public Policy,* ed. Walter Burnham and Martha Weinberg, pp. 307–35. Cambridge: MIT Press.

Ribaudo, Marc. 1989. *Water Quality Benefits from the Conservation Reserve Program.* Agricultural Economic Report no. 606. Washington, DC: Economic Research Service, U.S. Department of Agriculture.

Ringquist, Evan. 1993. "Instrumental Rationality and Policy Failure in Water Development." Paper presented at the annual meeting of the Southwest Political Science Association, New Orleans, LA. March 18–21.

Ripley, Randall, and Grace Franklin. 1986. *Bureaucracy, Politics, and Public Policy.* 3d ed. Boston: Little, Brown.

Rosenbaum, Walter. 1977. *The Politics of Environmental Concern.* 2d ed. New York: Praeger.

———. 1985. *Environmental Politics and Policy.* Washington, DC: Congressional Quarterly Press.

———. 1989. "The Bureaucracy and Environmental Policy." In *Environmental Policy and Politics,* ed. James Lester. Durham, NC: Duke University Press.

———. 1991. *Environmental Politics and Policy.* 2d ed. Washington, DC: Congressional Quarterly Press.

Rosenthal, Alan. 1988. "Better Legislatures: Poorer Results." In *State Government,* ed. Thad Beyle, pp. 93–95. Washington, DC: Congressional Quarterly Press.

———. 1989. "The Legislative Institution: Transformed and at Risk." In *The State of the States,* ed. Carl E. Van Horn, pp. 69–101. Washington, DC: Congressional Quarterly Press.

Rourke, Francis E. 1984. *Bureaucracy, Politics, and Public Policy.* 3d ed. Boston: Little, Brown.

Rowland, L.K., and Roger Marz. 1982. "Gresham's Law: The Regulatory Analogy." *Policy Studies Review* 1:3, pp. 572–80.

Russell, Clifford S., Winston Harrington, and William J. Vaughan. 1986. *Enforcing Pollution Control Laws.* Washington, DC: Resources for the Future.

Sabatier, Paul. 1975. "Social Movements and Regulatory Agencies." *Policy Sciences* 17:3, pp. 301–42.

———. 1977. "Regulatory Policy Making: Toward a Framework of Analysis." *Natural Resources Journal* 17:3, pp. 415–60.

———. 1986. "Top-Down and Bottom-Up Approaches to Implementation Research: A Critical Analysis and Suggested Synthesis." *Journal of Public Policy* 6:2, pp. 21–48.

Sabatier, Paul, and Dan Mazmanian. 1983. *Can Regulation Work? The Implementation of the 1972 California Coastal Initiative.* New York: Plenum.

Sabatier, Paul, and Neil Pelkey. 1987. "Incorporating Multiple Actors and Guidance Instruments into Models of Regulatory Policy Making: An Advocacy Coalition Framework." *Administration and Society* 19, pp. 236–63.

Sabato, Larry. 1983. *Goodbye to Goodtime Charlie: The American Governor Transformed.* 2d ed. Washington, DC: Congressional Quarterly Press.

Sagoff, Mark. 1988. *The Economy of the Earth: Philosophy, Law, and the Environment.* Cambridge: Cambridge University Press.

Salisbury, Robert H. 1968. "The Analysis of Public Policy: A Search for Theories and Roles." In *Political Science and Public Policy,* ed. Austin Ranney. Chicago: Markham.

———. 1984. "Interest Representation: The Dominance of Institutions." *American Political Science Review* 78:1, pp. 64–76.

Sanford, Terry. 1967. *Storm over the States.* New York: McGraw-Hill.

Savage, Robert. 1985. "When a Policy's Time Has Come: Cases of Rapid Policy Diffusion, 1983–84." *Publius* 15:3, pp. 111–25.

Schattschneider, E.E. 1960. *The Semi-Sovereign People: A Realist's View of Democracy in America.* New York: Holt, Rinehart, and Winston.

Schlotzman, Kay Lehman, and John T. Tierney. 1986. *Organized Interests and American Democracy.* New York: Harper and Row.

Schneider, Keith. 1991a. "EPA Forces States to Adopt Toxic Pollutant Regs." *New York Times,* October 7, sec. A.

———. 1991b. "States Join Suit Challenging EPA Ozone Standard." *New York Times,* October 22, p. B–4.

———. 1992a. "Courthouse a Citadel No Longer." *New York Times,* March 23, sec. B.

———. 1992b. "EPA Sued over Toxic Pollutant Regs." *New York Times,* February 2, p. L–28.

———. 1992c. "Pushed and Pulled, Environmental Inc. is on the Defensive." *New York Times,* March 29, sec. 4.

Schoenbaum, T. 1972. "The Efficiency of Federal and State Control of Water Pollution in Interstate Streams." *Arizona Law Review* 14.

Scholz, John T., and Feng Heng Wei. 1986. "Regulatory Enforcement in a Federalist System." *American Political Science Review* 80:4, pp. 1249–70.

Schwarz, John. 1988. *America's Hidden Success.* 2d ed. New York: W.W. Norton.

Sharkansky, Ira. 1967. "Government Expenditures and Public Services in the American States." *American Political Science Review* 61:4, pp. 1066–77.

Sharkansky, Ira, and Richard Hofferbert. 1969. "Dimensions of State Politics, Economics, and Public Policy." *American Political Science Review* 63:3, pp. 867–79.

Sheehan, Reginald, William Mishler, and Donald Songer. 1992. "Ideology, Status, and the Differential Success of Direct Parties before the Supreme Court." *American Political Science Review* 86:2, pp. 464–71.

Sierra Club v. *Ruckleshaus.* 344 F. Supp. 253 (D.D.C. 1972).

Sigelman, Lee, and Roland E. Smith. 1980. "Consumer Legislation in the American States: An Attempt at Explanation." *Social Science Quarterly* 61:1, pp. 58–70.

Smith, Richard, Robert Hirsch, and James Slack. 1982. *A Study of Trends in Total Phosphorus Measurements at NASQUAN Stations.* USGs Water Supply Paper 2190. Washington, DC: U.S. Geological Survey.

Smith, Richard, and Richard Alexander. 1983. "A Statistical Summary of Data from the U.S. Geological Survey's National Water Quality Networks." *U.S. Geological Survey Open File Report 83–533.* Reston, VA: U.S. Geological Survey.

Smith, Richard, Richard Alexander, and M. Gordon Wolman. 1987. "Water Quality Trends in the Nation's Rivers." *Science* 235:12, pp. 1607–15.

Smith, Zachary. 1992. *The Environmental Policy Paradox.* Englewood Cliffs, NJ: Prentice Hall.

Stanfield, Rochelle. 1984. "Ruckleshaus Casts EPA as 'Gorilla' in State's Enforcement Closet." *National Journal* (May 26), pp. 1024–38.

————. 1988. "Out-Standing in Court." *National Journal* (December 13), pp. 388–91.

Stevenson, Richard. 1992a. "California to Use Market Approach in Controlling Air Pollution." *New York Times,* January 30, sec. A.

————. 1992b. "Monitoring Pollution at Its Source." *New York Times,* April 8, sec. D.

Stewart, Richard. 1975. "The Reformation of American Administrative Law." *Harvard Law Review* 88, pp. 1667–813.

Stigler, George. 1971. "The Theory of Economic Regulation." *Bell Journal of Economics and Management Science* 2:1, pp. 3–21.

Stone, Deborah A. 1988. *Policy Paradox and Political Reason.* Glenview, IL: Scott, Foresman.

Stonecash, Jeffrey M. 1987. "Inter-Party Competition, Political Dialogue, and Public Policy: A Critical Review." *Policy Studies Journal* 16:2, pp. 243–62.

Sullivan, John. 1972. "A Note on Redistributive Politics." *American Political Science Review* 66:4, pp. 1302–5.

Svoboda, Craig. 1992. "Examining State Air Pollution Regulations." Paper presented at the annual meeting of the Southern Political Science Association, November 5–7, Atlanta.

Sylves, Richard. 1982. "Congress, EPA, the States, and the Fight to Decentralize Water-Pollution-Grant Policy." In *Environmental Policy Implementation,* ed. Dean Mann, pp. 109–26. Lexington, MA: Lexington Books.

Sylvester, Kathleen. 1990. "Global Warming: The Answers Are Not Always Global." *Governing* (April), pp. 42–48.

Teske, Paul. 1991. "A Comparative Analysis of State Regulation Studies." Paper presented at the Midwest Political Science Association Annual Meeting April 18–20, Chicago.

The Almanac of American Politics. 1989. Washington, DC: Barone.

Thomas, Clive, and Ronald Hrebenar. 1991. "Nationalization of Interest Groups and Lobbying in the American States." In *Interest Group Politics,* ed. Allan J. Cigler and Burdett A. Loomis, ch. 3. Washington, DC: Congressional Quarterly Press.

Thomas, Robert. 1976. "Intergovernmental Coordination in the Implementation of National Air and Water Pollution Policies." In *Public Policy Making in a Federal System,* ed. Charles Jones and Robert Thomas, pp. 129–47. Beverly Hills: Sage.

Thompson, Frank, and Michael Scicchitano. 1985. "State Enforcement of Federal Regulatory Policy: The Lessons of OSHA." *Policy Studies Journal* 13:3, pp. 591–98.

Tobin, Richard. 1984. "Revising the Clean Air Act: Legislative Failure and Administrative Success." In *Environmental Policy in the 1980s,* ed. Norman Vig and Michael Kraft. Washington, DC: Congressional Quarterly Press.

————. 1992. "Environmental Protection and the New Federalism: A Longitudinal Analysis of State Perceptions." *Publius* (Winter), pp. 93–107.

Truman, David. 1951. *The Governmental Process.* New York: Knopf.

Tuchman, Jessica, ed. 1991. *Preserving the Global Environment.* New York: W.W. Norton.

Udall, Stewart. 1963. *The Quiet Crisis.* New York: Holt, Rinehart, and Winston.

U.S. Congress. Senate. 1984. *Implementation of the Federal Clean Water Act: Hearings before the Subcommittee on Investigations and Oversight of the Committee on Public Works and Conservation.* 98th Congress. Second session.

U.S. Council on Environmental Quality. (U.S. CEQ) 1980. *The Global 2000 Report to the President.* Washington, DC: GPO.

————. 1983. *Environmental Quality 1983: 14th Annual Report of the Council on Environmental Quality.* Washington, DC: GPO.

————. 1989. *Environmental Trends.* Washington, DC: GPO.

U.S. Department of Agriculture (USDA). 1977. National Agricultural Statistics Service Report: *Acreage.* A92.24/4–2:977.

————. 1987. *Second RCA Appraisal: Analysis of Conditions and Trends.* Washington, DC: GPO.

————. 1990. National Agricultural Statistics Service Report: *Acreage.* A92.24/4–2:990.

U.S. Department of Commerce, Bureau of the Census. 1971–82. *Environmental Quality Control, Government Finances: FY 1970–1981.* Washington, DC: GPO.

————. 1974–91. *Statistical Abstract of the United States* 94th through 111th editions). Washington, DC: GPO.

————. 1982. *Survey of Current Business* (February). Washington, DC: GPO.

————. 1984. *Census of Manufacturing Industries: 1982.* Washington, DC: GPO.

————. 1985–88. *Annual Survey of Manufacturers: 1984 to 1987.* Washington, DC: GPO.

U.S. Department of Commerce. Bureau of Economic Analysis. 1981. *Survey of Current Business* (February). Washington, Dc: GPO.

————. 1992. *Survey of Current Business* (June). Washington, DC: GPO.

U.S. Department of Commerce. Economics and Statistics Administration. 1982–92. *Federal Expenditures by State.* Washington, DC: GPO.

U.S. Department of Energy. 1989. *State Energy Data Report: Consumption Estimates, 1960–1987.* Energy Information Administration, DOE/EIA–0214(87). Washington, DC: GPO.

U.S. Department of the Treasury. 1974–81. *Federal Aid to the States.* Washington, DC: GPO.

U.S. Environmental Protection Agency (U.S. EPA) 1975–1990. *1973–1988 National Emission Report* (second through fifteenth editions). Washington, DC: GPO.

————. 1983. *National Water Quality Inventory: 1982 Report to Congress.* Washington, DC: GPO.

————. 1987a. *National Water Quality Inventory: 1986 Report to Congress.* Washington, DC: GPO.

————. 1987b. *Unfinished Business: A Comparative Assessment of Environmental Problems.* Washington, DC: Office of Policy Analysis.

————. 1988a. *Environmental Progress and Challenges: EPA's Update.* Washington, DC: U.S. GPO.

————. 1988b. "NPDES and Pretreatment Spotlight." Staff Report, Office of Water Enforcement and Permits, December.

————. 1988c. *Water Quality Standards Criteria Summaries: A Compilation of State/Federal Criteria.* Washington, DC: Office of Water Regulation and Standards.

————. 1989a. "Briefing on NMP Effectiveness Study." Staff Briefing Paper, Office of Water Enforcement and Permits, January 9.

————. 1989b. "Draft: FY 1989 EPA and State Enforcement Summary." Office of Enforcement and Compliance Monitoring.

————. 1989c. *Water Quality in the Middle Great Lakes.* Chicago: Great Lakes National Program Office.

————. 1990. *National Water Quality Inventory: 1988 Report to Congress.* Washington, DC: EPA Office of Water.

————. 1991a. *Fish Kills Caused by Pollution 1977–87.* Washington, DC: Office of Water Regulation and Standards.

————. 1991b. *Toxics in the Community: The 1989 Toxics Release Inventory National Report.* Washington, DC: Office of Toxic Substances.

U.S. General Accounting Office (U.S. GAO). 1986a. *The Nation's Water: Key Unanswered Questions about the Quality of Rivers and Streams.* Washington, DC: U.S. General Accounting Office.

————. 1986b. *Water Quality: An Evaluation Method for the Construction Grants Program.* Volumes 1 and 2. Washington, DC: U.S. General Accounting Office.

U.S. National Acid Precipitation Assessment Program. (NAPAP) 1987. *Joint Report to Bilateral Advisory and Consultant Group: Status of Canadian/U.S. Research in Acidic Deposition.* Washington, DC: GPO.

———. 1990. *NAPAP 1990 Integrated Assessment Report.* Washington, DC: NAPAP.

U.S. Office of Management and Budget (OMB). *Budget of the United States Federal Government.* Fiscal years 1980–93. Washington, DC: GPO.

Van Horn, Carl. 1978. "Implementing CETA: The Federal Role." *Policy Analysis* 4:1, pp. 159–83.

———. 1979. *Policy Implementation in the Federal System: National Goals and Local Implementors.* Lexington, MA: Lexington Books.

———, ed. 1989. *The State of the States.* Washington, DC: Congressional Quarterly Press.

Vaughan, William, and Clifford Russell. 1982. *Recreational Freshwater Fishing: The National Benefits of Water Pollution Control.* Washington, DC: Resources for the Future.

Vig, Norman, and Michael Kraft, eds. 1984. *Environmental Policy in the 1980s: Reagan's New Agenda.* Washington, DC: Congressional Quarterly Press.

———. 1990. *Environmental Policy in the 1990s.* Washington, DC: Congressional Quarterly Press.

Viscusi, W. Kip. 1984. *Regulating Consumer Product Safety.* Washington, DC: American Enterprise Institute.

Wald, Mathew. 1991a. "Nine Northeastern States and DC Agree to Stricter Auto Pollution Standards." *New York Times,* October 30, sec. A.

———. 1991b. "Connecticut Refuses to Adopt Stricter Emission Standards." *New York Times,* November 8, sec. B.

———. 1991c. "California Adopts Tough New Gasoline Standards." *New York Times,* November 23, sec. L.

———. 1992a. "To Fight Smog, 8 Northeastern States Adopt New Curbs on Power Plants." *New York Times,* April 3, sec. A.

———. 1992b. "States Sue EPA over Lack of Clean Air Rules." *New York Times,* April 14, sec. B.

———. 1992c. "Clean Air Battle: Unusual Cast of Courtroom Foes." *New York Times,* April 25, sec. A.

———. 1992d. "Utility Is Selling Right to Pollute." *New York Times,* May 12, sec. A.

Walker, Jack. 1969. "The Diffusion of Innovation among the American States." *American Political Science Review* 63:3, pp. 880–99.

———. 1983. "The Origins and Maintenance of Interest Groups in America." *American Political Science Review* 77:2, pp. 390–406.

Warren, Charles. 1982. "State Government's Capacity: Continuing to Improve." *National Civic Review* 71:5, pp. 34–39.

Warwick, Donald. 1975. *A Theory of Public Bureaucracy.* Boston: Harvard University Press.

Waxman, Henry. 1992. "The Environmental Pollution President." *New York Times,* April 29, sec. A.

Webb, Lee, and Jefferey Tryens, eds. 1984. *An Environmental Agenda for the States.* Washington, DC: The Conference on Alternative State and Local Policies.

Weidenbaum, Murray. 1979. *The Future of Business Regulation: Private Action and Public Demand.* New York: Amacon.

Welborn, David. 1977. *Governance of Federal Regulatory Agencies.* Knoxville: University of Tennessee Press.

Wenner, Lettie McSpadden. 1982. *The Environmental Decade in Court.* Bloomington: Indiana University Press.

————. 1983. "Interest Group Litigation and Environmental Policy." *Policy Studies Journal* 11:4, pp. 671–83.

————. 1989. "The Courts and Environmental Policy." In *Environmental Politics and Policy,* ed. James Lester, pp. 238–60. Durham, NC: Duke University Press.

————. 1990. "Environmental Policy and the Courts." In *Environmental Policy in the 1990s,* ed. Norman Vig and Michael Kraft, pp. 189–210. Washington, DC: Congressional Quarterly Press.

White, Lawrence. 1982. "U.S. Mobile Source Emissions Regulation: The Problems of Implementation." *Policy Studies Journal* 11:1, pp. 77–87.

Wildavsky, Aaron. 1984. *The Politics of the Budgetary Process.* 4th ed. Boston: Little, Brown.

Williams, Bruce, and Albert Matheny. 1984. "Testing Theories of Social Regulation: Hazardous Waste Regulations in the American States." *Journal of Politics* 46:2, pp. 428–59.

Wilson, Graham K. 1981. *Interest Groups in the United States.* New York: Oxford University Press.

————. 1986. "American Business and Politics." In *Interest Group Politics,* ed. Allan J. Cigler and Burdett A. Loomis. Washington, DC: Congressional Quarterly Press.

Wilson, James Q. 1973. *Political Organizations.* New York: Basic Books.

————. 1980. *The Politics of Regulation.* New York: Basic Books.

Winters, Richard. 1976. "Party Control and Policy Change." *American Journal of Political Science* 20:4, pp. 597–636.

Wonnacott, Thomas, and Ronald Wonnacott. 1981. *Regression: A Second Course in Statistics.* Somerset, NJ: Wiley and Sons.

————. 1987. *Regression: A Second Course in Statistics.* Malabar, FL: Krieger.

Wood, B. Dan. 1988. "Principles, Bureaucrats, and Responsiveness in Clean Air Enforcements." *American Political Science Review* 82:1, pp. 213–34.

————. 1990. "Does Politics Make a Difference at the EEOC?" *American Journal of Political Science* 34:2, pp. 503–30.

————. 1991. "Federalism and Policy Responsiveness: The Clean Air Case." *Journal of Politics* 53:3, pp. 851–59.

————. 1992. "Modeling Federal Implementation as a System: The Clean Air Case." *American Journal of Political Science* 36, pp. 40–67.

Wood, B. Dan, and Richard Waterman. 1991. "The Dynamics of Political Control of the Bureaucracy." *American Political Science Review* 85, pp. 801–28.

Wood, Floris, ed. 1990. *An American Profile: Opinions and Behavior, 1972–1989.* New York: Gale Research.

Worsham, Jeffrey. 1991. "The Political Economy of Banking Deregulation." Doctoral dissertation, University of Wisconsin-Madison.

Wright, Gerald C., Jr., Robert S. Erikson, and John McIver. 1985. "Measuring State Political Ideology with Survey Data." *Journal of Politics* 47:2, pp. 469–89.

————. 1987. "Public Opinion and Policy Liberalism in the American States." *American Journal of Political Science* 31:4, pp. 980–1001.

Yandle, Bruce. 1989. *The Political Limits of Environmental Regulation.* Westport, CT: Quorum.

Ziegler, L. Harmon, and Hendrik van Dahlen. 1976. "Interest Groups in State Politics." In *Politics in the American States: A Comparative Analysis,* ed. Herbert Jacob and Kenneth Vines, pp. 93–138. 3d ed. Boston: Little, Brown.

Zwick, David, and Mary Benstock. 1971. *Water Wasteland.* New York: Grossman.

Index

White, Lawrence, 9, 128
Wildavsky, Aaron, 95, 98, 152*n*
Williams, Bruce, 10, 11, 89, 105, 107, 113, 132, 202
Wilson, Graham, 113
Wilson, James Q., 26, 85, 87, 95, 164, 165
Winters, Richard, 82, 83, 84, 104, 105
Wisconsin Air Toxics Task Force, 70–71
Wisconsin Power and Light, 52
Wise Use, 30
Wonnacott, Ronald, 124n, 152*n*

Wonnacott, Thomas, 124n, 152*n*
Wood, B. Dan, 6, 36, 38, 68, 73, 87, 95, 99, 132, 136
Worsham, Jeffrey, 87
Wright, Deil, 66, 98
Wright, Gerald, 84, 104, 105, 108, 109, 110, 120
Yandle, Bruce, 13, 128, 200, 202
Zellner, Richard, 152*n*
Ziegler, L. Harmon, 89, 156
Zupan, M.A., 90
Zwick, David, 5

Evan J. Ringquist is Assistant Professor of Political Science at Florida State University. Born in Minneapolis, Minnesota, Dr. Ringquist received undergraduate training in political science, economics, and biology at Moorhead State University and his M.A. and Ph.D. in Political Science and graduate training in Environmental Studies at the University of Wisconsin-Madison. He taught previously at the University of Wisconsin-Milwaukee and Texas Tech University, where he was Coordinator of the Graduate Program in Environmental and Natural Resources Administration.